Theodor Storm

Interpretations of Storm's life and work have been a faithful barometer of dominant ideological trends in Germany from 1850 to the present. This new study argues that the various "legends" have obscured Storm's true significance and artistic stature as a champion of democratic-humanitarian traditions and aspirations. This commitment and its literary manifestations are studied in a variety of contexts from the 1830s to the late 1880s. The book highlights Storm's critique of Christianity, his vision of capitalism, and his probing analysis of class relationships. The study contends that his literary forms, techniques, and strategies were shaped by the need to respond to specific socio-political constraints and the prejudices of publishers, editors, and readers. It throws new light on Storm's attitude to love, marriage, the family, women, sex, and education. In its advocacy of new approaches and its use of much unpublished primary material this challenging book offers new insights into the problems and preoccupations of nineteenth-century Germany.

David A. Jackson is a lecturer in the School of European Studies, University of Wales, Cardiff.

MONOGRAPHS IN GERMAN LITERATURE

General Editors:
Keith Bullivant, Professor of German, University of Florida, Gainesville
and
Jeffrey L. Sammons, Professor of German, Yale University

HEINRICH HEINE: POETRY IN CONTEXT
A Study of *Buch der Lieder*
Michael Perraudin, Lecturer in German, University of Birmingham

In Preparation:

"WHERE I AM, THERE IS GERMANY"
Thomas Mann in America, 1938–1952
Hans Rudolf Vaget, Helen and Laura Shedd Professor of German Language and Literature, Smith College

Theodor Storm

The Life and Works of a Democratic
Humanitarian

By David A. Jackson

BERG
New York / Oxford

Distributed exclusively in the U.S. and Canada by
St. Martin's Press, New York

Published in 1992 by
Berg Publishers, Inc.
Editorial offices:
165 Taber Avenue, Providence, RI 02906, U.S.A.
150 Cowley Road, Oxford OX4 1JJ, UK

**A CIP catalogue record for this book is available
from the British Library.**

Library of Congress Cataloging-in-Publication Data
Jackson, David A., 1934–
    Theodor Storm: the life and works of a democratic humanitarian/
by David A. Jackson.
        p.   cm.
    Includes bibliographical references and index.
    ISBN 0-85496-593-9: $44.00
    1. Storm, Theodor, 1817–1889. 2. Authors, German—19th century
—Biography. I. Title.
PT2528.Z5J3   1992
833'.8—dc20
[B]   91–44737
                                                                CIP

Printed and bound in Great Britain by
Billing and Sons Ltd, Worcester

*For my father and in memory
of my mother (1911–1991)*

Contents

Acknowledgments

Scholarship is a collaborative venture, and without the labors of Storm scholars, past and present, this book could not have been written. I am indebted to the works, editions, articles, and words of encouragement of Clifford Bernd, Brian Coghlan, Peter Goldammer, Gerhardt Jaritz, and Hamish Ritchie. Karl-Ernst Laage and Dieter Lohmeier and their respective staffs at the Storm House in Husum and the State Library in Kiel have been very supportive. David Hanley, Jim Reed, Alfred White, and my wife offered their critical thoughts on various chapters, and my wife checked the manuscript. But my greatest debt is to Chris Weedon for her unstinting help.

I am grateful to the State Library in Kiel for permission to use unpublished material; to Gottfried Honnefelder of Insel Verlag for the right to cite the new critical edition; and to Ellinor Kahleyss of the Erich Schmidt Verlag for permission to make ample use of the new critical editions.

Research in Husum and Kiel was made possible by a research grant awarded by the German Academic Exchange Service (DAAD) (1982) and by the School of European Studies in Cardiff (1990). Katharina Tietz, Martin Weber, Johannes Jung, Jörg Kobarg, and Ansgar v.d. Osten provided invaluable practical help.

Finally my thanks are due to Marion Berghahn for having been ready to back the book.

The remaining faults and idiosyncracies are my responsibility alone.

DAVID JACKSON

Introduction

This study of Theodor Storm (1817–88) interprets his work as a response, albeit a very individual one, to major nineteenth-century social and political issues. It discusses the various ways in which the complexion of state and society influenced the options and scope available to him as a writer and considers the effect of both the market and cultural and literary traditions on the forms and functions of his works. One of the book's prime concerns is to explore the reasons why certain elements from contemporary life feature in his work while others do not and why those that do appear are presented in particular ways.

At the present time a synthetic overview seems inappropriate. Much quarrying and processing of biographical raw material remains to be done, and information on institutional and ideological issues is still often sketchy.[1] But what, above all, should deter any attempt to write a definitive study is the fact that the 1980s have seen a stimulating plurality of approaches to Storm's

---

1. The editions of Gertrud Storm (listed in the bibliography) are notoriously unreliable. Letters and passages in letters which she considered detrimental to her father's memory were frequently omitted entirely. In other cases the transcriptions simply do not correspond to modern editorial standards. Since the passages I quote from letters to his parents, fiancée/wife and children largely come into the excised category, I give details of the addressee and the date and, unless otherwise indicated, refer the reader to the originals in the Schleswig-Holsteinische Landesbibliothek in Kiel. If there is one area of Storm scholarship where new editions are needed, it is here. In contrast, the new critical editions appearing in the Erich Schmidt Verlag are invaluable tools. Volumes in this series are referred to in the abbreviated form, e.g. *Storm-Heyse* 1. The edition of Storm's works cited is the new 4-volume critical edition, Theodor Storm, *Sämtliche Werke*, ed. K.-E. Laage and D. Lohmeier, Frankfurt, 1987–88 (LL 1, 2 etc.). Other abbreviations: *Blätter der Freundschaft* = *Blätter der Freundschaft. Aus dem Briefwechsel zwischen Theodor Storm und Ludwig Pietsch*, ed. V. Pauls, 2d ed., Heide, 1943; *Briefe* 1, 2 = Theodor Storm, *Briefe*, ed. P. Goldammer, 2 vols., Berlin and Weimar, 1972, 1984²; SHLB = Schleswig-Holsteinische Landesbibliothek; *Storm-Keller* = *Der Briefwechsel zwischen Theodor Storm und Gottfried Keller*, ed. P. Goldammer, Berlin, 1960; *Storm-Mommsen* = *Theodor Storms Briefwechsel mit Theodor Mommsen*, ed. H.-E. Teitge, Weimar, 1966; STSG = *Schriften der Theodor-Storm-Gesellschaft*; ZSGH = *Zeitschrift zur Geschichte Schleswig-Holsteins*.

writing. It would be sad were that debate to be foreclosed. Chapter 1 discusses Storm's reputation during his lifetime and the uses to which his work was subsequently put. Chapter 2 examines Schleswig-Holstein in the early nineteenth century, while Chapter 3 focuses on Husum and the Storm and Woldsen families. Its climax is the account of Storm's involvement in the Schleswig-Holstein Rising (1848–51) and of his attempts to use literature to further the democratic cause. Chapter 4 falls into two halves. The first analyzes the implications for an oppositional writer of conditions in Prussia in the 1850s; the second revolves around the tension between Storm's consciousness of the social, political and economic backwardness of the duchies and much of Germany and the qualified optimism fostered by contemporary developments. His misgivings about the middle classes and his resistance to certain aspects of Poetic Realism are discussed as the focus moves between marital, domestic and sexual topics and wider socio-political and ideological issues. Chapter 5 considers Storm's return to Schleswig in 1864 and his reactions to the Prussian annexation.

Within very obvious limitations, Chapter 6 sketches the Bismarckian settlement and the dilemmas facing Storm in the Second Empire. A condensed glimpse of his "hidden biography" brings out its implications for the quality and quantity of his later work. His recourse to Heinean and Hoffmannesque techniques is discussed together with his other experiments in the early 1870s. Chapter 7 looks at the great continuities in his work and analyzes his use of historical subjects. It offers tentative thoughts on the dilemmas which faced anyone criticizing aspects of middle-class life at a time of growing concern about the spread of socialism. It suggests that literature offered a realm where one could adumbrate taboo topics, provided one observed certain aesthetic rules. Chapter 8 considers the issue of heredity and its impact on Storm's definitions of guilt and tragedy before looking at his aesthetic crisis. Remarks on his presentation of "the social question" in *Bötjer Basch* and of the stigmatization of an ex-convict in *Ein Doppelgänger* lead to the final section, a detailed study of *Der Schimmelreiter*.

Storm never witnessed a democratic, humanitarian Germany. In many respects his life from the 1848 revolutions, via the Schleswig-Holstein Rising of 1863/64, the Prussian annexation of the duchies in 1867 and the creation of the Second German

Empire in 1871, to his death in 1888 is a history of frustrated expectations. On a personal, family level so many of the hopes of the 1840–65 period had been destroyed. Nevertheless, I hope that readers will not feel a dread sense of fatalism, a feeling – which historians enjoying the mixed blessing of hindsight often convey – that winners and losers were predetermined and that only fools supported the latter. Perhaps Storm's democratic humanitarianism will emerge as more than a mere historical petrifact.

1

Traditions and Legends

Storm criticism, like Storm's reputation, mirrors developments in Germany from the 1840s to the present.[1] Before his works were even conceived, expectations already existed which shaped both his own view of them and the responses of contemporaries. These theories, articulated, for example, by G. G. Gervinus in his *Geschichte der poetischen Nationalliteratur der Deutschen* (1835–42),[2] claimed that German literature could flourish again only in a free, united Germany. In this view, Goethe had achieved all that could be achieved as long as the so-called *Kunstperiode* lasted. After his death Germany's pettiness and provincialism had reproduced themselves in epigonal artifacts.

The year 1848 was greeted as the dawn of the new age. But the euphoria fast evaporated, and Storm achieved his literary breakthrough in a repressive environment when it was an advantage not to have a known radical past. His good fortune was that the novella *Immensee* (1849) became a best seller with the well-to-do ladies who comprised the clientele of a Berlin publisher, Alexander Duncker. Their reading of it reflected the post-revolutionary mood. Preoccupied as he was with securing recognition as a lyric poet, Storm was glad of any favorable mention and happy

---

1. For an informative, succinct overview see P. Goldammer, "Theodor Storm und die deutsche Literaturgeschichtsschreibung," *Aufbau*, vol. 12, 1956, pp. 963–72.
2. G. G. Gervinus, *Geschichte der poetischen Nationalliteratur der Deutschen*, 5 vols., Leipzig, 1835–42. The final vol. (5th ed., 1853) ends, p. 667: ". . . wir wollen nicht glauben, daß diese Nation in Kunst, Religion und Wissenschaft das Größte vermocht habe, und im Staate gar nichts vermöge. Aber freilich müssen wir es in die Hände des Schicksals geben, ob es jene enthusiastische Energie, die allem unserem ersten Beginnen eigen ist, einmal nach dieser Richtung lenken werde. Was an uns liegt, ist, ob wir die Winke der Zeit verstehen, die Zersplitterung unserer Thätigkeit aufheben und unser Wirken nach dem Punkte richten wollen, nach dem die ungestümsten Wünsche am lautesten geworden sind. Der Wettkampf der Kunst ist vollendet; jetzt sollten wir uns das andere Ziel stecken, das noch kein Schütze bei uns getroffen hat, ob uns auch da Apollon den Ruhm gewährt, den er uns dort nicht versagte."

to apply Gervinus's condescending categories[3] to his prose works. The general mood also encouraged him to emphasize the idyllic, humorous elements in his work. But this labelling was a mixed blessing.[4] Thus, Paul Heyse, while commending him for being "an artistic reactionary" hostile to the pre-1848 *Tendenzdichter*, criticized him for providing only genre pictures and still-lifes.[5] Increasingly, demands were made for a "realist" literature that would affirm the economic strength and moral virtues of the middle classes. These qualities, not radicalism and revolution, would, it was argued, achieve national unity and liberal–constitutional freedom. A new classical era in German culture evoked before 1848 could then dawn. With the advent of the New Era in Prussia in 1858, Storm suffered from having been associated in the public's mind with so-called "gold-leaf literature."[6]

3. See Storm to H. Brinkmann, *Storm-Brinkmann*, p. 27: "Bei dem Ausdruck 'Situationen' in der Dedication habe ich an eine Stelle in Gervinus Literaturgeschichte B. V. p. 697 gedacht, wo er sagt, die Novelle sei wesentlich Situation, und als solche geeignet, der großen Gattung subordinirter Conversationspoësie, dem Roman, der sich im Geleise des modernen socialen Lebens bewege, eine poëtische Seite abzugewinnen durch Beschränkung und Isolirung auf einzelne Momente von poëtischem Interesse, die sich auch im dürftigsten Alltagsleben finden." In the original, Gervinus himself makes it clear that he has simply adopted a term coined by Georg von Reinbeck (see A. Wierlacher, "Situationen," Zu Storm früher Prosa," *STSG*, vol. 21, 1972, pp. 38–44). In September 1881 Storm wrote to Erich Schmidt (*Storm-Schmidt* 2, 46f.): "Gervinus sagt in seiner Geschichte der poet Nationalliteratur Bd V 2te Aufl. S. 359: Nachdem die schöne Prosa alle großen Gegenstände des öffentlichen Lebens berührt hatte, so bemächtigte sie sich nun auch im ganzen Umfange aller der kleinen Gegenstände der engern Gesellschaft und des Privatlebens. In diese Gebiete folgt die Literaturgeschichte nicht – Sie haben also dennoch diese Gebiete betreten. Aber die Schriftsteller, welche G im Auge hat, sahen wohl nur die kleinen Dinge, weil sie keine Dichter waren; das lag aber an ihnen, nicht an der Region, wo sie ihre Stoffe suchten; 'wo der Mensch mit seinem Leben ist, da ist auch Poesie, triffst du nur das rechte Wort'; und das *Haus* ist das Fundament des Staates, und die Strahlenbrechungen des ganzen Volkslebens sind auch dort. Die schönen Reflexionen des sel. G aus dem höheren Gesichtspunkt sind doch mitunter recht seichte Redereien." Gervinus had in fact gone on: "Sie hat es mit dem zu thun, was auf dem öffentlichen Boden der Nationalkultur, zur rechten Zeit gesäet, als erzielte Pflanzung darin aufgeht; das Unkraut, das von selbst dazwischen wuchert, geht sie nicht weiter an . . ."
4. See I. Schuster, "Theodor Storm und der Publikumsgeschmack seiner Zeit," in *Analecta Helvetica et Germanica. Eine Festschrift zu Ehren von H. Böschenstein*, Bonn, 1979, pp. 247–65. For a very detailed study of the whole period from 1850 to 1890, see R. Fasold, "Die Rezeption der Dichtung Theodor Storms in Zeitungen, Zeitschriften und buchmonographischen Veröffentlichungen zwischen 1850 und 1890," dissertation, Leipzig, 1983.
5. Paul Heyse, "Theodor Storm," *Literaturblatt des deutschen Kunstblattes*, 28 December 1954, pp. 203–4.

Although he threw himself into the fray with a gusto which alienated Duncker, this period of renewed national, democratic hopes was too brief to dislodge the public's image of him. Once Bismarck began uniting Germany "from above," Storm's democratic notions swiftly seemed a relic of the past, and by the late 1860s his career had apparently petered out. In 1870–71 his alienation from the prevailing mood prevented him boosting his reputation by composing patriotic lyrics. In addition, he rashly provoked the influential critic Rudolf Gottschall into launching an attack on his lyric poetry which confirmed the picture of him as a purveyor of genre pictures and "miniature feelings."[7]

For Bismarck's supporters the benefits of the new Empire were universal, and it was assumed that its cultural purveyors would produce fitting tributes to the new age. The largely middle-class readers, for whom Storm catered in *Westermanns Monatshefte* and the *Deutsche Rundschau*, may have savored other writers' presentations of heroes, geniuses and national, ethnic struggles; but they also had less august needs. His growing reputation was built, not on works held in high esteem today, like *Aquis submersus* (1876) or *Carsten Curator* (1878), but on the continuing popularity of the early works and on optimistic, humorous or idyllic ones, like *Beim Vetter Christian* (1874), *Viola tricolor* (1874), and *Die Söhne des Senators* (1880). In fact, critics, readers, and friends registered disapproval whenever sordid and ugly elements seemed to call socio-political arrangements into question.

New national and international forces gradually transformed the constellation of socio-economic interests which had underlain the ideology of the new state since 1866. The alliance between Bismarck and the National Liberals ended; the appeal of laissez-faire capitalism waned; the agrarian Junkers and heavy industrialists demanded protection from international competition; socialists envisaged the overthrow of the capitalist system. Great Britain's economic dominance no longer went unchallenged; its imperial dominions aroused envy. The German Empire seemed on the threshold of a new era of world-historical power.

Now that national impotence and division were only memories,

6. See L. Pietsch, *Aus jungen und alten Tagen. Erinnerungen,* Berlin, 1904, pp. 167 ff.

7. See LL 4, pp. 881 ff.

Germany's provincial past took on a bittersweet attractiveness as people experienced the speed with which industrialization, urbanization, and bureaucratic regularization were destroying the old fabric of society and unmaking the identities of individual regions. This ambivalent amalgam of affection for a vanishing Germany and a sense of Germany's limitations informs the picture of Storm painted in the 1880s by his friend and correspondent, the dynamic young professor Erich Schmidt.[8] Echoing the view that 1870–71 was a great watershed in German history, Schmidt talked about lethargic, resigned heroes needing a touch of cold steel and of heroes with more iron in their blood clenching their fists and putting their shoulder to the wheel.[9] However, he still concentrated on Storm, the creator of still-lifes, vignettes, and genre paintings devoted to a cult of the family, of family traditions, houses, and furniture. Sharply focused, probing studies, either of the past or the present, were allegedly far from Storm's mind: "Sonst wird gern verschwiegen, was die Menschen im bürgerlichen Leben sind und was sie treiben. Ihr Beruf ist gleichgiltig. Die Fluten der Welt bespülen kaum ihr kleines Erdreich ... Die Personen leben so ganz in der Sphäre des Gemüths, daß man am Ende nicht weiß, ob sie gescheit oder stumpf, gebildet oder ungebildet sind ..."[10]

The backlash, when it came, was fierce. It is true that in the 1880s representatives of the naturalist movement recognized elements in Storm with which they had affinities, and a socialist critic, Johannes Wedde, commended his sympathy for *die kleinen Leute*.[11] On the other hand, Karl Bleibtreu described both Keller and Storm as overrated miniaturists. Storm, he wrote, could only be described as an excellent artist, a master of the novella, if one meant by that petty genre pictures. Only philistine German nightwatchmen with the small-time in their blood could acclaim such a narrow spirit as a first-rate author.[12] Such criticism had little effect on public consumption. In 1888, the year of Storm's death, readers of the magazine *Daheim* were enjoined to savor

---

8. E. Schmidt, "Theodor Storm," *Deutsche Rundschau*, vol. 24, 1880, pp. 31–56.
9. Idem, *Charakteristiken*, 2d ed., vol. 1, Berlin, 1902, p. 431.
10. Ibid., pp. 408, 417f.
11. J. Wedde, *Theodor Storm, Einige Züge zu seinem Bilde*, Hamburg, 1888, pp. 20f.
12. K. Bleibtreu, "Theodor Storm," *Die Gesellschaft*, vol. 5, 1888, p. 337.

his poetic transfigurations of "the German home," of "a woman's quiet sway in narrow confines."[13] Storm's genre paintings were commended for presenting the good old times with such sunny humor and intimate coziness. A crucial phase for writers' survival and reputation is the period after their death. The surge of immediate posthumous interest over, a deafening silence or terminal collapse often sets in. That was to be the fate of Storm's friend, the Nobel Prize winner Paul Heyse. Storm's case was more complex. He slipped from the first rank in the literary hierarchy to a lower one. Once he was dubbed a *Heimatdichter*, it confirmed critical spirits in their rejection of much of his writing. They could cite Theodor Fontane, who in the mid–1890s made *Husumerei* a byword for absorption in a narrow personal round and myopic provincialism.[14] By 1900 ethnic categories permeated official ideology, and Storm was by now mentioned in the same breath as Jensen, Frenssen, and Tim Kröger. Many of his letters, as well as crucial secondary material, like his daughter Gertrud's two-volume biography,[15] appeared during these years. The centenary of his birth in 1917 was used to enlist him in the attack on western, democratic humanitarianism.[16] Thomas Mann continued the push in his *Betrachtungen eines Unpolitischen* (1918).[17]

The balance was not redressed during the Weimar Republic, for by now Storm had long been annexed by the right. What did profoundly affect interpretations of Storm well into the postwar period was the emergence of new brands of radical conservatism. Various types of elitist, heroic tragic existentialism became the haven of those opposed to humanitarianism, democracy,

13. R. König in *Daheim*, no. 43, 1888, p. 686.
14. T. Fontane, *Von Zwanzig bis Dreißig*, Berlin, 1898. The chapter devoted to Storm had in fact first appeared in the *Deutsche Rundschau* in 1896. See also P. Goldammer, "Storms Werk und Persönlichkeit im Urteil Th. Fontanes," *Fontane Blätter*, vol. 1, 1968, pp. 247–63; idem, "Er war für den Husumer Deich, ich war für die Londonerbrücke. Fontanes Storm-Essay – und die Folgen," in *Theodor Fontane im literarischen Leben seiner Zeit. Beiträge zur Fontane-Konferenz vom 17. bis 20. Juni in Potsdam*, Berlin, 1987, pp. 379–96.
15. G. Storm, *Theodor Storm, Ein Bild seines Lebens*, 2 vols., Berlin, 1912–13.
16. See F. Düsel, ed., *Theodor Storm, Gedenkbuch zu Storms hundertstem Geburtstage*, Brunswick, 1916.
17. T. Mann, *Betrachtungen eines Unpolitischen*, Berlin, 1918, in T. M., *Politische Schriften und Reden*, ed. H. Bürgin, vol. 1, Frankfurt, 1968, pp. 86ff. Mann later made some amends. See T. M., "Theodor Storm," in *Leiden und Größe der Meister*, Berlin, 1935, pp. 181–207.

socialism, and Marxism but unwilling to advocate a return to pre-war structures. Once these groups threw in their lot with Nazism, it was no longer enough to be a worthy German burgher; one had to transcend oneself and attain a deeper grasp of reality, a more heroic, tragic concept of fate. In his *Bürgerlichkeit und Stammestum in Theodor Storms Novellendichtung*,[18] Wolfgang Kayser claimed that Storm entered this dimension after 1870. The Nazi film industry adapted *Der Schimmelreiter* and *Immensee* to its purposes.[19]

After 1945 it was relatively easy for scholars to excise Nazi jargon from their publications and issue a revised version of the tragic existentialism of the late 1920s and early 1930s. Franz Stuckert's war-time study of Storm was reprinted, unchanged, in 1952.[20] By the time his critical biography appeared in 1955,[21] the Nazi slogans had gone, but the underlying stance was little changed. Fritz Martini's criticism[22] of Fritz Böttger's East-German, Marxist study[23] epitomized Cold War attitudes. The sections on Storm in his history of German literature from 1848 to 1898 blended in well with the vogue of existentialism in Western Europe and America.[24] The latter dominated western Storm criticism in the 1960s.

In the German Democratic Republic, Böttger's study was complemented by Peter Goldammer's edition of Storm's works[25] and his selection of letters.[26] Goldammer's vision of a democratic, humanitarian Storm found greater resonance in the west in the wake of the student unrest in the later 1960s. Thus, in the early 1970s, Hartmut Vinçon[27] challenged the old "Storm-leg-

---

18. W. Kayser, *Bürgerlichkeit und Stammestum in Theodor Storms Novellendichtung*, Berlin, 1938.
19. See H. G. Kästner, ed., *Theodor Storm im Film. Die Kino- und Fernsehverfilmungen seiner Werke*, Lübeck, 1987.
20. F. Stuckert, *Der Dichter in seiner Welt*, 2d ed., Tübingen, 1952.
21. Idem, *Theodor Storm, Sein Leben und seine Welt*, Bremen, 1955.
22. F. Martini, "Deutsche Literatur in der Zeit des bürgerlichen Realismus," Ein Literaturbericht', *Deutsche Vierteljahrsschrift*, vol. 34, 1960, pp. 639f.
23. F. Böttger, *Theodor Storm in seiner Zeit*, Berlin, n.d. (1958 or 1959).
24. F. Martini, *Deutsche Literatur im bürgerlichen Realismus 1848 bis 1896*, 2d ed., Stuttgart, 1964, pp. 286–94, 630–64.
25. Theodor Storm, *Sämtliche Werke*, 4 vols., Weimar and Berlin, 1956, 1967², 1972³.
26. Theodor Storm, *Briefe*, 2 vols., Berlin and Weimar, 1972, 1984².
27. H. Vinçon, *Theodor Storm in Selbstzeugnissen und Bilddokumenten*, Reinbek, 1972.

end" in a volume in the popular Rororo series. During the later 1970s and the 1980s a more tolerant plurality of critical opinions has gradually emerged. Now, for example, Marxists and socialists are not alone in stressing "the critical Storm."[28]

28. K.-E. Laage, *Der kritische Storm*, Heide, 1989.

2

The Old Times

2.1 Schleswig and Holstein

Storm was born on 14 September 1817 in Husum, a small coastal town in the duchy of Schleswig.[1]

Schleswig and Holstein formed part of the Danish Helstat or Gesamtstaat.[2] Like other absolute rulers, the Danish monarch introduced administrative, legal, and economic reforms at the end of the eighteenth century. The challenge of the French Revolution to the principles of the old régime accelerated this process. The abolition of serfdom in 1805 was a landmark. In Copenhagen the influence of German nobles and officials was strong; the officials of the intermediate authorities for the duchies were overwhelmingly Germans, as were important royal officials, the lawyers, pastors, and teachers in the duchies. A separate Schleswig-Holstein Chancellery, itself virtually independent of the other government colleges, supervised administration, police, church, and schools. Even in financial matters, the duchies were accorded special treatment. Although a small number of educated people stressed national identities and popular culture, ethnic nationalism was a thing of the future. Nobody demanded closer links between Schleswig and Holstein as the means of safeguarding a German identity – much less that the duchies should become an autonomous state. Even more remote from people's minds was any talk of their becoming part of a unified

---

1. Hard data about Schleswig-Holstein and Husum only found their way into studies of Storm late in the day via historians and sociologists. Especially important were J. Jensen, *Nordfriesland in den geistigen und politischen Strömungen des 19.Jahrhunderts*, Neumünster, 1961, and I.E. Momsen, *Die Bevölkerung der Stadt Husum von 1769 bis 1860*, Kiel, 1969.

2. The following remarks rely heavily on W. Carr, *Schleswig-Holstein 1815–48. A Study in National Conflict*, Manchester, 1963. Other useful works are: O. Brandt, *Geistesleben und Politik in Schleswig-Holstein um die Wende des 18.Jahrhunderts*, Berlin and Leipzig, 1925; O. Klose and C. Degn, *Die Herzogtümer im Gesamtstaat 1720–1830*, Neumünster, 1960.

German state. Cosmopolitanism, not nationalism, befitted educated, cultured people. The officials, teachers, and pastors regarded the institutions of enlightened absolutism as a far safer vehicle for promoting material and moral progress than any alliance with aristocratic or radical factions. The loyalties of the vast majority of people were still very local.

The Napoleonic Era ended the duchies' prosperity. The Continental Blockade was ruinous for trade and shipping, even if individual ports profited. Thus Husum temporarily became a point of entry for British goods and an export center. Storm was later to suggest the confusions of this period in the novellas *In St. Jürgen* (1868) and *Carsten Curator* (1878). Farmers, often recently liberated serfs, were unable to pay rising land rents and repay mortgages. Having, as Napoleon's ally, suffered the full rigors of war and occupation, the Helstat went bankrupt in 1812–13. Even then, the overwhelming majority of people remained loyal to it.

The Danish royal house had never assimilated the duchies into a centralized, unitary monarchy. In Denmark itself, on the other hand, under the Kongelov or Lex Regia, the monarch's power was absolute: the nobility's powers had been curtailed; all elective bodies had been abolished; the Ämter (the primary administrative subdivisions) were firmly under royal control, while Dansk Lov provided a single, coherent legal code. In Schleswig and Holstein, in contrast, the Landtag, although not convoked since 1721, had never been abolished. Various local jurisdictions – Danish, Saxon, Roman, Löbsch, and Common Law – competed with each other. The duchies had their own coinage, their own note-issuing bank, and their own customs and excise. The fact that female issue could succeed in Denmark, but not in the duchies, was to cause grave problems.

The administrative and structural arrangements blended idiosyncratic elements that had grown up over the centuries with a superimposed absolutist administrative framework.[3] The uniform structures of a modern unitary state were still far away. Thus both duchies consisted of a number of districts or Communen divided into four "orders": firstly, counties (Ämter) and districts (Landschaften), towns, noble estates, monasteries and nunneries,

---

3. See N. Falck, *Handbuch des Schleswig-Holsteinischen Privatrechts,* 5 vols., Altona, 1825–48.

and polders built by royal concession; secondly, various types of parish (Harden in Schleswig, and Kirchspiele in Holstein), lesser districts (Landschaften and Birken); thirdly and fourthly, villages and larger villages (Flecken), and in rare cases individual houses and farms or groups of them.

In the counties or districts royal power was vested in an Amtmann or Oberbeamter who might head several authorities. Responsible for supervising judicial and administrative matters, he was commonly assisted by an Amtsverwalter or Amtsschreiber in charge of levying dues and taxes, a Hausvogt in charge of roads and transport, and a Hardesvogt or Landvogt. The former had only policing duties while the latter combined these with judicial ones. These civil servants had their assistants (Gehülfen, Officianten and Subalterne).

A different system applied in the towns, of which there were thirteen in Schleswig and fourteen in Holstein. There authority rested with the Magistrat, a body composed of one or two mayors, the Ratsverwandte/Ratsherren (in Husum: Senatoren) and the secretary. The mayor, who sometimes combined this office with that of secretary and chief of police, as he did in Husum during Storm's boyhood, headed the town council with its Deputierte; policing was entrusted to the Polizeimeister who had his own court; the town clerk or cashier was in charge of levying municipal taxes and dues.

The principle of civic autonomy had long been infringed. Thus, although in theory the Magistrat was freely elected, in actual practice – with the exception of Kiel – mayors and secretaries were royal appointees. The Magistrat's powers were limited, and even if it elected senators from the general body of town councillors, here, too, the duke's confirmation had to be sought or the authorities at least notified. Husum was not among the few towns where the Bürger elected the councillors direct: the latter elected any replacements. In Husum some councillors were elected for life, others for a limited period. The system was a far cry from democratic local government and municipal autonomy.

At the level of Helstat and duchy the same pattern was repeated. Towns, districts, and individuals did enjoy certain rights to petition the king, to submit supplications and send deputations; but there was no parliamentary, representative assembly and no constitution. The Helstat was still structured on the principle of estates, and each estate was invested with its particular privileges, freedoms and duties. Any abstract notion of "freedom" was alien to a system based on liberties specific to individuals, corporations and estates and acquired in the course of history, laid down in charters and granted by rulers. In the economic field any relaxing of the regulations governing the activity permitted to the respective estates, its organization and location was slow to take effect. Moves toward a more liberal, open society ran up against the weight of tradition.

In both Schleswig and Holstein the nobility continued to enjoy great power. The princely estate (Fürstenstand) and, below it, the knightage (Ritterschaft) both constituted "privileged estates." In 1820 there were some 300 noble estates in Schleswig; in Holstein, where they were larger, there were even more. Owning some 25 per cent of the total land in the duchies, the knights retained considerable privileges and jurisdictional rights on their estates, especially in East Holstein. In Prussia a similar system prevailed east of the Elbe. If one is to understand the passion with which men like Storm attacked the aristocratic principle, one has to grasp that they were no Don Quixotes tilting at windmills.

This society was marked by infinite gradations of rank and honor. "Honor," far from being some vague, moral entity, corresponded to precise social indicators. Strict regulations extended to far less esoteric issues than entitlement to attend the royal court or to seating arrangements at the royal table. In the later eighteenth century, as Storm's novella *Im Saal* (1848) points out, dress regulations meant that only aristocrats could sport moustaches. On every occasion, in meeting of bodies and corporations, social gatherings or processions, rigid rules determined who had precedence. "Esteem" and "dignity" derived from one's social status or office. The annual official *Königlich-Dänischer Hof- und Staats-Kalender* informed Räte, Etatsräte, Kammerherren, etc., of their precise position in terms of rank and honor.

Within the individual estates there were finely calibrated distinctions. Thus there was no "peasant," only a complex range of rural proprietors and tenants, as well as a whole hierarchy of farm workers. One has to be aware of these complexities if one is to understand fully *Der Schimmelreiter*. At the bottom of this pyramid were the "dishonorable" professions, the knacker, the executioner and the servants of the law with whom "decent," "honorable" persons would not sit or drink and whom nobody was eager to bury. This group figures in Storm's *Wie den alten Husumern der Teufel und der Henker zu schaffen gemacht* (1872) (LL 4, 244f.) in which he sought to convey society's gradual emergence from medieval conditions. As *Pole Poppenspäler* (1874) makes clear, traveling players and entertainers often fell into the "dishonorable" category. Vagabonds and beggars, criminals and prostitutes were, of course, beyond the pale of honorable society. One has to bear in mind this complicated network of rank, dignity, honor, and status if one is to appreciate how revolutionary it was for Enlightenment thinkers to champion a concept of human dignity and moral nobility, which had nothing to do with corporate, sectional status, and privilege. A huge divide separates such pre-democratic states and societies from their modern liberal-democratic counterparts. Here, in theory at least, every member of society enjoys certain inalienable, universal human rights. If social and economic injustices and inequalities still exist in the best of liberal democracies, few would justify them in terms of a God-given station. Only somebody as intimately acquainted with these structures and mentalities as Storm was could grasp the huge conditioning power of social origins and circumstances. In his fiction he would evoke the daunting external and internal barriers that frustrated anyone seeking to formulate stifled human aspirations and translate them into reality.

The church played a key role in this system.[4] Lutheranism, the religion of Denmark and the duchies, had always been a conservative force, with the principle *cuius regio, eius religio* enshrining the regents' right to determine their subjects' religion. Obedience to divinely appointed authority was high on the Lutheran agenda. In return for sanctifying the temporal authority, the state church was invested with power and privileges. Thus every subject had to be brought up in the state religion and pass through the obligatory stages of baptism, religious education at school, confirmation, church marriage, and church burial. Civil marriage did not exist; it was virtually impossible to be classed as not belonging to any church; and a secular education was unavailable. Studying theology at university was not just a means of entering the church and thus, as a pastor, occupying a key ideo-

---

4. See D.A. Jackson, "Storms Stellung zum Christentum und zur christlichen Kirche," in B. Coghlan and K.-E. Laage, eds., *Theodor Storm und das 19.Jahrhundert*, Berlin, 1989, pp. 41–99.

logical position in a still overwhelmingly illiterate society; it was also a recognized qualification for becoming a grammar-school teacher – even if teachers often entered the church because of the better salaries. Since Lutheranism was the state church, all other faiths and sects were technically heresies, and it was not until 1818 that the regulation was altered requiring Catholics and Calvinists to seek prior official permission before taking up residence in towns other than Altona, Glückstadt, Rendsburg or Friedrichstadt. For their part, Jews – referred to as *Mosaische Glaubensgenossen* – were confined to a few specific towns, like Friedrichstadt, until well into the nineteenth century. They were debarred from the civil service and all civic posts.

Rationalism had bitten deep into Lutheran orthodoxy. At the end of the eighteenth century the authorities introduced a new ritual and a new hymn book. In 1815 they added a revised version of the Lutheran Bible, the so-called Altona Bible. The resultant protest was so fierce that it had to be withdrawn. The rationalism found among many pastors and in the urban upper and middle classes contrasted with the orthodoxy of the rural population. Pietism, a form of Protestantism which reacted against "dry" orthodoxy and emphasized the need for an intense, personal experience of the workings of faith and providence, had never died out. After 1815 its emotional fervor fused with a renewed stress on the doctrines of Lutheran orthodoxy to produce a strong revivalist movement akin to those which flourished in Hamburg and other German states like Baden and Württemberg, and to which the young Conrad Ferdinand Meyer was exposed in Zürich. In 1817, in imitation of Luther's action in 1517, Claus Harms, Deacon of the Nikolaikirche in Kiel, published his ninety-five theses which epitomized the new movement. Whereas rationalist theology stressed the reasonableness and perfectibility of human beings and assumed that reason was compatible with an ethical Christianity, Harms underlined the sinfulness of human nature, demanding that sinners should repent and throw themselves on the mercy and grace of God which Jesus Christ had secured for humanity by his sacrificial death on the cross. The clash between the Enlightenment tradition and this new blend of orthodoxy and pietism was to affect Storm's entire life and work.

Rationalism in religious matters was, however, only one part of a much wider Enlightenment movement which affected the

fabric of everyday life as much as it did philosophy, politics, and
aesthetics. Its influence in the duchies lasted well into the nineteenth century. The influence of Empfindsamkeit (the literature
of Sensibility) had remained strong, too. Thus Klopstock, after
leaving Copenhagen in 1771, had gone to live in neighboring
Hamburg. Prominent members of the Hainbund, a circle of poets
based in Göttingen in the years 1772 to 1774, were Schleswig-
Holsteiners by birth and returned to live and work there. Friedrich von Stolberg became Vizehofmarschall in Eutin in 1781; J.H.
Voss joined him as headmaster of the grammar school there in
1782; H.C. Boie became headmaster in Meldorf. C.H. Esmarch,
the father of Storm's father-in-law, had been associated with this
group, and, as students in Heidelberg, Storm's father and father-
in-law had later visited Voss. Poets like Klopstock, Claudius,
Bürger, and Hölty, whom Storm was to cite and refer to in several
of his works, continued to be read here much longer than elsewhere. Thus Klopstock's poems were still on the sixth-form
syllabus in Husum in 1866. In contrast, Weimar Classicism,
Romanticism and the national-romantic literature of the anti-
Napoleon movement and the Wars of Liberation did not put
down any such deep roots. Schleswig-Holstein "made a leap, so
to speak, from the Enlightenment and anacreontic Empfindsamkeit to militancy and political enthusiasm; itself produced
crucial literary works and inspired the national enthusiasm in
the whole of Germany without – like southern or central Germany – ever having seriously come to grips with classicism, not
even the classicism of a Wieland or Schiller. It sounds strange,
but is true: the Enlightenment was followed by the Vormärz."[5]

2.2 Husum

In 1800 Husum had a population of less than 4,000.[6] Its heyday
as a port long past, it was important as an administrative, legal
and judicial center and as a market town.

---

5. See R.S. Elkar, *Junges Deutschland in polemischem Zeitalter. Das schleswig-
holsteinische Bildungsbürgertum in der ersten Hälfte des 19.Jahrhunderts*, Düsseldorf,
1979, p. 316. See also F. Kopitzsch, "Lesegesellschaften und Aufklärung in
Schleswig-Holstein," *ZSHG*, vol. 108, 1983, pp. 141–70; idem. "Aufklärung und
Schule. Zur Sozialgeschichte der Bildung und Erziehung in Norddeutschland,"
Siegener Studien, vol. 26, 1979/80, pp. 71–83; H. Lohmann and D. Lohmeier, eds.,
Aufklärung und Pietismus im dänischen Gesamtstaat 1770–1820, Neumünster, 1983.

Administratively the town was distinct from the Amt of Husum, i.e. the enclave formed by the castle and the eight surrounding parishes. The Amtmann with his secretaries and clerical assistants was complemented by a Schloß- und Zollverwalter, an Amtsverwalter and a Landvogt. Storm himself would be Landvogt from 1864 until the Prussians abolished the post in 1867. There was also a Postmaster and a Dike Inspector for the northern Marsch district. The villainous hero of the novella *Der Herr Etatsrat* (1881) is based on the Husum dike inspector in Storm's boyhood and youth, C.F. Salchow. The town administration comprised two mayors, four senators and eight town councillors. On Storm's maternal side, members of the Woldsen and Feddersen families had been senators. The Polizeimeister, with his own court, was in charge of the nightwatchman and the knacker. Until the turn of the century the town had had its own executioner. The Armenvogt or Armendiener, who was responsible for providing support to the poor, aged and needy, was in charge of the Poor Hospital and the Gasthaus zum Ritter St. Jürgen, an almshouse which figures in the novella *In St. Jürgen* (1868); he supervised the work house, the orphanage, and the almshouses, and also organized foster places for orphans in private houses – a system open to abuse and described in *Waldwinkel* (1874). At a time when a state old-age pension, state national insurance, and social security were unheard of, it fell to the towns and parishes – and to a lesser extent to the church – to look after the aged, the sick, and the orphaned, and to supplement the income of the needy by grants or loans. As rural poverty and dislocation increased, towns and parishes sought to restrict support to those born within their boundaries or who had acquired various rights after settling there. Meticulous distinctions were made between Heimatsrecht and Bürgerrecht and between Einheimische, Eingesessene, Beisassen, Schutzverwandte, and

---

6. Useful information on Husum is contained in: E. Erichsen, "Das Bettelwesen und Armenwesen in Schleswig-Holstein während der ersten Hälfte des 19.Jahrhunderts," *ZSHG*, vol. 79, 1955, pp. 217–56, and vol. 80, 1956, pp. 93–148; F. Hoffmann, *Das alte Husum zur Zeit des jungen Storm*, Kiel, 1957; idem, "Volksleben und Volkswesen im Husum vergangener Zeiten," *ZSHG*, vol. 74/75, 1951, pp. 296–319; T. Mügge, *Streifzüge in Schleswig-Holstein und im Norden der Elbe*, Frankfurt a.M., 1846; J.A. Petersen, *Wanderungen durch die Herzogthümer Schleswig, Holstein und Lauenburg*, Kiel, 1839–47, *Dritte Sektion: Nordfriesland*, 2d ed., 1844; M. Voß, *Innungen und Zünfte in Husum*, Husum, 1896.

Landeseinwohner. Any male wanting to earn his living in the town (*bürgerliche Nahrung treiben*), to acquire a house or occupy a civic office *had* to become a burgher since then he was liable to municipal taxes and duties. On the other hand, civil servants, clerics, and soldiers did not enjoy citizen-status and were exempted.[7]

The town catered for the rural hinterland, i.e. the wealthy Marschbauern on the rich, lower-lying land, and the Geestbauern on the poorer, higher land. In addition to the local markets and the Whitsun and Michaelmas markets, two cattle markets were held annually. The sailors and dockworkers were complemented by the usual range of craftsmen from dyers and tanners to coopers and smiths. Artisans were still organized in guilds, although non-guild craftsmen were beginning to establish themselves in the town. Outside the town craftsmen escaped guild regulations and undercut guild prices. Masters had their Gehilfen, i.e. journeymen and apprentices, although some trades had only Knechte and Mägde. There was a whole range of domestic servants, cooks and maids. Many inhabitants still kept animals, and with its manure heaps and its often poorly cobbled, unlit streets, Husum was far from being the gleaming tourist center it is today. One-storeyed, often thatched dwellings, like those described in *Auf der Universität* (1863) and *Ein Doppelgänger* (1887), and basement dwellings alternated with the proud patrician houses near the town center.

In terms of mechanization and industrialization, Schleswig-Holstein, like the rest of the German states, lagged behind Great Britain. In Husum, establishments classed as factories did exist, but they were tiny compared with their British counterparts. The state strictly regulated economic activity. Thus factories were not allowed in the country, and in towns and small towns (*Flecken*) tobacco and chicory factories could only be set up after obtaining a special royal privilege. In the late 1760s Friedrich Woldsen, Storm's great-grandfather, had opened a sugar refinery adjacent to the house in which Storm grew up in the 1820s. It finally folded in 1822. The Woldsens had not made the transition to modern capitalist entrepreneurs. Without rail links, good, metalled roads, and good port facilities, Husum was marooned in its own backwardness, a town reliant on a range of traders and

7. Falck, *Privatrecht*, vol. 4, pp. 152ff.

merchants, from the larger wholesalers and corn- and cattle-merchants down to the small shopkeepers and hucksters who sold textiles, ironmongery, household utensils and groceries.

The educated middle class, i.e. those whose profession required a university training, was small. It comprised civil servants, lawyers, doctors and pastors. They tended to reproduce themselves from their own ranks, and the sons of officials and pastors were massively overrepresented in higher education. As in most enlightened autocracies with underdeveloped capitalist economies, these families tended to seek status and respectability for their sons in the state service or the professions rather than in trade and commerce. They could aspire to all but the most senior posts in the administration. These, like diplomatic positions and the higher ranks in the army, remained almost exclusively the preserve of the nobility.

2.3 The Family Background

Storm's father, Johann Casimir Storm (1790–1874), was born in Westermühlen in the parish of Hohn near Rendsburg.[8] Originally Lower Saxons, the Storms had settled here as farmers and millers. Storm distinguished them from feudal serfs by referring to his grandfather as a heritable leaseholder and proprietor. Storm's grandmother, like her own mother, was a pastor's daughter. These links with the educated classes, concern about splitting up their land holdings, and possibly the fact that farmers' sons who studied avoided conscription may have all helped mold the decision to send Storm's father to the grammar school (Gelehrtenschule) in Husum and then to university rather than have him attend only the bottom class or classes. It is tempting to see his career as typifying the gradual liberalization of trades and increasing social mobility. Indeed, Storm presents the hero of the novella *Im Schloß* (1862) in this light. For ideological purposes, too, the hero's ancestors are turned into serfs. In fact, the career of Storm's father conforms to an older pattern. If the

---

8. The essential autobiographical information is contained in LL 4, pp. 415–30 and in K.-E. Laage, ed., *Theodor Storms Welt in Bildern. Eine Bildbiographie*, Heide, 1987. Storm's letter to E. Kuh of 13 August 1873 (*Briefe* 2, 632ff.) is particularly important.

absolutist state was to man the expanding administration, it had to recruit additional civil servants and integrate them within existing structures. Storm's father studied law, the entrance ticket to the administrative professions in the Helstat, and, after a brief spell in state employment, opened his own practice in Husum after 1815, setting the seal on his social ascent by marrying into the patrician Woldsen family. He may have indulged memories of his childhood, retained his dovecote, and insisted on speaking Low German at a time when High German, the language of school, church, and administration, was the hallmark of the educated, professional classes, but he had every reason to feel grateful to the Helstat. He steadily increased his property holdings and capital. Having in the 1830s first become a member and then secretary of the Schleswig Estates, he was made a member of the Dannebrogorden by the Danish king in 1840. While opposing the demands of Danish nationalists, he did not share the younger generation's desire to break with the Gesamtstaat and he retired from politics before 1848.

Although as a child and young man Storm visited the rural world of Westermühlen, its impact on his work is slight. The much-quoted episode in the novella *Im Schloß* has less to do with any concern to capture autobiographical details than with consolidating the work's ideological thrust. The hero Arnold's experience of existential loneliness, while it may parallel a boyhood experience in Westermühlen, also has nothing specifically rural or peasant about it; its significance is as part of the novella's corresponding stress on the need for human love and support. In the 1840s Storm admired the *Oberhof* section of Karl Immermann's novel *Münchhausen* (1838–39) with its depiction of the life of traditional, prosperous Wesphalian farmers. He even named his daughter Lisbeth after the heroine. In the 1850s and 1860s he recognized how important it was, if the democratic cause were to succeed, that the peasantry should have a proud sense of its own dignity and identity *vis-à-vis* aristocratic pretensions. This concern is central to *Im Schloß*. However, as he lost his confidence in the democratic potential of the *Volk,* he grew more critical of the peasantry's ignorance, superstition, and deference. The situation and mentality of farming communities in *Draußen im Heidedorf* (1872) and *Der Schimmelreiter* (1888) are not sentimentalized or held up for imitation. In the 1880s Storm's response to the problem of modernization and industrialization was not to advocate a *Blut und Boden* ideology, and although his work as a lawyer and judge brought him into close contact with farmers and their problems, he remained an urban, educated burgher. After 1870 there was also a perceptible shift in his view of his paternal ancestors. As he ruminated on the possible role of hereditary and ethnic elements in the downfall of his eldest son Hans, he adopted a family legend according to which his grandmother's father had been a hard-drinking Polish pastor with two equally hard-drinking officer brothers (LL 4, 420f.). In Storm's view, two of his father's brothers and his own son had inherited alcoholism, or at least a predisposition to it, whereas he and his father had escaped.[9]

In religious matters Storm's father was a rationalist who never attended church and did not insist on his sons attending either. Storm later praised him on this score. In contrast, he was critical of other aspects of his temperament and lifestyle. His smoking and card-playing apart, he incarnated the spirit of Protestant inner-worldly asceticism. Lacking the *joie de vivre* and elegance of the Woldsens, he was uninterested in *belles lettres*, read only legal and historical books, and disapproved of his son's literary ventures. On several occasions, Storm stressed his father's total lack of any need for beautiful surroundings or cultured contacts, seeing this as a trait inherited by his own sons.[10]

His critique of his father's cult of humorless hard work and resigned self-discipline never wavered. He singled out his fear of showing emotion and his inability to express affection to his children. These traits reinforced similar tendencies in his wife, with the result that throughout his life Storm sought in friendship and love an emotional security denied him as a child. When lent intellectual legitimacy by thinkers like Ludwig Feuerbach, this concern with alternative values prompted him to analyse the causes of such emotional impoverishment and to envisage ideologies and institutions which would enable individuals to relate to their own and others' needs in more fulfilling ways.

He criticized his father's authoritarian behavior, especially when, as a fledgling lawyer, he depended on his support in the early 1840s. During those years he began to formulate his ideal

---

9. Storm to Karl Storm, 31 October 1883; to H.v. Byern, 17 March 1886; to Otto Storm, 22 December 1883.
10. Storm to Karl Storm, 27 October 1881.

of the non-authoritarian marriage and family. Even his sense of gratitude to his father for providing financial support until his death in 1874 bred ambivalent feelings. It was humiliating to need loans and gifts, and his father's financial acumen only heightened a sense of his own inadequacies. To the end relations with his father frustrated his emotional needs.

If one looks at Storm's attitude to the maternal side of the family, a different picture emerges. The knowledge that his great-grandfather, Friedrich Woldsen (1725–1811), had been Husum's last great merchant, had owned his own fleet of ships, and had slaughtered an ox for the poor at Christmas (LL 4, 416), boosted his morale in Potsdam in the early 1850s when he was suffering from homesickness and a humiliating loss of status. But this patrician past did more than shore up his self-identity. As a child Storm lived with his parents in his widowed grandmother's patrician house in the Hohle Gasse and visited the house of great-grandmother Feddersen. Both women's stories, as well as their furniture, dresses, and jewelery introduced him to a world based on values very different from those of his father's generation. In the 1840s and early 1850s he came to regard elements of this patrician past as valuable parts of a broken tradition. They were to be integrated into a future democratic scheme of things. Not that he blinded himself to other features. In the novellas *Im Saal* (1848) and *Im Sonnenschein* (1854) the great-grandfathers are authoritarian fathers demanding that sons and daughters subordinate their aspirations to the firm's interests and to exclusive class notions. In contrast, the generation of Storm's own grandfather and grandmother exhibits a new *joie de vivre*. Qualities, which at that time had been frustrated by dominant fathers, caste prejudices and the economic vicissitudes of the Napoleonic period and which were lacking in the next generation, could, Storm hoped, be reborn in his own generation. The democratic age would incorporate such patrician values rather than be built on middle-class industriousness and self-denial. In 1874, in the novella *Beim Vetter Christian*, he could still paint an idyllic variant of what was originally a pre-revolutionary, Vormärz vision. But from the late 1860s onward he also began to emphasize negative aspects of the Woldsen legacy. As his sons seemed bent on self-destruction, he suspected that this might be the result of hereditary family traits, such as a certain effeteness, an irresponsible nonchalance, and a lack of moral fiber and will-power.[11]

Storm's presentations of his mother, Lucie Woldsen, highlight her inability to show affection to her children. Thus, in the early 1870s, he emphasized to Emil Kuh that he could not remember having ever been kissed or embraced by her.[12] Being the eldest in a family of some thirteen children, of whom six survived to adulthood, he clearly felt starved of love, and the fear that love and friendship could suddenly be withdrawn was a lifelong trauma. He sought compensatory affection from his great-grand-mother and his grandmother, but especially from Magdalena Jürgens, the fictional "Lena Wies," the unmarried daughter of a baker, with an inexhaustible stock of stories. She came to epito-mize for him the popular soul, and his affection for her influ-enced his lifelong sympathy for *die kleinen Leute*. He was also particularly attached to his younger sister Lucie (1822–29), with whom he shared a bed. Her death prompted him to write his first poem, and his preoccupation with the incest theme from his first, unpublished prose work *Celeste* (c. 1840) via the poem "Ges-chwisterblut" (1853) to the novella *Eekenhof* (1879) is probably related to this early experience. It may also explain his fascina-tion with the child, Bertha von Buchan (see p. 31).

2.4 Restoration and Reaction

In the 1800s German national feeling had grown among a small number of intellectuals, professors, and students in response to the humiliations inflicted by Napoleon. However, there was no room in the Act of the German Confederation (1815) for nation-alism, liberal constitutionalism, republicanism, or democratic notions of popular sovereignty. The provisions for representa-tive bodies in the individual German states were seldom hon-ored. Professors and students continuing to advocate a united, free, German fatherland were dismissed, relegated, or impris-oned.

Student unrest barely touched the duchies.[13] Few demurred when the Danish king joined the German Confederation as Duke

---

11. Storm to Karl Storm, 11 June 1880.
12. Storm to E. Kuh, 13 August 1873, *Briefe* 2, p. 68.
13. See L. Andresen, ed., *Kieler Studenten im Vormärz*, Kiel, 1940.

of Holstein and Lauenburg, whereas Schleswig was left outside. It is true that F.C. Dahlmann, a professor in Kiel, demanded that the duchies should be regarded as a single German state in personal union with Denmark and that any constitution granted to Holstein on the basis of the 1815 treaties should also apply to Schleswig. But his ideas found little resonance outside a small circle in Kiel. His researches had, however, unearthed a document dating from 1460 in which Christian I pledged "dat se (i.e. the duchies) bliven ewich tosamende ungedelt." The slogan was to have a great future; but nationalism was as yet a mere fledgling.

Although pre-publication censorship had not existed in the Helstat since 1770, the fear of confiscation after publication acted as a deterrent.[14] Anyone found guilty of attacking the Kongelov and disseminating hatred of and discontent with the absolutist system of government could be punished with death, exile, convict prison, ordinary prison on bread and water, and stiff fines. Pre-publication censorship was reintroduced in 1819 when the Diet of the German Confederation suppressed student and radical activities after the murder of the dramatist Kotzebue by the student Sand. The new laws automatically applied in Holstein. Here two censors were appointed; all books under twenty sheets had to obtain written consent before they could be published; unacceptable manuscripts were to be returned to the author with an explanation. From 1820 all dailies and weeklies needed a royal "privilege." If they appeared in Altona or Kiel, they had to be submitted to the censors; elsewhere, to the local police. Books had to exhibit the author's name; papers and periodicals his name and the editor's, otherwise an edition could be confiscated. In Schleswig, from 1820 onward, all printers were required to send copies of any book under twenty sheets to the Polizeimeister or police official before putting it on sale or distributing it. A book not exhibiting the name of both author and printer could be confiscated and passed on to the High Court in Gottorf. Weeklies and gazettes (*Tageblätter*) needed a "privilege" and were subject to police censorship. There were as yet no dailies (*Zeitungen*) in Schleswig at all. In both duchies it was forbidden to include

14. See Falck, *Privatrecht*, vol. 2, pp. 524 ff; A. Scharff, *Schleswig-Holstein und die Auflösung des dänischen Gesamtstaates 1830–1864/67*, Neumünster, 1975–, pp. 130ff.

political news without having obtained special permission in the original "privilege."[15]

Organized political parties were a thing of the future, and in a town like Husum political activity was non-existent. The *Husumer Wochenblatt*, whose professed purpose was to entertain, welcomed contributions of all sorts – provided they were not insulting or political. Much later Storm himself wrote of this period:

Zweimal in der Woche kam die Post von Hamburg; dann war 'Posttag' und die Kaufleute saßen bis spät in ihren Kontoren am Schreibtisch; sie brachte auch den Altonaischen Mercur, der eben aus Kleinoktav in Kleinquart Format übergegangen war; viel mochte die Zeitung damals nicht zu berichten haben; es war in der langen Friedenszeit nach Napoleons Sturz. Die Fürsten und ihre Minister regierten wieder; die in der Not versprochenen Verfassungen wurden nicht gegeben; wie aus blauem Himmel fiel dann und wann den Leuten eine Verordnung oder ein Reskript auf den Kopf; doch wurde es bei uns wohl mäßig damit gehalten. Derweilen saßen die klugen Leute am Sonntag nach der Kirche im Weinhaus, kannegießerten eine Weile und gingen dann zum Sonntagsbraten. Es war eine praktisch unpolitische Zeit; die französische Revolution und das Kaiserreich nahmen auf Jahrzehnte die Gedanken der Menschen in Anspruch; aber meistenteils nur als Vergangenheit, wie eine ungeheuere Tragödie (LL 4, 436).

In Storm's boyhood Husum had no bookshop; an outside bookseller sold books at the Michaelmas market. Only gradually did bookbinders like Delff and Thomsen begin to act as intermediaries, retailing books and providing a lending service. On the other hand, the Gelehrtenschule prided itself on its extensive library; a reading circle had been founded in 1813; in 1827 the Harmony Society was founded in order to stimulate social intercourse among the citizenry; in 1838 a Civic Association with its own library was set up to encourage economic activity; and in

15. *Verordnung wegen einer Censur für die Bücher, die nicht über zwanzig Bogen im Druck haben, so wie für die Schriften, welche heftweise oder in der Form täglicher Blätter herauskommen*, 9 November 1819, no. 120, in *Chronologische Sammlung der im Jahre 1819 ergangenen Verordnungen und Verfügungen für die Herzogthümer Schleswig und Holstein*, Kiel, 1820, p. 155; *Verfügung, die erforderlichen Maßregeln zur Verhütung des Mißbrauchs der Presse im Herzogthum Schleswig betr.*, 22 February 1820, no. 21, and *Kanzleipatent, betreffend die Herausgabe von Zeitungen, Wochen- und Tageblättern*, 4 March 1820, no. 23, in *Chronologische Sammlung 1820*, pp. 24, 29.

the 1840s Meyler, the publisher of the *Husumer Wochenblatt*, set up a reading circle.[16] But these were not fronts for organizations struggling to outwit the authorities. Looking back at this period after 1870, Storm was sure that later generations would find it difficult to imagine the absolute powers of the royal officials. But by then even the paternal absolutism of J.C. Lüders, the mayor during his boyhood, was attractive compared with the bureaucratic system imposed by the Prussians.

In economic terms, the years in which Storm grew up were difficult ones. The British Corn Laws of 1815 and the heightened competition from Hamburg and Britain in shipping and trade hit the town hard.[17] After his late grandfather's sugar refinery had folded, another operated briefly, and attempts were made to operate chicory-processing factories like the one described in *Ein Doppelgänger* (1887). Salt, tobacco, and textile factories are also recorded. Such an economy did not generate pressure for social or political changes. Husum lacked a bourgeoisie eager for the advantages of a national market, the liberalization of trades and other legal measures conducive to capitalist development. Although road links improved, port facilities were inadequate. Husum was not linked to the emergent rail network. The novella *Drüben am Markt* (1860) would capture this economic backwardness.

Whereas rising agrarian prices helped farmers, they increased poverty in the larger villages and towns. On the other hand, whenever prices fell, this affected farmers' ability to pay off debts and mortgages. Storm later stressed clients' gratitude to his father for his counsel during this time of falling land prices,[18] and the economic decline of a once-proud landed patrician family is at the core of the novella *Auf dem Staatshof* (1858). In the 1830s cereal prices and cattle exports rose. In *Auf dem Staatshof* Claus Peters is depicted as a prosperous beef exporter to Britain. But a sustained growth in the size of the population, coupled with rural dislocation, led to the pauperism and vagabondage also evoked in the novella. Fears of overpopulation led people to consider raising the age for confirmation and thus raising the

---

16. See Hoffmann, *Das alte Husum*, pp. 68, 87, 114; Petersen, *Wanderungen*, p. 40.
17. Elkar, *Junges Deutschland*, pp. 23ff.
18. Storm to E. Kuh, 13 August 1873, *Briefe* 2, p. 64.

age at which people could marry.[19] There was talk of following the example of certain German states and granting parishes wide powers to prohibit marriages. In fact, socio-economic arrangements already played a major role in deterring them. Clerks, servants, maids and cooks were still often expected to "live in" and could not acquire the means to marry and set up independently. This problem is at the heart of the novella *Abseits* (1863). The idea was mooted of forming a German-American colonial society to promote emigration,[20] and relatives and acquaintances of Storm were among those seeking a new life overseas. Throughout the pre-1870 period, the growth in the population plus the growing pressure from machines and factories made it increasingly difficult for journeymen to achieve master status or even retain their journeyman status. Masters, for their part, had to struggle to keep their heads above water and retain their independence. The novella *In St. Jürgen* (1868) explores some of these problems.

The year 1830 saw the first challenge to the settlements of 1815 on a European scale. In France the Bourbons were toppled and replaced by the "citizen king," Louis Philippe. In 1832 Britain's aristocracy defused the *haute bourgeoisie*'s frustration by extending the franchise to encompass it. In the German states, on the other hand, the authorities stamped out unrest in those states where it occurred. However, Metternich deemed it politic for member states of the German Confederation to grant the constitutions promised in 1815. They could, after all, be toothless bodies. Although Uwe Lornsen, the Sylt Landvogt, had caused a momentary stir in the duchies with his publication, *Über das Verfassungswerk in Schleswig-Holstein* (1830), it was only under pressure from the Frankfurt Diet that the Danish king in 1831 granted a constitution which provided for four provincial Estates, two for Denmark and two for the duchies. Several years elapsed before they met. Their function was purely advisory; the high property qualifications restricted the franchise to a tiny percentage of the population; sessions were closed; reports of debates could appear only in the official gazette and could be censored; members did not enjoy legal immunity.

---

19. Erichsen, *Armenwesen*, vol. 80, pp. 106f.
20. Ibid., p. 101.

A further clampdown on the press soon followed. In 1834, again in response to pressure from Metternich, the Copenhagen Chancellery instructed the relevant authorities to vet with the utmost care not only newspapers and pamphlets but also works written for young persons and ordinary folk (*das Volk*). Particular attention was to be paid to the form and tone of the language. If the thrust was pernicious, works were to be banned. No published material was to offend against decency and morality, or endanger or injure the dignity and security of the German Confederation and the individual states. Respect for the ruling houses and the maintenance of peace and internal order in Germany were, it declared, of paramount importance. No articles were to be published which aimed at establishing any other focus of unity for the German nation than the German Confederation or which advocated a democratic transformation of federal arrangements. All works were forbidden which attacked the validity of the present constitutional provisions or sought to overthrow the "legal and lawful" status quo. Offending books from the rest of Germany or Paris were banned.[21]

More was to follow. In 1835 the Federal Diet banned the writings of the so-called Young Germans, Heinrich Heine, Karl Gutzkow, Ludwig Wienbarg, Heinrich Laube, and Theodor Mundt as unchristian and blasphemous, declaring that they trampled underfoot all morality, modesty, and decency. An official Danish report declared that these works undermined all previous notions of Christianity, authority, property, and marriage. They would, it went on, spread baneful anarchy in all social arrangements and pave the way for a general revolution.[22] In Kiel student fraternities were vetted and banned. The Husum student and later friend of Storm, C.U. Beccau, was among those not allowed to take their exams because of belonging to a fraternity.

In 1835 Storm was completing his studies at the Husum Gelehrtenschule and about to move to the Katharineum Gymnasium in Lübeck. He was eighteen on 14 September 1835.

---

21. Scharff, *Schleswig-Holstein und die Auflösung*, p. 135.
22. Ibid., p. 142.

2.5 Storm's Education

In 1814, regulations[23] came into force which affected the whole school system. They required parents to send their children to school at the age of six or seven. Many were, however, deterred by poverty or because the children were needed to work on the land or in cottage industries. Schools were divided into three categories: the Gelehrtenschulen (grammar schools) for those intending to study at university; the Bürgerschulen, divided into Aufsichts-, Elementar- and Hauptschulen, whose brief was to produce, not *Gelehrte*, but good, skilled citizens and righteous Christians; and Landschulen. Schools were subject to supervision by the church, and the Schulkollegium or Board of Governors typically included either the superintendent, the provost, or the pastor. All would-be teachers in Bürgerschulen had to be vetted by the provost and then introduced by him. He and the Amtmann decided on appointments and dismissals. The School inspectors themselves were often clerics. Acts of worship played an important part in the weekly timetable, with attendance at divine service and catechism compulsory until confirmation. All confirmed pupils had to attend communion at least once a year with the teachers, and the latter were expected to set a good example by attending church. In country schools the teacher was expected to take the pupils through the sermon on Mondays.[24]

The authorities made efforts to keep liberal-democratic and German-national aspirations out of all schools. Respect for law and order, obedience and self-fulfillment within the limits of one's estate were the virtues enjoined on pupils. Any reforms had to come from above. Rektor J.B. Friese in Kiel, who had been headmaster in Husum, and in 1831 likened developments in 1813–1815 to a "non too fragrant ferment," demanded that pupils should be protected from all revolutionary ideas. No school was to tolerate

23. *Allgemeine Schulordnung 1814*, 24 August, no. 76, in *Repertorium der für die Herzogthümer Schleswig und Holstein erlassenen Verordnungen und Verfügungen*, vol. 1, *Systematische Übersicht der allgemeinen Verordnungen*, Kiel, 1840, pp. 112ff. See also E. Erichsen and H. Sellschopp, *Die allgemeine Schulordnung für die Herzogthümer Schleswig und Holstein vom 24. August, 1814*; F. Kopitzsch, ed., *Erziehungs- und Bildungsgeschichte Schleswig-Holsteins von der Aufklärung bis zum Kaiserreich*, Neumünster, 1981.

24. The standard and most comprehensive general study of the whole field of education is still F. Paulsen, *Geschichte des gelehrten Unterrichts auf den deutschen Schulen und Universitäten vom Ausgang des Mittelalters bis zur Gegenwart*, 2 vols., Berlin and Leipzig, 1919–21.

a spirit of reform since this would destroy venerable antiquities and endanger the status quo.[25]

The gap yawned wide both between town and rural schools and, in the towns themselves, between the various types of school. As late as 1769 Husum enjoyed only a Gelehrtenschule or grammar school, a Poor School and various other small private nursery schools (Winkel-, Warte- or Klippschulen). The first Bürgerschule consisted of a reading and writing class attached to the grammar school – a system described in *Pole Poppenspäler* (1874). In Storm's childhood this system was modernized by creating two primary schools to feed two single-sex Hauptschulen. His own formal education began at the age of four in a Klippschule run by an old Hamburg woman. He was later critical of the corporal punishment she employed and the humiliating system of dunces' caps (LL 4, 427f.).

At the age of nine he was sent to the grammar school, which had been founded in 1527 by the reformer Hermann Tast. There were ten such schools in the duchies. Their function was to feed into Kiel University and provide the state with the law and theology students needed to man the administration, the church and the higher reaches of the teaching profession. A select number of grammar schools known as Gymnasien acted as half-way houses between school and university. The Mommsen brothers attended such a school in Altona, and the Katharineum in Lübeck, which Storm attended from 1835 to 1837, was of this type. Girls were excluded from higher state education, and of the male population itself only a small percentage enjoyed the privilege of a grammar-school education. Farmers' and artisans' sons rarely progressed beyond the lowest class or classes. In contrast, the sons of academically educated fathers were massively over-represented. If one considers the sectional identities and cultures, the social divisions produced and reproduced in Britain by the division of schools into elementary and grammar schools from 1871 to 1945 and nowadays into private ("public") schools, grammar schools and comprehensives, one can form some idea of the impact of this system. The *Gelehrte(n)* or *Gebildete(n)*, as they tended to call themselves, had a great sense of their status. The label *ein Gebildeter* was not based on conforming as an individual to some vague notion of what constituted a cultured, educated

25. Elkar, *Junges Deutschland*, p. 193.

person: it denoted that one belonged to the *Stand* or estate of educated people. This *Bildung* – grammar school and university education supplemented by continuing personal and social self-cultivation – served the educated middle class as a means of establishing its identity *vis-à-vis* the aristocracy. The latter, for its part, tended to employ private tutors well into the century. Storm's later friend in Heiligenstadt, the Landrat Alexander von Wussow, did so in the 1860s, and the hero of *Im Schloß* (1862) is a middle-class tutor in an aristocratic family. At university noble students formed exclusive corps as opposed to the normal frater-nities.

Storm's sense of belonging to the *Stand der Gebildeten,* together with the aesthetic, linguistic, and ideological values acquired in the course of classical education, had far-reaching effects on his life and work. His later evocations of his own schooldays may highlight certain deficiencies but their main purpose is to draw favorable comparisons between the old system and that imposed by the Prussians after 1866. German language and literature, history, and geography lagged behind Latin, Greek, and religion on the syllabus. Modern languages, science, and mathematics received even less attention. While grammar school scholars were expected to be able to translate from and into Danish and from French into German, oral proficiency in Danish was left to pri-vate tuition, as were English and Italian. The emphasis was on proficiency in the *gelehrte Sprachen,* i.e. Latin, Greek, and – in the case of future theology students – Hebrew. Although in 1848 attempts would be made to move someway toward a Realgym-nasium, i.e. one emphasising modern languages and, later, the sciences, the champions of the old ideal remained undeterred. In 1867, Heinrich Keck, who became headmaster in Husum after 1870, still stressed that the syllabus had to be centered on clas-sical antiquity.[26] This classical education imparted distinctive norms and principles; it encouraged particular ways of conceiv-ing socio-political, ethical, and religious issues. It also transmit-ted definite views about literature's nature and function. The individual genres' respective status in the aesthetic hierarchy, the registers of language, the treatment befitting particular sub-jects – these were all matters at the heart of Latin and Greek

26. H. Keck, *Ueber das Wesen der Bildung und den Anteil des Gymnasiums an derselben,* Schleswig, 1867.

lessons. They also governed the treatment of German language and literature. Modern German poets like Heine may have played no part in the curriculum; a teenager like Storm thrilled to them outside school. But poets like Heine were part of the classical tradition, and readers appreciated them through classically trained eyes and ears.

Instruction in Latin and Greek followed a rigid scheme.[27] One progressed from spelling, simple grammar, and syntax to essay-writing – conceived of as a means of practicing more complex syntax – to declamation and rhetoric. In the *Prima*, pupils were encouraged to express themselves, but only on standard topics and in prescribed ways. German was taught according to the same principles. On completing his grammar-school education, the *Primaner* gave a public address in Latin or German on a chosen subject. Storm performed twice: once on the standard topic, "The decline of states," and once, to the tolerant incomprehension of the headmaster, in verse, on "Mattathias, the Liberator of the Jews" (LL 4, 165ff.). Later he would attack the continuing influence of the rhetorical tradition on lyric poetry (see p. 74), and, in *Der Herr Etatsrat* (1881), would poke savage irony at the bombast encouraged by it in Wilheiminian Germany.

The classical tradition did not emphasize "genius," inspiration, and unique creative processes; nor did it confine literature to any triad of epic, drama, and lyric. Paradoxically, despite its rigid prescriptions and conventions, it allowed a greater range of possibilities than would the Poetic-Realist aesthetic after 1848. It only stipulated that the genre and treatment chosen should be appropriate to the subject.

27. Elkar, *Junges Deutschland*, pp. 196ff.

3

The Road to Revolution

3.1 University Years

Storm began studying law in Kiel in 1837, spent a short spell in
Berlin, and, having returned to Kiel in 1839, completed his studies there in 1842.

For the whole of that time he was in love with Bertha von
Buchan (1826–79) whom he first got to know as a ten-year-old in
Hamburg in 1836.[1] Although she was still at school and uncon-
firmed, he wanted to get engaged to her in 1841. The episode
illustrates his immaturity and insecurity. Repressed sexual longings loomed large in his fantasies. His first known prose work,
the "fantasy" *Celeste* (LL 4, 265ff.) revolves around a young man
and a young woman shipwrecked on an island. To the girl's
dismay the hero offers to be her brother, and there is much play
on "brother," "sister," *Weib,* "virgin." As he watches over her in
a grotto during the night, his sexual desires increase when she
clings to him in fear of the howling hyenas. Although their
howling dies away, his own predatory passions threaten to
overwhelm him. The fantasy ends with him waking from his
dream. Storm continued to send Bertha copies of his works for
years to come. As a student, Storm sowed his wild oats and is
therefore to be regarded as a typical instance of the nineteenth-
century middle-class male torn between pure, platonic love of
the beloved and satisfaction of sexual needs with lower-class
girls. Closing that gap would be a major concern in his writing.

His first impression of student life in 1837 had been negative.
He had divided students into two categories: the drinking,
duelling fraternity students with their girlfriends, and those
immersed in their studies and oblivious to all else (LL 4, 495).
This hostility pervades *Immensee* (1849), *Auf der Universität*
(1863), and *Der Herr Etatsrat* (1881). He would consistently view

---

1. See E.O. Wooley, "Storm and Bertha von Buchan," in: E.W., *Studies in Theodor Storm*, Bloomington, 1942, pp. 11–46.

31

universities in terms of their place in the scheme of social repro-
duction and concentrate on analyzing the values they fostered.
During his second period of study in Kiel (1839–42), as a close
friend of Theodor Mommsen and a member of the so-called
"clique," Storm enjoyed an intellectual stimulus which his law
studies did not afford him.[2] Having in Lübeck read Goethe, Heine,
and Eichendorff, he now added Mörike to his lyric mentors. He
also read works by the Young Germans, a loose group of progressive writers whose heyday in the early 1830s had been cut
short by the ban imposed on their writings in 1835. They were
followed after 1840 by a group of writers and thinkers espousing
left-Hegelian categories and committed to radical change. The
latter claimed that the future lay with philosophy since it possessed the dialectical, "scientific" key to history. Scholars like
D.F. Strauss, L. Feuerbach, and B. Bauer had supposedly revealed
the true nature of religion. Having progressed from a religious
childhood to a literary youth, humanity was entering its philosophic maturity. Philosophy itself would move from a contem-
plative, analytic role to an active one.

Literary repercussions were inevitable. Thus Goethe was
denounced as olympian, "indifferent," and aloof from politics.
He had allegedly cultivated elitist notions of art and culture. In
the search for literary models, Ludwig Börne with his ethical,
radical commitment was a much more congenial figure to the
group than Heinrich Heine with his supposed "immorality" and
lack of seriousness. The Young Germans were considered a frivo-
lous, immoral coterie whose works were unscientific and divorced
from the "people." It became a badge of shame to be considered
steeped in the salon culture of the *ancien régime.* Instead, art was
to communicate the new philosophical insights and stimulate
action. Writers had to address the *Volk*; the lyric poet had to
"take sides" *(Partei ergreifen).*[3]

Mommsen, Storm's intellectual mentor at the time, took a more
balanced view of the Young Germans. He had read widely in
their works[4] and probably introduced Storm to them.[5] Despite

---

2. See L. Wickert, *Theodor Mommsen*, vol. 1, pp. 133ff.

3. J. Hermand's two Reclam vols., *Das Junge Deutschland* (1966) and *Der deutsche
Vormärz* (1967) offer a good first introduction to the subject. J. Sammons offers
insight into Young German preoccupations in his *Six Essays on the Young German
Novel*, Chapel Hill, 1972.

4. See Wickert, *Mommsen*, pp. 73ff.

the attacks made on the Young Germans by post-1840 *Vormärz* writers, their positions often overlapped. They were, after all, both responding to the same structures and mentalities which frustrated the aspirations of young middle-class males; and they were both conscious of developments in other Western-European countries. Many of their key ideas and positions return in Storm's work: the juxtaposition of the old and new times; the evocation of Germany's backwardness; the emphasis on modernity and the need for literature to broach controversial social, religious, and ethical issues; the Saint-Simonian, positive attitudes to sex.

Theodor Mommsen, his brother Tycho, and Storm all had literary ambitions. They decided, therefore, to embark on a joint literary venture, *Das Liederbuch dreier Freunde* (1843).[6] Storm's callow contributions show him bent on becoming an *Erotiker*, or love poet. In contrast, the altogether more sophisticated Theodor Mommsen indulged in literary polemic and set out his views on political poetry. Faced by poets as different as Mörike, Herwegh, and Freiligrath, Mommsen refused to adopt an exclusive stance. The sonnet "Eduard Mörike" illustrates his awareness of the contrast between centers of trade and commerce like Hamburg and the Elbe, on the one hand, and the secluded valleys of Swabia, on the other.[7] But while recognizing that literature was responding to these developments, he was not prepared to follow Gervinus and declare that Germans should turn to "prose," i.e. the practical matters which would supposedly bring about a united, free Germany.

> In dieser Zeit ist's nicht genug, wenn uns ein Lied geraten;
> Politisch soll der Dichter sein, das heißt man Liedertaten.
> Es ist die Welt doch weit genug und viel kann drinne wohnen,
> Und sind doch nicht bloß Pressen drin und Konstituzionen.

---

5. Information on which works Storm read is scarce. We do know that he went to a performance of Gutzkow's *Zopf und Schwert* and that he read Willkomm's *Die Europamüden*, but that is probably only the tip of the iceberg. See Storm to Constanze Esmarch, 15 November 1845 and September 1846(?): "Europamüde sind die Menschen, denen die Hohlheit und Lügenhaftigkeit unsrer gesellschaftlichen Zustände zu wieder ist, und die sich aus dem gebildeten Europa heraus nach Urzuständen sehnen oder einfach nach rücksichtsloser Wahrheit."

6. Theodor Mommsen, Tycho Mommsen, T. Storm, *Liederbuch dreier Freunde*, Kiel, 1843.

7. "Eduard Mörike," ibid., p. 157.

Man liebt und phantasiert so fort, und das ist keine Schande;
Im Herzen hat gar Vieles Raum noch bei dem Vaterlande.[8]

Despite praising – and imitating – Herwegh's *Lieder eines Lebendigen*, Mommsen had doubts, first, about the political poets'
assumption that state and society were in a pre-revolutionary
situation and, secondly, about the usefulness in practical terms
of their enthusiasm and rhetoric. In his view, political poets could
only play a meaningful role if the time was ripe and if they had
a genuine grasp of politics. Mommsen's ideas influenced Storm.
Even at times when he was actively involved in politics, Storm
would never lose the sense that, compared with Mommsen or
even Fontane, he was "unpolitical" and had best preface any
political opinion with that disclaimer.[9] He would keep away from
political poetry except at junctures when it did, indeed, seem
timely.

3.2 Radicalization

Storm returned to Husum in October 1842 and remained there
until 1853. It is tempting to assume that in this "backwater" he
was divorced from the socio-economic and ideological tensions
of the 1840s. Yet here, paradoxically, he was at least as likely to
be receptive to critical ideas as he would have been had he enjoyed
the relative freedom of a metropolis. In fact, these years gave
him an intimate insight into provincial life. As a notable, he had
access to the highest reaches of society, while as a lawyer, he
encountered a wide cross-section of people and problems. The
distinctive feature of his attitude toward provincial life is that it
blends affection with criticism.

A poem like "Die Jungen" (1843) may be inspired by typical
Vormärz sentiments:

Sieh, wie vor den alten Kanzlern und Räten
Die Leute sich bücken, gehorsamst betreten!
Pfui, wie sie den grämlichen Alten hofieren!
Will uns denn niemand respektieren? –

8. "Exodus," ibid., pp. 168f.
9. E.g. Storm to Fontane, 15 June 1853, *Storm-Fontane*, p. 36.

Das Haupt entblößt! Respekt, ihr Leut'!
Wir sind die Kanzler der werdenden Zeit. (LL 1, 223)

But it was only gradually that Storm's definition of the impending struggle gained clarity and substance. Although a member of
the committee organizing the great choral festival held in Bred-
stedt in 1844 as one of a series of mass concerts to popularize the
Schleswig-Holstein cause, he attended in a musical capacity and
was sceptical of the speakers' rhetoric, of the way in which they
catechized the listening farmers from the platform, and of their
illusions about their audience's level of political consciousness.[10]
By 1845 he was refusing to betray his convictions by servilely
lauding the Danish king on his visit to Husum. In 1846 German-
national feeling in the duchies was inflamed by the publication
of the Danish king's Open Letter declaring that the same rights
of succession would in future obtain in the duchies as in Denmark. Storm felt impelled to write a political poem. Although at
this stage he got no further than the first three stanzas (see LL
1, 818), the poem's emphasis on the natural resurrection of spring
and its vision of a revitalizing political springtime put it firmly
in the Vormärz tradition. By 1847 he was writing poems highly
critical of the alliance between Throne and Altar ("Gesegnete
Mahlzeit"), of the domination of politics and policy-making by
the established powers ("Kirschen") and of the aristocratic principle ("Zwiesprach," "Beim Tanz," and "Halbe Arbeit"). The latter
runs:

Leibeigenschaft war nur der Rumpf;
Nur halb erlegte man den Drachen,
Der noch aus dem feudalen Sumpf
Zu uns herüber reckt den Rachen.
Behalten blieb es bessern Tagen,
Das freche Haupt herabzuschlagen.
(LL 1, 252)

Only "Gesegnete Mahlzeit" could be published. By this time,
too, he was also highly critical of the church and Christianity.
What had prompted this development?

---

10. Storm to Constanze, 11 June 1844, *Briefe* 1, pp. 65f.

On his return to Husum, Storm, who had incurred gambling debts in Kiel, found his father insisting on self-discipline, respectability, and thrift. He had no alternative but to submit. However, he attached great importance to enjoying an elegant, cultured life-style and, having become engaged to his cousin, Constanze Esmarch, in 1844, resented the thought of having to embark on married life in cramping circumstances. Overcoming the material – as well as the cultural and ethical – constraints of provincial life become a key element in his vision of the full life. This aspiration informs works like *Späte Rosen* (1859) or *Von Jenseit des Meeres* (1865).

But his attitude toward other aspects of provincial life was much more ambivalent. Thus, in the early 1840s, his stance *vis-à-vis* patrician and aristocratic behavior was by no means as critical as it would be in the later novellas *Drüben am Markt* (1860) and *Auf der Universität* (1863). The aristocratic Amtmann residing in the castle represented the nub of royal power and the center of social and cultural life. The mayors, the patrician families and senators were lesser centers without in any way challenging this pre-eminence. The sons and daughters of the notables were groomed in the social skills at dancing classes. Elegant balls, with an entrance fee to cover the cost of the music and illuminations, were held at the Town Hall. Apprentices were sometimes excluded from them, and separate dances were organized for journeymen.[11] Storm took a full part in the social round of Husum's patrician and well-to-do families with their dinner dances and card-playing, helping to organize balls at the castle and writing and acting in pantomimes and masquerades. But he also tried to inject a new modern spirit into social activities by promoting chamber music and founding a choral society which performed both classical works and works by modern composers like Mendelssohn and Schumann. He also sought to extend the range of the Harmony Society's library. Modest though they were, these were attempts to promote modern ideas and modern sensibility.

Yet, whereas Constanze was reluctant to have dealings with people who were condescending and patronizing, Storm was flattered to consort with aristocrat families like that of the mayor,

11. See Hoffmann, *Das alte Husum,* pp. 79f., 101.

von Kaup. In the poem "Aus Großkrähwinkel. Die Beamten-
töchter" (later part of "Vom Staatskalender"), which was based
on the behavior of Amtsverwalter Setzer's daughters toward those
of Senator Jensen, he satirized the airs adopted toward a merchant's daughter by the daughters of a civil servant who has
acquired aristocratic rank and privileges; but he was prone to
agree with his aspiring friend, the Amtssekretär Hartmuth Brinkmann, and distinguish between superior/aristocratic (*vornehm*)
natures and vulgar/common ones. Such distinctions had, he
claimed, nothing to do with social rank. He did, however, add:
". . . obgleich oft jenes Gefühl der vornehmern Persönlichkeit
ziemlich hohl ist und lediglich auf dem Bewußtsein des höhern
Ranges oder Reichthums oder Umgangs mit Höheren beruht."[12]
How true this was soon became apparent when he found that
Sophie Setzer, with whom his cousin Ernst Esmarch was in love,
was prepared, as he put it, to sell her young body to a repulsive
fellow, Heinrich Tetens.[13] Almost thirty years her senior, Tetens'
asset was his rank of Counsellor of Justice (Justizrat). Sophie's
sister Mathilde was married off in similar fashion to the Syndic
of Kiel, Friedrich Witte. Storm's letters brim over with revulsion
at this "profanation of love." Brinkman, himself in love with
Laura Setzer, realized that he was viewed as a less than desirable
brother- and son-in-law. Storm's part in stiffening his resolve
and intriguing on the lovers' behalf incurred Setzer's displeasure. It is worth dwelling on the incident because it illustrates
how immediate and personal were the forms taken in these circles
by the tensions between the old and the new times.

What turned many young middle-class professionals and
students into revolutionaries in 1848 was frustration with aristocratic privileges and exclusiveness and with the older generation's
dominance in virtually all areas. The works of the Young Germans and Vormärz writers fuelled this frustration at being
dominated by "old men," old ideologies, and old institutions.
"Modern" and "young" were key slogans. Today it may not seem
revolutionary to challenge parental authority and vindicate the
rights of love; in fact these young men were disturbing one of
the cornerstones of a society which still thought in terms of
separate estates, rank and honor. The concerns which had fuelled

---

12. Storm to Constanze, 4 May 1846. See *Storm-Brinkmann*, p. 12
13. Storm to Constanze, 17 May 1846, ibid., pp. 13f.

Storm and Stress dramas and the "middle-class tragedy" of the eighteenth century were still on the agenda precisely because state and society had changed so little in the interim. Henceforth the issue of aristocrats refusing to regard commoners as potential sons- or brothers-in-law was to be central to Storm's rejection of the aristocratic principle. *Im Schloß* (1862), *Aquis submersus* (1876), and *Zur Chronik von Grieshuus* (1884/85) all return to the theme.

His denunciation of such marriages of convenience for conflicting with modern notions of the sanctity and chastity of body and soul would not have been so violent had he not been convinced that love was the key to true human happiness. In April 1844 he wrote to Constanze: ". . . ist denn die Liebe nicht eine göttliche Offenbarung? bist du vorher so gewesen, wie jetzt? hast du je das gefühlt und gewußt? hast du es denn aber gelernt? kams dir nicht auf einmal wie vom Himmel herab? glaub es immer, Liebe ist unmittelbare Gottheit, Liebe ist Andacht, ja Liebe ist schon Religion."[14] Increasingly he judged institutions and ideologies in terms of whether they promoted, prevented, or perverted this ideal.

Once one asks whether individual writers or thinkers pointed Storm in this direction, one is faced by a frustrating situation. Although the consensus nowadays is that Storm's work is decidely Feuerbachian, Storm never once mentions the philosopher Ludwig Feuerbach (1804–72), and nobody has been able to adduce hard evidence that he definitely read his works – much less, which.[15] Did he, one asks, encounter Feuerbach's ideas at second or third hand? And when? Until recently Storm was deemed such a provincial *ingénu* that he could only have taken cognizance of modern philosophical ideas after 1848. That view no longer holds, and although, for example, it was not until 1848 that Gottfried Keller responded to his ideas, Feuerbach had a major impact in the early 1840s. By the mid-1840s Storm was adopting humanitarian positions and propounding a cult of love which are Feuerbachian. There is no marked or sudden change after 1848.

14. Storm to Constanze, 24–28 April 1844.
15. See P. Westra, "Theodor Storm en Ludwig Feuerbach," *De Gids,* vol. 113, 1950, pp. 268–87; M. Bassler, "Die ins Haus heimgeholte Transzendenz. Theodor Storms Liebesauffassung vor dem Hintergrund der Philosophie Ludwig Feuerbachs," *STSG,* 36, 1987, pp. 43–60.

Feuerbach's philosophy was so compelling because it was so simple and promised such a short, straight road to an earthly paradise. He argued that religion originated in human needs and aspirations and that Christianity could be divided into positive and negative elements. The positive element was the universal human need for love, sympathy, and support, the negative the metaphysics and theological dogmas fabricated by the church. These perverted human aspirations and perpetuated human alienation. Human beings had projected supreme human qualities on to non-existent deities. They now had to repossess their true humanity from these phantasmagoria. The dictum "God is love" had to be turned into "Love is divine." According to Feuerbach, incomplete, individual human beings could become whole in the sexual and spiritual oneness achievable in marriage. Human beings were social beings dependent on their fellows for love, care and support, and the quality of their lives depended on the relations obtaining in the family, in society, and in the state. Only democratic structures with strong communitarian and social elements could provide an ideal framework. Storm's concept of alienation, his critique of Christianity, and his cult of human love are very much in the Feuerbachian mold. Yet these ideas only had such a deep and lasting effect on him because they corresponded to his own fundamental needs. To somebody craving love and security, they held out the promise of fulfillment. His novellas would return again and again to the need for individuals to recognize their true human needs and seek to fulfill them, whatever the contrary pressures.

In Storm's letters to his fiancée, communication emerges as a prime value. In a Christian, theist scheme the revealed Word of God, prayer, and confession are of paramount importance. In contrast, once relations between human beings replace a supposedly illusory relationship between believer and deity, the quality of communication, especially between partners and spouses, moves center stage. Storm became obsessed with the issue. Thus he castigated Constanze for letters which were sloppily formulated, used jargon, contained spelling mistakes, were short or only dealt with practical, "trivial" matters, denouncing them as inimical to communication and unworthy of an educated person.[16] Letters which did not assure him about the ineffable nature of their love

---

16. E.g. 3–4 May 1845, 26 December 1845.

and her eternal devotion, or which were simply slow in arriving plunged him into doubts about her love in particular and love in general.[17] This pattern remained constant until her death in 1865; thereafter Storm transferred his obsessions to his dealings with his sons.

This cult of love was egocentric and male-oriented. He assumed that a bride and wife would find fulfillment in devoting herself to her lover and husband. But in order to be an ideal intellectual companion and soul-mate, she needed opportunities to acquire *Bildung*. Therefore Storm demanded that his father-in-law should allow Constanze more time off from acquiring domestic skills in order to read German literature, especially Goethe. She was not, however, to read corrupting French novels like those of Eugène Sue which he himself was reading![18] He was also far too insecure to want to challenge existing gender roles and advocate real independence for women. Thus he was horrified by the idea that Constanze could have an existence outside the home and outside his orbit by helping at the local nursery school. Only women without a home and without love, he declared, ran public institutions: charitable work outside the home was an unfeminine folly, a Schleswig-Holstein plague, a piece of modern nonsense.[19] And yet, compared with his parents' marriage, Storm's own ideal was undoubtedly progressive:

> Mein Geist is zu leichtbeweglich, zu feurig, um mit solchen Frauen leben zu können. Dazu kommen noch die ewigen Haushaltungsgespräche, die zur guten Haushaltungsführung ganz überflüßig sind; denn Mutter ist gar nicht einmal sparsam; dann die Verdrießlichkeit, wenn man einmal bemerkt, daß die Gurcken verdorben sind – daß Vater nicht bei seiner Frau sein mag, ist begreiflich; denn Mutter ist wirklich bis zum Exceß langweilig, vielleicht hat er (his father) sie selbst dazu gemacht, – Nein Dange das ist nichts solche Ehe; Gott schütz uns davor![20]

Storm stressed that they would share everything, including money, and that he would not dole out housekeeping money to her like a gift or alms: "Du hast ja gleiches Recht daran; es ist ja

---

17. E.g. 24 June 1846.
18. Storm to E. Esmarch, between November 1844 and January 1845, *Storm-Esmarch*, p. 18; Storm to Constanze, 23 June 1846.
19. Storm to Constanze, 3 September 1845.
20. Storm to Constanze, n.d.

nicht mehr meins wie deins . . ."[21] In order to appreciate the progressive elements in this ideal, one has to remember that at this time the husband was the legal head of the family and that the wife was on a par with the children or the servants. A husband had a claim on a wife's help, support and service; he could demand her compliance and obedience; he could punish her; he could represent her in court. In contrast, she could neither represent herself nor engage somebody to do so against her husband's wishes. A wife's *Beruf* was to run the household. Yet even this was only a commission entrusted to her by her husband. In areas where Saxon Law prevailed, the husband became the marital guardian of all his wife's movable and immovable assets, could enjoy the income from them and could even sell the former without her consent. The legal position of a father *vis-à-vis* his children was no more progressive. He had complete power over them, had the right to respect and obedience, could choose their future professions and castigate them – provided he did not occasion them serious injury.[22]

Storm's religion of love involved him in an ever widening conflict with the establishment. When his father and father-in-law demanded that he and Constanze should live apart until their marriage and that the marriage should be delayed for two years until his practice was on a sound footing. Storm denounced this as philistinism, an inability to see the essence of things for petty considerations of convention.[23] But he had to submit. Tensions grew to the point that he described his father as "ein gar zu rücksichtslos egoistischer Mann" who dominated conversation and made all his son's interests seem "heresies": Mit einem Wort, im Herzensgrunde sind wir uns gegenseitig so recht durch und durch zuwider. Daß ich mich in der Nähe eines solchen Mannes, zumal ich von ihm abhänge und mich ihm daher unterordnen muß, unbehaglich fühle, ja daß ich nie rein gestimmt sein konnte, ist leicht begreiflich.[24]

As a self-styled modern man convinced of the primacy of love, Storm had had sexual intercourse with Constanze early in their

---

21. Storm to Constanze, 20 June 1846.
22. Falck, *Privatrecht*, vol. 4, 392ff.
23. Storm to Constanze, before 19 April 1844: "Welche Philister – das heißt Leute, die das Wesen der Dinge vor kleinen Conventionssachen nicht sehen – sind doch eigentlich unsere Eltern!"
24. Storm to Constanze, n.d.

relationship and commended her for this:"... so will ich dir es wiederholen, daß ich dich unbeschreiblich liebe, daß ich dich verehre wegen deiner großen Hingebung und dich deshalb höher achte und schätze, als wenn du dich mir in allem zimperlich entzogen hättest, bis das Wort des Priesters zu allem recht-fertigte."[25] Enthusiastically he quoted from Wilhelm Heinse's novel *Ardinghello* (1787), endorsing its stress on the duty of individuals "von reiner Empfindung und klarem Begriff" to pur-sue their happiness even when outwardly conforming to the rules and conventions obeyed by the great mass of people.[26] Fortunately for the quality and subtlety of his fiction, Storm did not subsequently write crude *pièces à thèse* or present utopian solutions. Instead he portrayed individuals entangled in conflict-ing aspirations and pressures. His own experiences also soon cured him of any illusions about achieving happiness by leading a double life.

Storm's rejection of Christianity and his affirmation of the divinity of love led him to criticize the Church's involvement in the regulation of love, sex, and marriage. He rejected its claim to legalize and hallow a relationship which was already "divine."[27] Although church marriage was mandatory, he took the radical step of refusing to comply. He was adamant that he would not tolerate this "barbaric" practice of exposing to public view what was an intensely personal, intimate matter.[28] Making use of an option not usually available in such cases, he thus paid the necessary fee to obtain a special concession permitting a *Haus-copulation*. He and Constanze were married, by a pastor, in her father's house, Segeberg townhall. None of the Storms attended. In 1866 he would similarly insist on marrying Doris Jensen, not in the church in Hattstet but in the vicarage. No pastor officiated at Constanze's funeral in 1865, and he stipulated that none should officiate at his own. Paradoxically, confronting the system in this way was something which he could not have done in a literary work. Had he done so, he would have faced criminal charges for undermining religion and morality.

From the mid-1840s onward Storm was convinced that a true marriage had to be built on sex and passion. If it was to perform

25. Storm to Constanze, 21 April 1844.
26. Storm to Constanze, 26 December 1845. *Briefe* 1, pp. 86ff.
27. Storm to Constanze, 19 July 1846.
28. Storm to Constanze, 29 August 1846.

its full humanizing function, sex had to be a genuinely shared experience. But contemporary society also shaped Storm's feelings in more problematic ways. Thus he feared that a woman who had yielded to male advances once might do so again; Constanze was to keep predatory males at bay and not allow them the slightest familiarity. He could not endure the thought of any other male touching, dancing with, or even just looking at her.[29] If his letters are right about the morals of married men in Husum, his fears were perhaps not unfounded. They, for their part, considered him prudish for not joining in their crude talk about marital sex.[30] After their marriage he and Constanze would, he hoped, shut themselves off entirely from all social contacts for a considerable period.[31]

Constanze was to conceal, not only every inch of her legs, but also of her soul; not even women friends or children were to see her naked since her body was his "exclusive property."[32] If she bared herself in their presence, she was denuding him, too. He forbade her to talk to any women friends about their relationship or even be affectionate toward them.[33] Such letters enable one to see the personal pressures behind Storm's hostility to the Catholic sacrament of confession in the novella *Veronica* (1861): a wife confessing marital secrets to a priest was, in his view, committing a form of adultery as reprehensible as physical adultery.

Gertrud Storm's edition of the letters omits many of Storm's ruminations on the fidelity he expected of a surviving partner and also his denunciations of second marriages.[34] The affirmations of eternal love are bound up with his fear of being replaced in his wife's affection, and his depictions of ideal loving relationships are also rooted in his needs and fears. The gap between art and life, between aspirations and reality is marked, and this distance is at the heart of Poetic Realism (see pp. 119–21). Storm belonged to a tradition which made it subjectively and objectively impossible to present certain topics in any but a positive fashion. What can be uncharitably labelled "humbug," often

---

29. Storm to Constanze, 20 August 1845.
30. Storm to Constanze, 19 November 1845, 6 July 1846.
31. Storm to Constanze, 22 November 1845.
32. Storm to Constanze, 14 August 1845.
33. Storm to Constanze, 6 November 1845.
34. Storm to Constanze, 24–28 April 1844, 27 June 1844, 29 December 1845.

sprang from unimpeachable motives – in this case the need to believe in the redemptive power of love. Like any ideal, the cult of love bred its own taboos and illusions.

Soon after his marriage Storm fell passionately in love with Doris Jensen, one of the daughters of Senator Peter Jensen. His own early marital sexual relations had not been rapturous. In contrast, he felt a strong sexual *rapport* with Doris. A *ménage à trois* was set up. Presumably they tried, in Heinsean fashion, to keep the arrangement secret. However, it is difficult to imagine that they could have concealed it from everyone in such a close-knit society. Certainly Storm's mother seems to have been aware of what was going on. In her case fear of the repercussions for all three families, were the affair to be brought out into the open, may have counselled silence. The decision to end the affair was not Storm's. Unable to cope with all the strains and feelings of guilt, Doris broke off the relationship and left Husum. Storm himself did not endorse this step and was to be tormented for years by doubts about whether, by not being more resolute, he had betrayed this unique opportunity to achieve true human happiness. The affair generated some of his finest love poems (see pp. 70–72), *Immensee* (1849) and *Angelica* (1855).

Whereas during the 1840s he was obsessed by love and its social implications, there is little evidence to suggest that he was equally concerned about the social and economic distress of these years, which culminated in the so-called Hunger Years of 1846/47. Publicists urged the need to develop industry in order to prevent further emigration and stem the poverty and pauperism which were growing like a cancer in Schleswig-Holstein.[35] Husum's notables hoped to revive the local economy by selling harbor modernization plans to the Danish crown and including Husum in the rail network. In his *Streifzüge in Schleswig-Holstein und im Norden der Elbe*, Theodor Mügge, whom Storm met when he visited Husum, spoke of a deprived proletariat and of pariahs desperate to find work on the dikes or dock schemes.[36] But apart from isolated comments about a destitute turner and young girls forced to beg, Storm is silent on all this.

---

35. *Volksbuch für die Herzogthümer Schleswig, Holstein und Lauenburg auf das Jahr 1844*, K.L. Biernatzki ed., p. 189.
36. T. Mügge, *Streifzüge*, pp. 306ff.

3.3 Literary Outlets: Communication and Survival Strategies

Once Theodor Mommsen abandoned his literary ambitions, Storm was left high and dry. Mommsen, who had acted as agent and go-between, also lost interest in their second joint venture, a collection of Schleswig-Holstein legends, fairy-tales, and folksongs, virtually ordering Storm to hand over all his material to another editor, Karl Müllenhof. An obvious, if modest outlet for his poems would have been the *Husumer Wochenblatt*. But his father forbade him to publish there. When a royal rescript banned choirs from exploiting the Schleswig-Holstein flag for propaganda purposes, he was eager that the poem "Aus Schleswig-Holstein" should appear in newspapers and acquire general popularity. He was delighted by rumors coming from Kiel that it had been put to music and looked set to rival Chemnitz's famous Schleswig-Holstein anthem, "Schleswig-Holstein, meerumschlungen." However, nobody was to know the identity of its author. In the event, his hopes came to nothing.[37]

Help came from an unlikely quarter. K.L. Biernatzki, half-brother of the popular, moral writer, J.C. Biernatzki, was founding his *Volksbuch für die Herzogthümer Schleswig, Holstein und Lauenburg* in order to serve the Schleswig-Holstein cause and promote a pietistic, evangelical Protestantism. Biernatzki, who later occupied important posts in the foreign and inner missions of the Protestant church in Berlin, welcomed articles which stressed sinfulness, grace and redemption. Homilies by pastors on the ravages of drink and moral stories about redemption by grace alternated with learned contributions on historical, social and economic questions. Storm, having been recruited to lighten the mix with humorous contributions, must have realized that Biernatzki would not publish anything which smacked of Young German extravanganzas or the ideas of Strauss, Bauer, or Feuerbach. He had no alternative but to adapt his message to the medium. A frontal attack on the norms of Biernatzki's readers would, in any case, have been futile. Storm had to find ways of maneuvring readers into endorsing positions at variance with their existing norms and prejudices. It was a question of building up a groundswell of support for new ideas and creating an alternative consensus.

37. See LL 1, pp. 956ff.

No oppositional writer in the 1815–48 period could afford to disregard the censor. The more subversive the ideological contraband was, the greater were the camouflaging skills required. Educated, sophisticated readers were adept at reading between the lines and in picking up "sub-texts," and the authorities and censors often colluded in this conspiracy, realizing that such a level of sophistication was well beyond the range of uneducated readers. Indeed it was politic to allow the educated classes a safety-valve. Such tolerance ceased if critical writers wrote shorter works, broadsheets and pamphlets which poorer people might afford and which were written in a popular, accessible style. Trying to outwit the censor and at the same time cater for unsophisticated readers was no easy task.

However, Storm's aesthetic categories (see p. 74) encouraged him to believe that he could nevertheless convey new ideas and norms to readers with very different reading skills and expectations since art, including literature, did not address itself primarily to the intellect – where disparities in education were marked – but to the imagination and the *Gemüt*, i.e. the feelings and emotions. These were deemed to be attributes common to all people regardless of sex, class, and education. Similarly, since faculties and senses were all part of finely tuned system of correspondences, a reaction produced in the imagination or feelings led to insights crystallizing in the intellect. Readers' educational levels might affect the quality and clarity of these conclusions; but, provided authors had translated their ideas into images and sequences which addressed the imagination and feelings, even unsophisticated readers would formulate unfamiliar insights.

The belief in the unique power of art to affect human beings in this way because of its concrete, pictorial qualities, its musical elements, and its ability to conjure up moods and atmosphere entailed rejection of more abstract, analytic techniques since they supposedly failed to utilize art's unique resources and could not therefore have a decisive impact on people's thoughts and feelings. Storm's theory and practice were well adapted to the repressive environment. It was much harder for a censor to point accusingly to a "situation," "image," or "general mood" than to an explicitly irreligious or politically subversive statement. The coded communication skills which he learned in the 1840s stood him in good stead in later decades. These constraints promoted an artistic subtlety which he might not have developed in a more liberal climate.

In the search for "situations," "motifs," narrative techniques, and levels of language capable of appealing to a wide audience, the notion of a *Volks- und Heimatsgeist* was highly attractive.[38] It enabled Storm to see himself as helping the *Volk* articulate its true needs. One could study artifacts produced by the *Volk*, strip away the alienated elements and distill the valid essence, i.e. the underlying human needs – just as Feuerbach had done in religion. The notion of universal human needs fitted in well with Storm's aesthetic assumptions about imagination and *Gemüt* being common to all people. Together they gave someone largely segregated from the lower class in social and educational terms the confidence that he could nevertheless articulate popular aspirations.

If a new body of secular humanitarian writings was to be created, subject matter, techniques, and language could not be adjusted to the expectations of readers used to low-brow romances. That would only perpetuate the alienation which the new literature sought to overcome. In the *Volksbuch* edition of *Marthe und ihre Uhr* (1847), the text is ironical about those "gebildete Damen der höheren Stände, welche gemeiniglich nur von Frau von Paalzov's van der Nees oder dem französischen Grafen von Monte Christo entzückt zu sein pflegen" (LL 1, 1012). The solution lay in employing popular forms. Storm's concern with collecting folklore was itself part of this attempt to break out of aristocratic and upper-class culture. A modern *Volkslied* (see pp. 73f.) seemed the genre suited to transmitting the new ethos. In prose fiction, fairy stories, and legends seemed equally propitious genres. On the other hand, if one were to use the novella, one would have to incorporate elements from the other popular genres. This Storm would attempt to do in *Immensee.*

---

38. In a letter to Mommsen, 13 July 1843, *Storm-Mommsen,* p. 49, Storm wrote of the "Pietät, die wir der Sage schuldig sind" and referred to its "Unverletzlichkeit als Emanation des ganzen Volks– und Heimathgeistes." To the end Storm hoped to be a *Volksschriftsteller.* He wrote to E. Schmidt, 23 December 1880, *Storm-Schmidt* 2, 27, of his satisfaction at having "written himself into the heart of the people"; but he lamented to Hermione von Preuschen that the great sorrow of his life was that, despite the recognition achieved by his novellas, his lyric poetry had remained as good as unknown among the people. See H.v.P, "Erinnerungen an Theodor Storm," *Deutsche Revue*, vol. 24, 1899, pp. 206f.

In the struggle for the minds and feelings of people outside the pale of grammar school education, Christian writers, besides enjoying official favor, had an easier task than radical ones in that they could work from material, norms, and sentiments already familiar to "simple" readers. A pastor like Jeremias Gotthelf or those writing in the *Volksbuch* could employ Biblical language and motifs inculcated in the home, at school and from the pulpit. (Even that did not, however, alter the fact that Gotthelf's didactic novels tended to be read by the educated middle classes wealthy enough to pay for them or subscribe to lending libraries.) Was not part of the solution to be flexible about High German, itself the privilege of the educated, and write in a regional language or dialect? Klaus Groth and Fritz Reuter opted for that course. Storm was not prepared to take such a step. In his case the refusal to write in Low German, except in very consciously "folksy" or often humorous genre pieces, sprang from the conviction that although Low German had a great vitality when it came to capturing popular life and painting genre pictures, High German, the language of administration, education, theology, and literature in the duchies, alone had the resources to cope with modern thought and sensibility and the issues facing state and society.[39] To have used Low German in a novella or novel would not only have restricted a work's appeal; it would have made reading a nightmare for those struggling into literacy or with limited reading skills. In elementary schools reading and writing were based on High German – as was church worship. The ability to savor renderings of dialect is a very sophisticated delight.

Storm had to adjust to his medium, and his first published story, *Marthe und ihre Uhr* (1847) outwardly seems a typical contribution to Biernatzki's *Volksbuch*.[40] A story describing the austere life of a dutiful daughter who uncomplainingly sacrifices herself to care for her parents was the very stuff of which edifying tales were made. The evocation of a simple, God-fearing family's Christmas celebrations and a moonlit death-bed scene in which the daughter clasps her dead mother's hand during a night-long vigil – these were motifs as congenial to Biernatzki's public as they were to the early Victorians. Storm's achievement

39. See LL 4, pp. 329, 348.
40. See D.A. Jackson, "Theodor Storm's *Marthe und ihre Uhr, Trivium*,"19, 1984, pp. 39–53.

was to use such familiar, reassuring ingredients while prompting the reader to draw critical conclusions about Marthe's life-style and the values underpinning it.

He recognized the artistic potential of the motif of an old clock and glimpsed that he could introduce a critical voice and contrasting values through a fictional narrator who, as a student, lodged with Marthe when she was forced to take in students in order to eke out a frugal existence. His very different upbringing, values, and prospects enable him to remain critical of her life-style while conveying genuine affection for her as a person. He explicitly attributes her frugality and contentment with her narrow round to her upbringing and the influence of a strict father whose own principles reflected his limited circumstances (LL 1, 281). Marthe is the daughter expected to remain single and stay at home to look after her parents in their old age. After their deaths she creates for herself a surrogate world inhabited by fictional characters, and she satisfied her need to be useful by looking after her lodgers. Altruism and self-sacrifice have ousted other needs.

Incapable of friendship and lacking contacts outside the house – she even withdraws from contact with a married sister and her family – she projects her needs for human company and conversation on to articles of furniture, especially an old Dutch clock. She invests these objects, which are all associated with her parents, with a pseudo-life by lending them parts of her soul. (LL 1, 282) But the alienation and essential loneliness remain. In order to function, she needs to imagine that the clock, this replacement father-figure, dictates to her with its hard, insistent tick. The text suggests that her father has prevented her from articulating her own deepest needs. It also ironically suggests that in buying this old Dutch clock at an Amsterdam fair in the late eighteenth century, he obeyed some repressed sexual longing. Certainly, with its mermaids with long flowing tresses and scaly fish-like bodies entwined round the clock face and its hands modeled like scorpions, it is not the clock one would expect such an austere figure to buy. Its mechanical defects and whims in its old age suggest the father's own. When Marthe compulsively has to help it to chime, the link is clear between this and her tending of her ailing parents. Cleverly, too, the text introduces a typical Vormärz slogan, "die neue Zeit" (LL 1, 283). The clock is interested in the old times.

Instead of joining family Christmas celebrations, Marthe stays in the lonely house and relives two past Christmases. The first, a childhood Christmas, underlines the austerity of her parents' world. This subdued, almost formal occasion is dominated by the father who remains stiffly seated as the children go, one by one, to kiss his hand. There are no toys, only useful gifts; no play, only prayers (LL 1, 284f.). Marthe's second memory is of the Christmas night when her mother died. Each Christmas she relives these memories; they are her life. It is not until the narrator returns from his very different Christmas celebrations that she is rescued from her frozen immobility. He moves on to new experiences, new people and new places while she remains entombed in the house, with the clock and her memories. In the final lines the text spells out what Marthe lacks: a true love of life (LL 1, 287). She may live to a ripe old age, but her life will remain alienated, unfulfilled.

3.4   Revolution

At a time when people of his generation were discreetly silent about their doings in 1848 or ironized them as naive youthful peccadillos, Storm in 1886 still spoke of 1848 as the year "when the world was rejuvenated" (LL 4, 429).[41] The Schleswig-Holstein Rising (1848–51) reflected a range of national and socio-economic interests akin to those found in other European states gripped by revolution in 1848.[42] What was peculiar to the duchies was that here the nobility allied itself with liberals and democrats through fear of being absorbed into a unitary, liberal Denmark. However, such was its opposition to a constitutional, liberal state or a democratic republic, whether at duchy or national level, that conflict was inevitable.

By 1848 the situation in Schleswig-Holstein was explosive. Christian VIII died in December 1847. At the end of February his son Frederik VII issued a rescript giving details of a new

41. In Wilhelminian Germany 1848 was demoted to a painful hiccup; 1870/71, in contrast, was elevated to a glorious caesura in German history. See H. Böhme, *Die Reichsgründung*, Munich, 1967.

42. The literature on the Schleswig-Holstein Rising is voluminous. Particularly useful is A. Scharff, *Wesen und Bedeutung der schleswig-holsteinischen Erhebung 1848–1850*, Neumünster, 1978.

constitution planned for the Helstat. These proposals satisfied neither the Eiderdanes, those Danes demanding a liberal Denmark extending to the Eider, nor Germans pressing for a separate constitution for Schleswig-Holstein as an independent state. In February news of the revolution in Paris reached Kiel; close on its heels came reports of disturbances in the German states. By mid-March a revolutionary situation existed in the towns. A deputation of members of both Estates set sail for Copenhagen to demand for the duchies a separate constitution drawn up by the Estates. Schleswig was to be allowed to join the German Confederation. As the Eiderdanes had already pressured the king into annexing Schleswig, the delegation returned empty-handed. But in the interim a Provisional Government for the duchies had been formed after rumors of the appointment of an Eiderdane ministry had overcome the hesitations of prominent members of the knightage. Reluctant to break with legitimist traditions, the knights insisted on the legal fiction of the "unfree Duke" whereby the new government was simply preserving law and order in Frederik's name and defending the rights of the duchies until he was again a free agent. Such niceties enraged those wanting a clean break with Denmark and eager to press ahead with reforms. Storm, like Theodor Mommsen, grew impatient with the Estates' lack of urgency and the continuing influence of the nobility. He wished that the devil would take the Estates if that body did not take itself, i.e. abolish itself and make way for a much more democratic representative assembly.[43]

In Husum the Magistrat, the citizenry, and the royal officials had all pledged their allegiance to the new government. Storm, who had become conductor of the Liedertafel, a male choir founded in 1844 to promote the duchies' German identity, also became secretary of the "Patriotischer Hülfsverein" set up to organize support for a candidate in the elections to the constituent German National Assembly in Frankfurt. The candidate was his wife's uncle, J.C. Esmarch. Storm's involvement soon acquired a further dimension. After the Provisional Government had proclaimed the freedom of the press, the Democrat leader, Theodor Ohlshausen, had recruited Theodor Mommsen to edit the *Schleswig-Holsteinische Zeitung*, the new government's quasi official organ. Mommsen recruited Storm as a contributor. His local

43. Storm to Mommsen, end of April 1848, *Storm-Mommsen*, p. 104.

reports, which only came to light in the 1960s, illuminate his stance on key issues.[44] Now that Mommsen's reservations about the timeliness of political poetry were no longer valid, Storm envisaged a role for himself as the "Tyrtaeus of democracy." Tyrtaeus had been a Greek lyric poet in the seventh century B.C. whose songs had inspired the Spartans in their struggle against the Messinians. This hope would resurface in 1863/64. His first sally forth was, however, a fiasco. He completed the political poem which had remained a torso since 1846, only to find that Mommsen rejected it as too unspecific for a political newspaper. "An der Westküste der Friesen" (later entitled "Ostern") is very much in the mold of Vormärz political poetry, and one's immediate reaction is surprise that someone so critical of hackneyed lyrics should himself have written such a piece.

. . .

Der Frühling zog prophetisch über Land,
Die Lerchen jauchzten und die Knospen sprangen. —

Entfesselt ist die urgewalt'ge Kraft,
Die Erde quillt, die jungen Säfte tropfen,
Und Alles treibt, und Alles webt und schafft,
Des Lebens vollste Pulse hör' ich klopfen.

Der Flut entsteigt der frische Meeresduft,
Vom Himmel strömt die goldne Sonnenfülle;
Der Frühlingswind geht klingend durch die Luft
Und sprengt im Flug des Schlummers letzte Hülle.

O wehe fort, bis jede Knospe bricht,
Durchström die Welt, du wonningliches Werde!
Entfalte dich du gottgebornes Licht,
Und wanke nicht, du feste Heimaterde!
(LL 1, 56f.)[45]

Echoing the Biblical account of the Creation, Goethe's *Faust* and Chemnitz's Schleswig-Holstein anthem, the poem greets 1848 as

---

44. Ibid., pp. 18ff.
45. The line "Durchström . . . Werde" was later replaced by "Daß endlich uns ein ganzer Sommer werde."

a portentous stage in the history of humanity's self-creation. Revolution will be universal; an age of dynamic vitality will replace the torpor of the *ancien régime*.

Storm had other more specific hopes. High on the list was the final abolition of aristocratic power and privilege. Thus he welcomed the prospect of posts monopolized by the aristocracy being open to other applicants, and urged his father-in-law to apply for the post of Amtmann in Husum.[46] In the autumn, the Husum Magistrat and councillors proposed a new *Städteordnung* whereby the mayor ceased to be a royal appointee. Instead the citizens would elect him, his deputy and the four senators in direct elections. Significantly, the existing civic officials and representatives did, however, propose excluding wage-earners from citizenship, thus denying them voting rights.[47]

The issue of how democratic the franchise should be was debated at local, duchy, and national levels. Liberals would have preferred the elections to the Frankfurt Parliament to have been based on a restricted franchise and an indirect system. Primary electors would have elected secondary electors, who would then have elected the parliamentary representatives. Even if combined with a universal male franchise, such a procedure was well-suited to maintaining the influence of the well-to-do. Storm supported the arrangements adopted, and his election report (LL 4, 317f.) stresses that the outcome was the same as it would have been had an indirect procedure been followed. A great mass of people, including dike-workers, had voted; not knowing the candidate, they had relied on the recommendations of those with whom they had dealings and in whom they had trust. This final comment is crucial for understanding Storm's position. He was convinced that the educated classes had to articulate the needs of the "people"; but he did not envisage the lower classes voicing demands hostile to middle-class interests, nor did he envisage any radical redistribution of wealth and property. He never questioned the principle of private property.

---

46. Storm to E. Esmarch, 26 May 1848, *Storm-Esmarch*, pp. 25f.
47. See J. Jacobsen, "Landesregierung und städtische Verwaltung in Schleswig-Holstein am Ende der dänischen und Beginn der preußischen Zeit, dargestellt am Beispiel der Stadt Husum," *Nordfriesisches Jahrbuch*, new series, vol. 10, 1974, pp. 143–57. See also *Allgemeine Städteordnung für die Herzogthümer Schleswig-Holstein*, 18 October 1848, Schleswig, 1848.

Sometime during 1848 he wrote the story *Im Saal*. It treats the theme of the old times and the new and considers which elements of the past deserve to be preserved. The story stresses that the room – a familiar Vormärz symbol – will not be radically redesigned: it will be restored to its original state. The grandson identifies with the *joie de vivre*, warmth, humour, and elegance of his grandmother and her generation, rejecting both the authoritarian behavior of her father and the earnestness of her children – the generation of Storm's parents. On the other hand, there will be no return to the hierarchical society of the grandmother's youth:

> "Es war damals freilich noch eine stille, bescheidene Zeit; wir wollten noch nicht Alles besser wissen, als die Majestäten und ihre Minister; und wer seine Nase in die Politik steckte, den hießen wir einen Kannegießer, und war's ein Schuster, so ließ man die Stiefeln bei seinem Nachbar machen. Die Dienstmädchen hießen noch alle Trine und Stine, und jede trug den Rock nach seinem Stande. Jetzt tragt Ihr sogar Schnurrbärte wie Junker und Kavaliere. Was wollte Ihr denn? Wollt Ihr alle mit regieren?"
>
> "Ja, Großmutter," sagte der Enkel.
>
> "Und der Adel, und die hohen Herrschaften, die doch dazu geboren sind? Was soll aus denen werden?"
>
> "O - - Adel - - "sagte die junge Mutter, und sah mit stolzen liebevollen Augen zu ihrem Mann hinauf.
>
> Der lächelte und sagte: "Streichen, Großmutter; oder wir werden alle Freiherrn, ganz Deutschland mit Mann und Maus. Sonst seh ich keinen Rat."
>
> (LL 1, 292f.)

If one pillar of the *ancien régime*, the nobility, was to disappear, so too was its second main support, the church. In his report on discussions about the separation of church and state and the emancipation of schools from ecclesiastical supervision, Storm insisted that any further meetings should be publicly advertised and open to the general public. From what is known of his previous attitudes, there can be little doubt that he hoped such deliberations would lead to the separation of church and state and the secularization of education. The Staatsgrundgesetz of September 1848, however, only went so far as to declare, in Article 103, that the administration of schools would be entrusted to a special authority and that a subsequent law would regulate clerical involvement in the supervision of schools.

In the early summer of 1848 hopes seemed justified that state policy would no longer be a matter of cabinet politics and dynastic interests. Instead, it would reflect popular, national considerations. Many liberals pointed to Prussia as Germany's savior. Propaganda about Prussia's vocation to unify Germany had grown since the 1830s. This propaganda, which underlay post-1870 "Borussian," *kleindeutsch* interpretations of German history, highlighted a range of areas: the reforms of Stein and Hardenberg; the efficiency of the Prussian bureacracy; the excellence of its schools and universities since Wilhelm von Humboldt's reforms; its championing of enlightenment and religious tolerance since Frederick II; its judiciary's proud independence; its armies' prowess, especially since the reforms of Scharnhorst and Gneisenau; its national role in the Wars of Liberation; and, finally, the stimulus to national unity and capitalist development provided by the Zollverein. Was not Frederick-William IV now a constitutional monarch with liberal ministers? Having already pledged his army to the Schleswig-Holstein cause, was he not about to embark on a truly national role? The truth was soon revealed. At the very moment when the Schleswig-Holstein cause was backed by the Frankfurt Assembly and by liberals and democrats all over Germany, the Prussian government, under pressure from the great powers, unilaterally concluded the Malmö Armistice with Denmark. It stipulated that the Provisional Government should be dissolved and its decrees annulled. Soon even national-liberal supporters of the duchies like J.C. Droysen, would support ratification rather than back Democrat demands that the National Parliament should impose its will on the separate states.

After the events of the summer of 1848 and the diplomatic machinations of the following three years, nothing could ever dislodge Storm's suspicions that the Prussian monarchy was wedded to the old times and that the Prussian Junkers would strive to retain their powers and privileges, whatever the national and popular interest. When he spoke of his distaste for "politics,"[48] he had in mind dynastically, sectionally motivated cabinet politics of this type. In 1863/64 a cause backed by the overwhelming majority of the people would again be stifled by external powers and by classes and groups hostile to popular democracy and

---

48. E.g. in the poem "Kirschen" (LL 1, p. 252) or in the remark to Brinkmann, 10 December 1852, on the poem "Oktoberlied" (*Storm-Brinkmann*, p. 76).

self-determination. The villain would again be Prussia. The role of the army in the state and the spirit pervading it were inevitably key issues for a democrat like Storm. In 1848 *Freischaren* or irregular volunteer corps formed on the model of those in the Napoleonic period. A *Freischärler* is portrayed in a very positive light in the novella *Abseits* (1864). A regular Schleswig-Holstein army was also created, with Husum becoming the garrison town for a fusilier corps and an infantry batallion. Since the new army had few officers, seconded Prussian officers had to fill the gap. Especially after the Malmö Armistice, friction grew between Schleswig-Holstein recruits fresh from civilian life and Prussian aristocrats with rigid notions of rank and discipline. Storm counselled and consoled a Captain Gantzer quartered with the Storms when he found it difficult to enforce Prussian drill.[49] Unrest grew.[50] In September and October Storm provided ironic reports on the attempts being made by the Conservative press to present Husum as a bed of republicanism, radical agitation and anarchy. Alleging that the republic had been proclaimed, the *Altonaer Merkur* demanded stern measures to eradicate all republican and radical elements in the army. Storm, on the other hand, presented the affair as a harmless incident which in no way warranted the sending of troops to Husum and the transfer or dismissal of several officers. His comments on the "republican spirit" deserve quoting in full:

> Dieser Geist läßt sich zwar nicht töten, aber doch einem Umsichgreifen des Übels vorbeugen, man kann ein Exempel statuieren und je höher die Bestraften stehen, desto mehr Wirkung hat's nach unten! Ein Bißchen Denunziation, ein bißchen Übertreibung, dabei gläubige Ohren, furchtsame Herzen, und – 2 Hauptmänner, leider! die, welche, beim Jägerkorps am meisten und vielleicht allein beliebt sind, werden in puncto republikanischer Umtriebe in Verhör gezogen, darauf versetzt oder aus schleswig-holsteinischen Diensten entlassen. . . . Der Soldat darf seinen Vorgesetzten nicht lieben, so wenig wie er denken darf, fürchten muß er seinen Offizier und Honneurs machen vor ihm und dann bei Gelegenheit sich allenfalls totschießen lassen. (LL 4, 321f.)

49. Storm to Ernst Keil, 29 September 1861, SHLB.
50. F. Schmeißer, *Eine westschleswigsche Stadt*, pp. 20ff.

It is language few would associate with Storm. If his novellas rarely exhibit this cutting irony, it is because external constraints and his definition of literature counselled other strategies. Storm may well have had contact with another disciplined officer, a Captain Möller or Müller, who had imbibed democratic ideas while in the U.S.[51] He commended a Prussian captain who had won the love and respect of his men by recognizing the spirit inspiring the young troops and trying to combine the seriousness demanded of military service with the *Humanität* demanded by "our" times (LL 4, 324). Storm's vision of an army imbued with civilian, democratic values returned in the Federal Republic as the ideal of the *Bürger in Uniform*.

Could these major changes, from the abolition of the aristocracy and the reorganization of the role of the church to the fostering of a new spirit in the army, be effected within a monarchical framework, or did they require a republic? Was the new, united duchy to have a duke, and was Germany to have an emperor? Storm did not fight shy of republicanism. Early in the Rising he had rejected Droysen's view that republicanism and anarchy were synonymous,[52] and Prussian policy in the summer of 1848 so disgusted him that he wrote: "Schade in der Tat, daß wir Husumer Bürger nicht gegen das Königtum opponieren, sondern nur mit ganz Deutschland uns über königlich-preußische Diplomatie höchlichst doch submissest zu verwundern uns erlauben, sonst hätten wir uns einen Namen machen können, wir wären die deutschen Pariser" (LL 4, 322). But republicanism was a minor creed among the middle classes.

Had the liberal ministries in the ascendancy in Germany in the spring and summer of 1848 remained in power, many democratic demands would have remained unfulfilled. At the same time, one has to recognize the progress that would have been made had the Schleswig-Holstein State Basic Law of September, 1848, and the Imperial Constitution of December, 1848, come into effect. However, the disadvantaging of women remained. The President of the Schleswig-Holstein Estates had declared:

Natur und Sitte haben ihnen einen anderen Wirkungskreis angewiesen als eine Teilnahme an dem politischen Treiben der Männer und

---

51. Ibid., pp. 20ff.
52. Storm to Mommsen, end of April 1848, *Storm-Mommsen*, pp. 103f.

an der Volksrepräsentation. Bei der Ordnung des Hauswesens und
der Erziehung der Kinder räume ich gern dem Weib Mitwirkung ein,
und wenn es sich darum handelt, die Regeln des Schicklichen und
Schönen zu bestimmen, überhaupt im Gebiet der Ästhetik, bin ich
nicht abgeneigt, dem Weibe den Vorrang zuzugestehen; aber nicht in
der Politik.[53]

The Schleswig-Holstein constitution represented a compromise
between legitimist principles and liberal, democratic ones. Thus,
despite the introduction of universal male suffrage and a one-
chamber system in which fifty of the members were elected by
simple majorities in individual constituencies, the other fifty
were to be elected on the basis of tax contributions on income
and property. Ten of these were to be elected by the biggest
landowners, i.e. the knights. It also has to be remembered that
whereas males over twenty-one enjoyed the vote in the Imperial
constitution, here the age requirement was set at twenty-five.
The knights and the moderate conservatives ensured that the
constitution, like its Prussian counterpart, was based on the theory
of an agreement between an as yet unspecified duke and his
people, not on any notion of popular sovereignty. On the other
hand, while a duke was to head the executive, the assembly had
supervisory powers. Similarly both assembly and duke could
initiate legislation, and, despite his veto, any bill passed with a
two-thirds majority in three different sessions would automatically become law. The duke also had to nominate responsible
ministers to run legally-defined ministries, and a stipulation not
contained in any other German constitution was that any change
in government personnel required the agreement of the parliament. In the area of finance, the minister responsible was to
present annual accounts, and parliament was to debate state
expenditure and taxation. The oath sworn by members of the
armed forces would be to both duke and parliament. In terms of
human and civil rights, the constitution's provisions resembled
those of the Frankfurt Constitution dealt with below. Property
and all private rights were declared inviolable.[54]

53. H.G. Skambraks, "Die Entstehung des Staatsgrundgesetzes für die Herzogtümer Schleswig-Holstein vom 15. September 1848," *ZSHG*, vol. 84, 1960,
pp. 121–208 and vol. 85/86, 1961, pp. 131–242, p. 157, note 105.
    54. See J. Krech, *Das Schleswig-Holsteinische Staatsgrundgesetz vom 15. Septem-
ber 1846*, Frankfurt, Berne, New York, 1983; G.C.v.Unruh, ed., *Das Schleswig-
Holsteinische Staatsgrundgesetz von 1848*, Husum, 1981.

As a democrat, Storm could not have been delighted by all these provisions. But, as he was later to do in 1863/64, he exhibited a certain pragmatism. Rather than support Ohlshausen's democratic break-away movement, he chose to remain loyal to the Provisional Government which had reluctantly accepted the ratification of the Malmö Armistice by the National Parliament. He thus signed a declaration sent from Husum on 16 October pledging loyalty to the State Assembly and declaring that sovereignty rested solely with this freely elected body.[55]

But by this time the revolutionary cause was failing: Vienna fell on 1 November, and in Berlin the Constituent Assembly was dissolved a week later. Ironically, the Frankfurt Parliament was at this moment framing a catalogue of legal, political, and human rights, which was remarkably progressive for the time. Its provisions included: the abolition of the nobility and all distinctions of estate; equality of all before the law; universal liability for military service; the inviolability of freedom of the person; abolition of the death penalty; inviolability of one's domicile; secrecy of correspondence; freedom of the press; freedom of belief and conscience; freedom of scholarship and research; civil marriage; secular education; obligatory primary education and free education; the right of assembly and the right to form political associations. All land was declared a saleable commodity, and so-called noble estates could no longer be protected by entail; serfdom and villeiny in all their forms were terminated. Patrimonial judiciary powers and policing powers on noble estates were also ended. Although it left little imprint on the constitution of Bismarck's creation, the North German Confederation, or its successor, the German Empire, the 1848 constitution helped shape the Basic Law of the modern Federal Republic.

Once the Austrian prime minister rejected a *Großdeutschland* that would exclude Austria's non-German territories, democrats had little option but to support the *kleindeutsch* solution. In return the parliament's powers would be strengthened and a democratic franchise guaranteed. Since a strong national framework seemed the surest means of protecting the duchies against

---

55. For a survey of Storm's involvement with petitions, etc, see D. Lohmeier, "Die Berichte der Husumer Behörden über Storms politische Haltung während der schleswig-holsteinischen Erhebung," *STSG*, vol. 34, 1985, pp. 39–48; J. Jensen, "Theodor Storms Auswanderung 1853," *Nordfriesisches Jahrbuch*, new series, vol. 1, 1965, pp. 133–43.

Denmark, Storm, together with another 138 Husum citizens on 21 January 1849 signed a petition to the Schleswig-Holstein State Assembly asking it to back this proposal.

On 27 March 1849, Denmark renounced the Malmö Armistice, and early in April the Prussian king rejected the Imperial crown. Tensions intensified between those still upholding the legal fiction of the "unfree" duke and the advocates of a clean break with Denmark. Storm joined 256 Husum inhabitants in unsuccessfully petitioning the Magistrat to refuse to recognize Frederik as duke and to press for the abolition of the personal union. The Danish authorities would attach particular importance to the fact that he had signed this petition.

In the other German states the last desperate democratic risings had been put down by the summer of 1849 – even if the reprisals were only beginning. In Schleswig-Holstein the suspense dragged on. Everything was now in the hands of the great powers, who attempted to impose an interim settlement. Storm was heavily involved in the campaign of civil disobedience in the course of which the Amtmann, the mayor, and Storm's friend Hartmuth Brinkmann, were all dismissed. Prussian hussars were sent to quell disorders and install hated new officials. When the State Basic Law was declared null and void, Storm was among 259 citizens who signed a protest condemning this as an act of pure caprice by an illegal body. He turned away clients wanting to use the courts and refused to co-operate with the new authorities and officials in any way. He also helped organize new elections to the State Assembly even though they had been declared illegal.

But on 2 July 1850 peace was concluded between Prussia and Denmark. Without Prussian or German-Confederate help the Schleswig-Holstein army was doomed. The Danish victory at the battle of Idstedt on 25 July delivered all Schleswig into Danish hands; Husum was occupied, and a state of siege declared; Schleswig-Holstein troops failed to retake neighboring Friedrichstadt despite a heavy bombardment and heavy civilian casualties. Storm commemorated those killed at Idstedt in the poem "Gräber an der Küste" (which could appear only in 1856), while his contempt for the "apostates," who collaborated with the Danes, inspired the poem "Im Herbste 1850." He was anxious for it to be widely circulated – with no reference to its author's identity. In November, at Olmütz, Prussia and Austria agreed that the German Confederation should, if necessary, force Schleswig-Holstein to recognize the Danish king. It was pointless to continue the struggle, and by 1 February 1851 the Rising was over.

Late in 1850 Storm had written the novella *Ein grünes Blatt*. It describes the encounter between Gabriel, a conscript going to join his unit, and Regine, a very allegorical "Genius der Heimat" (see LL 1, 1047). Like *Immensee*, it is a modern fairy tale without fairy-tale solutions. Gabriel imagines himself the fairy-tale Hans whose kiss redeems the princess turned into a serpent (LL 1, 335). A dreamer, he turns the encounter with Regine into a poetic memory. Only at the end of the story, when told that she, her great-grandfather and the wood are in enemy hands, does he realize that he is no fairy-tale hero, that she is no mere poetic vision, and that he must fight to recapture the lost territory and turn his dream of love into reality. Then his fairy-tale princess (*regina*!) will become a true loving woman. This Gabriel is no divine messenger bringing tidings of great joy: he informs Regine of the war and the reasons for it. The heath, the wood, Regine's great-grandfather and the cottage are presented in the stylized terms of the idyll; but it is an endangered idyll: the rumble of cannon fire disturbs the stillness. Even Gabriel finds it uncanny that Regine and her great-grandfather should be so ignorant of events in the world outside: "es litt ihn nicht länger in der ahnungslosen Stille dieses Ortes" (LL 1, 343). Contrary to what they believe, the war does affect them, and the grandfather's confidence that the house is in God's hands is shown to be an illusion. At the end it is stressed that it is in enemy hands and that only human effort can liberate it.

Official investigations were already underway into the reasons why Storm had suspended his practice. On resuming it, he was soon embroiled in wrangles with the civil and military authorities as he defended farmers and ordinary folk subjected to physical violence and arbitrary measures. The program of linguistic Danization began; so, too, did the victimization of those involved in what the Danes now termed the Insurrection. Police surveillance increased; books were checked for content, and, if necessary, banned; the Provost and his assistant, the headmaster of the grammar school and various teachers were dismissed; a compliant Magistrat was formed. To Storm's disgust the Amtmann introduced a new pastor to his congregation by emphasizing that he should teach the schoolteachers blind obedience; they in their turn should enjoin it upon their pupils.[56] The Gelehrtenschule would soon be downgraded to a höhere Schule. In 1851 Storm and his father had both complied with the requirement that those given or confirmed in offices and privileges by Christian VIII before 1848 should apply for confirmation. Nothing further had been heard. But in 1852 the Amtmann was instructed to submit reports on the activities of the Husum lawyers. In November 1852 Storm was notified of the authorities' decision: non-confirmation.

Confident that he would soon find employment elsewhere, he put out feelers in Gotha, whose Duke was a prominent national liberal, and applied for the post of mayor in Buxtehude – but to no avail. Family contacts in high places encouraged him to take soundings in Berlin. However, no firm offer of employment was forthcoming. He even applied – to his mortification and again to no avail – for the job of administrator of Kloster Preetz, an aristocratic educational establishment in Holstein. Finally it was intimated to him from Berlin that he stood a better chance of joining the Prussian judiciary if he expressed a readiness to work with a court for a minimum of six weeks as an unpaid volunteer. He complied. More anxious months went by before he at last learned that he had been assigned to the county court in Potsdam.

3.5 *Immensee*

It may seem paradoxical that someone so concerned about the revolutionary struggles should have written a fairy story, *Hinzelmeier*, in 1850. In the 1850s the advocates of True or Poetic Realism stressed that prose writers should capture the positive essence of contemporary reality in the realist mode. While legends never went entirely out of favor since they could further the national cause, the *Märchen* lost status and became a genre for children. While disliking the esoteric, cerebral nature of Novalis's *Kunstmärchen*, Storm saw tapping into the *Volksseele* as a means of promoting new values. Democratic writers could first isolate commendable aspirations in folk material and then feed them back into the popular imagination via genres like the *Märchen*

---

56. Storm to Brinkmann, 22 March 1852, *Storm-Brinkmann*, p. 57.

and the *Volkslied*. Modern fairy stories would not rely on super-natural agencies; nor would they engineer happy endings where none were available. But they could lend momentum to the search for alternatives by making readers of all cultural and educational levels conscious of the defects of existing norms and institutions. In Storm's view it was both a failure to recognize literature's specific *modus operandi* and a betrayal of its rich variety and potential to imagine that only certain genres and modes could do this.

In fact, being able to write a fairy tale almost became, as it were, the litmus test of a writer's democratic, popular qualifica-tions. It proved whether one was attuned to the *Volksseele*. Typically, at the height of the Schleswig-Holstein crisis in 1863/64, Storm felt impelled to write a fairy tale, *Die Regentrude*. Born of his frustration with the machinations of the great powers, it reflected his belief that the popular cause would triumph like some irresistible natural force. This fairy story was followed by two more, *Bulemanns Haus* and *Der Spiegel des Cyprianus*. Indeed at one stage he hoped to write a whole series. To his dismay he discovered that the public no longer relished *Märchen*. Conse-quently, when the three stories were reissued, any reference to *Märchen* was dropped. Market forces also affected his produc-tivity in other genres. Thus the public's waning interest in lyric poetry in the 1850s helped to depress his lyric output. Similarly, although in the 1860s he could still defend ghost stories against Julian Schmidt's dismissive attitude (see LL 4, 610), he had to recognize that the genre had no commercial future. He also had to accept that his vision of the *Volk* delighting in wholesome folk material was an illusion.

Such insights lay ahead. At the end of the 1840s there seemed no reason why alienation could not be presented in various genres provided their characteristics were respected. *Immensee* has the same theme as *Hinzelmeier*: that of the wasted life, of the wrong options chosen. But a fairy story about the choice between the philosopher's stone or the rose maiden offered only limited pos-sibilities. Storm therefore created a modern fairy tale based on familiar folklore motifs but in a contemporary, "social realist" setting.[57] In it he explored definitions of gender roles, the family,

57. See D.A. Jackson, "Daniel in the Lions' Den. Theodor Storm's *Immensee*," *Oxford German Studies*, vol. 14, 1983, pp. 8–34.

educational goals, attitudes to sex, courtship and marriage, etc. He opted for a series of short "situations," which range from the idyllic to the dramatic and lyrical and in which, at crucial moments, the prose is broken by folk songs. Themes and leitmotifs link these "situations" to form a tightly-knit artistic whole.

The opening scene in the inner story (LL 1, 296ff.) illustrates the degree to which two small children are already subject to the pressures of parents, school, and church. Enjoying two unexpected days off from school, Elisabeth and Reinhardt may revel in the freedom of the garden and the meadow; but their every response is already being conditioned by the adult world, and the scene ends with adults calling them back to the house. Away from school, Reinhardt tells Elisabeth fairy stories, folk tales and legends; but they play no part in the school curriculum. Nor are their values those taught in the home and at school. One of these stories, that of the poor man in the lion's den, is central to the novella. It is not referred to as the Biblical story of Daniel in the lion's den, the implication being that this is only one version of of a much more widespread popular motif enshrining universal needs – albeit in an alienated form. Details from the story – the lion, the den, the trembling fear, the approach of morning and light, the radiance suffusing the angel, the act of looking up to find a figure standing in front of one, the beckoning and leading away to safety – all act as leitmotifs. For Storm the challenge was to convince his readers that deliverance had to come from other, human agencies. Although Reinhardt may not believe in angels, he cannot explain why Elisabeth's mother and teachers nevertheless expect her to believe in them, and he himself is credulous in other areas.

This opening "situation" implicitly contrasts a Rousseauistic vision of childhood innocence and natural potential with the constraints of middle-class life. Whereas the children build a play house, in adult life setting up house will be a complicated operation. The motif of the seat returns (LL 1, 319). Although the seat on Erich's estate enjoys a splendid view over the lake, a distraught Elisabeth can only fleetingly sit on it in the rain and darkness. Other themes are adumbrated, like the possibility of emigrating to a country like India, should happiness be incompatible with social arrangements in Europe; and the topic is introduced of children's dependence on parents and the need for them to assert their own needs. Whereas Reinhardt accuses Elisabeth of lacking this courage, the ending will suggest otherwise. The motif returns much later in *Pole Poppenspäler* (1874) (LL 2, 208, 215).

The following "situations" examine various aspects of middle-class socialization. Denied any secondary or higher education, young women like Elisabeth must wait until they are "rescued" by a respectable, wealthy suitor. Boys, in contrast, complete their grammar-school education, study, and concentrate on their careers. Emotional and sexual relationships with their female social peers play no part in this scheme. The picnic to mark Reinhardt's departure for the university (LL 1, 298ff.) illustrates the values transmitted to these young people. An old man exhorts them in Biblical fashion to go to the East and to the West in search of strawberries – and remain honest. Their knowing looks show what honesty will amount to, especially as they have been forewarned that dry bread awaits those who return empty-handed. The reader is invited to make the link between strawberries, money, and sexual possession. Reinhardt helps Elisabeth through the undergrowth whereas other young males rush off in pairs; but he does not find any strawberries. They abandon the search and rejoin the company on its terms.

The "situation" contains one of those rare moments when alienated human beings glimpse or are on the verge of glimpsing the true essence of life. Such incidents belong to the great continuities of Storm's work. Reinhardt's "revelation" is that Elisabeth, i.e. a natural human being, is the true "queen of the woods." He senses that this "symbol of everything delightful and wonderful in his young life" is entrusted to his protection. However – and this again is typical of so many of Storm's novellas – this fleeting recognition of his deepest human needs – and of the preconditions for poetic creativity – is quickly obscured by other social norms and pressures.

In its depiction of the role played by universities in the socialization process, *Immensee* anticipates works like *Auf der Universität* (1863) or *Der Herr Etatsrat* (1881). It criticizes their impact both on the young women left behind and also on the male students themselves. Denied sexual access to girls of their class, middle- and upper-class students satisfy these needs with musicians and singers in student pubs. Contact with the aristocracy also brings the danger of feudalization. In the original version of the novella (LL 1, 1026ff.), which was more outspoken in its critique of fraternity life, it is suggested that an intoxicated Reinhardt does indeed have sex with the gypsy-like zither girl. Hostile critical reactions made Storm revise the scene. But even in the final version sexual relations in this lions' den remain predatory. If Reinhardt spurns the girl, his chastity is not presented as a virtue. The text suggests that because she is genuinely attracted to Reinhardt she refuses to play for the Junker even though he offers her money. In a finite, mortal world her readiness to savor the present, despite knowing that the affair cannot last, is a more commendable response than the students' exploitative sexuality and emotional bankruptcy. In Reinhardt's case, fear of any intimate relationship is linked, here and later, to suggestions of impotence.

On this Christmas Eve Reinhardt is delivered, not by any messiah and Christian good tidings, but by the "Christ child," Elisabeth, her letter, and her presents. His poem, with its allusion to the Daniel story, captures this insight: "Er wäre fast verirret/Und wußte nicht hinaus;/Da stand das Kind am Wege/Und winkte ihm nach Haus!" (LL 1, 308). The young beggar girl – like the zither girl later – serves as a contrasting doppelgänger. Reinhardt's charity is no solution to the social problem, and the girl could become the prey of the next generation of students.

While Reinhardt studies, Elisabeth is exposed to the schemes of her mother and the wealthy suitor Erich. Whereas Reinhardt on his return home cannot understand the strains now affecting his relationship with Elisabeth, the text enables the reader to do so. It also suggests that his inability to forge a true relationship with her suits his professional ambitions. It is altogether safer and socially more acceptable to collect and classify botanical specimens with her rather than pick other flowers. Storm could not be more explicit than that. Such symbols protected him against any charge of prurience while making his meaning clear to discriminating readers. This dual function of both cloaking and exposing was vital. Reinhardt's twisted, repressed emotions are conveyed in the scene describing his departure (LL 1, 312f.). Although he has an alarming vague sense that his entire future is at stake, this Prince Charming cannot find the "redeeming word." He simply speaks of a secret he will reveal in two years' time. Elisabeth is expected to wait till then without visits or letters. Bowing to her mother's pressure, she finally gets engaged to Erich and marries him. Reinhardt does nothing. Indeed it is only when Erich invites him to Immensee to give Elisabeth a nice surprise (!) that he sees her again.

The "situations" set on Erich's estate (LL 1, 314ff.) abound in echoes of fairy stories. Despite all its splendor, Immensee is a castle under an evil spell. Elisabeth is the Sleeping Beauty whom Reinhardt alone can rouse. The text hints at how unfulfilled, perhaps even unconsummated, this marriage is. The child so full of vibrant life is now a pale, quiet, girlish figure who looks at Erich with sisterly eyes. The radiant queen of the woods has become the spectral White Lady roaming by the lake in the rain and darkness. Symbolically Erich drives away the stork. In terms of Storm's attitude to capitalism at the time it is revealing that the text presents the agroindustrialist Erich as a smug, calculating, insensitive philistine. His factory is not a plant manufacturing utilities, but a brandy distillery. In order to appreciate fully the significance of this detail one has to know that brandy drinking was a serious problem in the duchies, one preoccupying social commentators. It returns in *Drüben am Markt*. Erich is hostile to popular culture and alienated from the *Volk*, dismissing folk songs as thingumajigs (*Dinger*) sung by journeymen tailors and barbers, i.e. suspect elements. In the original version Elisabeth's mother commented: "Was hier die Leute bei der Arbeit singen, ist eben nicht für verwöhnte Ohren" (LL 1, 1033). Reinhardt's views on the origins of *Volkslieder*, on the other hand, echo Storm's own: "Sie werden gar nicht gemacht; sie wachsen, sie fallen aus der Luft, sie fliegen über Land wie Mariengarn, hierhin und dorthin, und werden an tausend Stellen zugleich gesungen. Unser eigenstes Tun und Leiden finden wir in diesen Liedern; es ist, als ob wir alle an ihnen mitgeholfen hätten" (LL 1, 320). In the original version the link was clear with the early scene in the wood and the Sleeping Beauty motif: "Das sind Urtöne ... sie schlafen in Waldesgründen. Gott weiß, wer sie gefunden hat ... " (LL 1, 1034).

The poem "Meine Mutter hat's gewollt" illustrates how apposite such modern folk songs are. The question the text poses is whether Reinhardt and Elisabeth will accept the girl's notion of "sin" or whether they will regard it as their duty to rescue Elisabeth from a marriage deemed inhuman and immoral. Should they do so, they will have to face material hardship and social opprobrium. The reality of what begging entails is brought out in the encounter with the zither girl (LL 1, 325f.). The text suggests that, spurned by Reinhardt, she became the Junker's mistress and began her descent into penury and mental derangement. But Elisabeth, too, is disturbed and impoverished in emotional and sexual, if not in financial terms.

The folk song, while producing in her a violent crisis, stimulates Reinhardt to swim out to the lily on the moonlit lake. The "situation" illustrates Storm's skill in exploiting the resources of his pictorial technique to treat taboo topics and produce "poetic" scenes. The sexual significance of the fairy-tale motif of the prince who has to pluck a flower in order to turn the spell-bound heroine back into a princess would be clear to many readers; on the other hand Storm could not be accused of explicitly advocating immoral behavior. Feeling himself swirled under the surface and entangled in the network of underwater stems, Reinhardt abandons his guest. Ultimately he is not prepared to confront his own or Elisabeth's sexuality; nor is he willing to struggle with all the difficulties that society would put in their way. It suits him better for Elisabeth to remain a pure lily.

Storm could not have presented Reinhardt directly suggesting to Elisabeth that they might have an adulterous affair. With a strange smile, he does, however, invite her to pick strawberries with him, only to be reminded that it is not the time for picking strawberries. When he rejoins that it will soon come, she shakes her head. Finally Reinhardt has to take the decision either to take up arms against society or to abandon Elisabeth. His nocturnal "agony" is rendered purely by means of symbols. Thus the nightingale gradually falls silent while the lark climbs high into the air. Typically he intends to communicate his decision in a short note and slip away while everyone is still asleep. The house cat – the lion's domestic cousin! – rubs its back against his hand; outside the sparrows pontificate away (*priestern*) that night is over.

The happy ending of the Daniel story is not repeated here. When Elisabeth learns he is leaving, never to return, she is described as looking at him with dead eyes. In contrast, the imagery makes it clear how confident he is that the big, wide world awaits him. In the original version he obtained an *Amt* and married. He found in his relationship to his son a novel sense of fulfillment: he could say tender things to his son which he had been unable to say to any woman (LL 1, 1037f.). Although the child dies, it is only thirty years later, as a widower, that his thoughts return to Elisabeth. After Tycho Mommsen found this ending prosaic, Storm amended it.

But the reader is still left in no doubt as to what has become of Reinhardt's confidence that he could lead a fulfilled, creative life without Elisabeth. He is a lonely old man, living far from his native region and estranged from the local community. In his retirement he pursues his scholarly researches, having never become a creative poet. A housekeeper bringing him his lamp, not the human angel, Elisabeth, rescues him as dusk and his memories threaten to engulf him.

Storm had to enter into a sort of collusive conspiracy with his public simply to survive as a writer. The more critical his stance, the more he had to guarantee that outwardly everything was reassuringly stable. It was one thing quietly to encourage readers to question conventions and social arrangements; it was quite another to depict characters flouting existing norms. While undermining taboos, Storm also had to support them. This "dual-track" approach was vital. Yet, by cloaking his message, he ran the risk of neutralizing it or even allowing readers to project their own preconceptions on to his story. Many of the upper-class ladies in Berlin who made *Immensee* into a best-seller would have identified with Elisabeth and remembered their own youthful love for a man close to them in age; many would have indulged bitter-sweet "adulterous" reveries. But that did not mean that they would tolerate depictions of actual adultery or be prepared to read about a German Nora who actually left her doll's house. Ultimately social "realities" and "moral" principles had to be upheld. A literary work which suggested that they could be resisted or flouted, was paradoxically more painful than one which enforced them since it denied the sense and "moral" value of their lives. Unlike Ibsen, Storm did not show men or women analyzing social arrangements and consciously deciding to break out of them.

3.6 Storm's Lyric Poetry

To the end of his life Storm believed that his main achievement was as a lyric poet.[58] The praise lavished on a poet like Emanuel Geibel, his lyric antipode, was always liable to touch a raw nerve,

---

58. For a stimulating discussion of Storm's place in the lyric tradition see F. Sengle, "Storms lyrische Eigenleistung. Abgrenzung von anderen großen Lyrikern des 19. Jahrhunderts," *STSG*, vol. 28, 1979, pp. 9–35.

and frustration at having been denied the recognition he deemed his due blighted even festive occasions. Storm saw himself as the last great German lyric poet. Few accepted such pretensions, either then or since. Critics for whom Goethe's *Erlebnislyrik* represented a *non plus ultra* dissented, as did critics who saw the 1880s as a watershed for lyric poetry. Storm's supposed rejection of C.F. Meyer's *Gedichte*(1882) was proof for them that his vision was narrow and backward-looking.

The key to understanding Storm's apparent hybris is the endangered status of lyric poetry after 1815.[59] Many believed that literature was irrelevant to the needs of contemporary state and society. The lyric poet was even more of a luxury than the prose writer. Not that the great tide of lyric poems ebbed. On the contrary, the public continued to love its anthologies, its Musenalmanachs, etc. Lyric poets often felt themselves to be epigones, heirs to a wealth of moods and techniques which they could imitate without ever finding forms and themes specific to their age. Poetry like that of August von Platen with its cult of beautiful form only fuelled attacks on dead formalism and aristocratic remoteness from the practical concerns of the day. At the end of the 1830s the nadir had been reached.

Everything was apparently reversed in 1840 with the resurgence of political poetry. A spate of collections followed Georg Herwegh's *Gedichte eines Lebendigen*. But this favor was conditional upon poets abandoning "subjective" moods and feelings. As we have seen, Mommsen demurred; so, too, did Friedrich Hebbel in the preface to his drama *Maria Magdalena* (1844). Storm, for his part, needed to convince himself and others that in writing love lyrics he could nevertheless be promoting the advent of the new times. His passion for Doris Jensen convinced him that his vocation was to seek to capture the miracle of love and convey its overriding claims. Thus he submitted the cycle *Ein Buch der roten Rose* to the magazine *Europa* early in 1848.[60] It was rejected. Once the revolutions had failed, there was even less likelihood of it finding a publisher. The poems had to be scattered between the two collections, *Sommergeschichten und Lieder* (1851) and *Gedichte*(1852). The poem "Frevel" – the crime is the woman's refusal to go further once the lovers' lips have brushed – had to be modified in tone and substance and given the new title "Die

59. Idem, *Biedermeierzeit*, vol. 2, 1972, pp. 467ff.
60. See LL 1, pp. 971f.

Stunde schlug" before it could appear. "Wir haben nicht Glück genossen" was never published in Storm's lifetime. The cycle erects love into a life-giving sacrament which must triumph over pudeur and feelings of guilt. There could, of course, be no suggestion that the lyric voice is that of a married man; but even without that the "immoral" message was clear enough.

Subsequently Storm may have emphasized that his lyric poetry conveyed experiences and emotions rather than reflecting on them; but, with few exceptions, these poems are not impressionistic, "realistic" *Erlebnisgedichte* evoking actual situations. In some cases Storm reworked motifs which arose in a quite different connection. Further, these poems have an almost programmatic character. Christian and classical symbols like the cup/chalice and the spark of life are lent a new humanitarian resonance. Originally a grand finale to the cycle, "Wir haben nicht das Glück genossen," affirms the supreme fulfillment afforded by passion and sex, whatever the preceding anguish and initial sexual disappointment:

> Wir haben nicht das Glück genossen
> In indischer Gelassenheit;
> In Qualen ist's emporgeschossen,
> Wir wußten nichts von Seligkeit.
>
> Verzehrend kam's, in Sturm und Drange
> Ein Weh nur war es, keine Lust;
> Es bleichte deine zarte Wange,
> Es brach den Atem meiner Brust;
>
> Es schlang uns ein in wilde Fluten,
> Es riß uns in den jähen Schlund;
> Zerschmettert fast und im Verbluten
> Lag endlich trunken Mund auf Mund.
>
> Des Lebens Flamme war gesunken,
> Des Lebens Feuerquell verrauscht,
> Bis wir aufs neu den Götterfunken(,)
> Umfangend, selig eingetauscht.[61]

61. For the history of the MS see LL 1, pp. 971f. Without the final stanza (see LL 1, 254) the whole thrust of the original poem is lost. Köster had no comma after *Götterfunken*. I have inserted one in order to prevent the confusion readers often fall into who imagine that *Götterfunken* is the object of *umfangend*.

The echoes of Goethe's "Ganymed" are intended. But, just as the poem "Größer werden die Menschen nicht" (see p. 257f.) is a Feuerbachian continuation of "Grenzen der Menschheit," so, too, this poem moves beyond pantheism. However, only by abstracting from "realistic" details and removing the *Erlebnis* to another plane, could Storm create for himself the space to articulate such sentiments at all. In order to get into print he had to adopt the tolerated codes of elevated, poetic language. The poem "Mysterium" (LL 1, 254) is bolder. But its account of how a young woman, a virgin, undresses to make love still requires that she should only agree to her lover's wishes because it is the night before they part; and the "mystery" – in the sense of religious mysteries – is that the girl is so exhausted with grief about their separation that she falls asleep in his arms before they can actually make love. There is a hint of a rococo *pointe* in this. Despite these precautions Storm still did not risk making the poem available for general consumption: an extra leaf was inserted in copies for trusted friends.

The counterparts to the "Buch der roten Rose," the three-part poem "Weiße Rose" and poems like "Wohl fühl' ich, wie das Leben rinnt," "Hyazinthen," or "Die Zeit ist hin" are very different in mood. They are free from the ideological insistence of the earlier cycle. Among Storm's finest poems, they convey the poet's jealous torment, frustration and grief as his lover separates herself from him. Delicately nuanced, they are permeated by a poignant sense of isolation and transience. But the implicit ideal remains the vision of fulfilled love. They are not simple *Erlebnisgedichte*. "Hyazinthen" may relate to feelings which Storm first experienced during his engagement; but the feelings and the motif could easily be transferred to Doris Jensen; and the poem was only completed after Storm had encountered Rosetta's song in Georg Büchner's comedy *Leonce und Lena*.

Storm's religion of love and his view of the German lyric tradition are interrelated. In his eyes, both were part of a general scheme of human development.[62] From the moment J.C. Günther glimpsed that the lyric was a medium to which one could entrust

---

62. Storm's theories on the lyric are contained in the prefaces to his anthologies, *Deutsche liebeslieder seit Johann Christian Günther* (1858) (LL 4, pp. 377–836), *Hausbuch aus deutschen Dichtern seit Claudius* (1870) (LL 4, pp. 390–407); in his various reviews in the early 1850s (see LL 4, pp. 329–74); and, especially, in the comments he provided for Hartmuth Brinkmann, 10 December 1852, to guide his review of his *Gedichte* 1852) (see *Storm-Brinkmann*, pp. 72ff.)

one's most personal feelings, it moved away from affirming the conventions and sentiments of a pre-democratic culture based on Christian orthodoxy. Poets began to articulate aspirations which this culture could not contain. Since he felt himself to be abreast of recent philosophic insights into human needs, endowed with a modern sensibility, and master of the techniques accumulated by past German poets, Storm judged himself well-equipped to take the German lyric tradition further along the road to a purely secular humanitarianism. His stress on individuality was itself only possible because he thought of the ideal modern poet as a truly representative figure. Earlier poets had, he claimed, all extended the range of emotions captured in poetry and refined the techniques with which to render them. Yet they had exhibited formal weaknesses and also not fully grasped the divinity of love. Goethe himself was not some unsurpassable model: he was part of a tradition that predated him and progressed beyond him.[63]

Yet if older poets were alienated in a Feuerbachian sense, aspects of *Empfindsamkeit* and pietism, for example, such as their intense inwardness and yearning for a consuming relationship with the deity, had enriched human sensibility. It was now a question of redirecting these emotions to their true object. In this respect none of Storm's lyric mentors could be models. Eichendorff, with his Catholicism and his view of sexual passion as the workings of a seductive Venus, belonged to the old times. Heine, in his middle phase, may have sketched a reconciliation of spirit and flesh, but he had devoted little of his poetry to evoking such a synthesis. Mörike, for his part, had endowed sexual love with a frustrating exotic magic. Sin, guilt and the fall permeate his Peregrina poems, and divine love still rises supreme above mere human love in poems like "Neue Liebe." The poet of the new age would have to progress beyond all three.

Without ever imagining that the *Volkslied* should become the sole or dominant *Lied* form, Storm did see the break with aristocratic, scholarly, or foreign forms as a crucial stage in the development of the German lyric. Modern folk songs like his

---

63. In the draft prefaces to the lyric anthologies the criticism of Goethe is much more pronounced than in the final versions. In a letter to Fontane, 25 May 1868, Storm highlights the supposed weaknessed in Goethe's lyrics. See *Storm-Fontane*, pp. 127f.

own "Meine Mutter hat's gewollt" could treat important contemporary questions. An alliance between poets and musical composers also offered exciting possibilities. In Storm's view, poetry
was not something to be consumed in isolation, but rather
something to be recited or sung in the family and at every type
of social occasion. Because of this it was well suited to creating
the new community of believers.

His view of the creation and reception processes encouraged
him in this belief. The true lyric poet rendered moods, feelings,
or ideas in such a way that they were reproduced in the reader.
But to achieve this, any experience, intellectual insight, or ethical
conviction had to pass through the poet's *Gemüt* and imagination. There it acquired warmth, color, bodily shape – in short,
achieved organic life. The poet translated feelings into words,
while, at the same time, employing the rhythm, movement and
tone color of the words to turn feelings into music and dissolve
them into the emotions in which they originated. Like music,
lyric poetry addressed the faculties of hearing and feeling; but,
like the fine arts, it addressed those of seeing and feeling, too.
This "total response" was crucial in assessing its strengths *vis-à-
vis* other genres.

Storm saw the lyric as the genre which addressed the *Gemüt*
and imagination without requiring the reader's intellect to make
any contribution. The poorly educated were thus not debarred
from enjoying it. But the lyric's impact did not simply end with
the arousal of feelings and *Stimmung.* If the feelings initially
aroused were the blossom, abstract concepts and conclusions were
the final fruit.[64] An idea or conviction which had enlisted the
energy of the feelings and the imagination in its support, was
more likely to become an essential part of the reader's or listener's
make-up than any dry philosophic idea.

It is not surprising to find that Storm was highly critical of
many of his fellow poets, accusing them of being inspired by
poetic reminiscences. Like sixth-formers, they sought to conceal
their lack of any real originality with pathos, slogans, rhetorical
devices, overloaded imagery, and hackneyed topoi. In their *Re-
flexionspoesie*, generalities and *aperçus* about life ousted its actual
presentation. The "Emanzipation von der Phrase" which Storm
advocated was a rejection of the whole classical rhetorical tra-

64. LL 4, p. 393.

dition of literature fostered in the grammar schools.[65] If, from the vantage point of today, he seems conservative in linguistic and technical terms, one should measure his lyrics, not against those of Goethe or the *Volkslied*, but against the rhetorical tradition epitomized by Geibel. It was after all Geibel whose poems appeared in edition after edition, not Storm's, and it was this rhetorical tradition that was the dominant one from 1850 to 1880 whatever the lip service paid to Goethe. Storm urged poets to strive for simplicity, brevity, and precision as the best means of capturing what Herder had defined as the *Naturlaut*. In the poem "Lyrische Form" (LL 1, 93) he enshrined his conviction that form could not be thought of as a beautiful golden vessel into which one poured golden content but rather as the contour of a living body.[66]

After 1848 market forces worked against the lyric. Whereas Duncker knew he could make money from novellas like *Immensee*, collections of poetry were a commercial risk. Having published a selection of Storm's poems in the *Sommergeschichten und Lieder*, he declined to publish a separate edition. Storm had to settle for a tiny press, Schwers, in Kiel. Predictably, the volume had little impact. The passion and anguish of the Doris Jensen affair once spent, Storm's productivity waned. In the post-revolutionary climate there was little scope for radical or morally subversive poems. The need to maximize his literary earnings impelled him more and more toward the novella, the paying public's favorite genre. In the 1850s and 1860s he did, however, still write longer programmatic poems (e.g. "Im Zeichen des Todes," "Ein Sterbender"). But poems like "An deines Kreuzes Stamm Jesu Christ" (see pp. 106f.), "Crucifixus" (see pp. 188f.) or "Größer werden die Menschen nicht" (see pp. 257f.) had either to be left unfinished and unpublished or could only be "smuggled" into print. In 1863/64, democratic political poetry briefly seemed on the agenda again; but Bismarck's annexation of the duchies

---

65. LL 4, p. 330.
66. "Lyrische Form," LL 1, p. 93. As late as 1885 he could still write in the *Braunes Taschenbuch*: "Für mich ist die Voraussetzung der schönen, insbesondere lyrischen Form das absolute Koinzidieren von Wort und Inhalt; kommt mir in einem Gedicht etwas Überflüssiges oder nicht ganz Deckendes, dann ist für mich die tiefere schöne Form verschwunden; vor der schönen Form des bloßen Klanges habe ich nicht den kleinsten Respekt, sie packt mich nicht, sie läßt mich völlig kalt" (See LL 4, p. 545).

soon terminated any hopes of a second spring. Although after Constanze's death in 1865 Storm attempted to blend the *Erlebnisgedicht* and the *Lehrgedicht* in "Tiefe Schatten," the general attrition continued. In 1870/71 he declined to swell the tide of patriotic lyrics. After a surge of lyric creativity in the early 1870s which produced the flawed *Neue Fiedellieder*, Storm fell virtually silent. The great exception is the late poem "Geh nicht hinein" which departs so strikingly from his previous lyrical principles. By that time, however, his financial survival depended on the novella.

He did, however, remain interested in developments in lyric poetry. It is true that he found the poetry of C.F. Meyer artificial, cold, and lacking in the genuine "tirra lirra of the soul." In his view it did not have the identity of emotion and expression which he considered the hallmark of the true lyric poet. However, statements in his letters[67] show that he acknowledged Meyer's achievement as a *Poet* if not as a *Lyriker*. His fear was, I suggest, that Meyer's type of poetry represented the abandonment of any attempt to harness the lyric to democratic, humanitarian goals. While Meyer did also write poems with a socio–political and ethical thrust, the symbolism of others was esoteric and narrowly personal. Storm sensed that if the lyric were to go down this road, it would move out of the mainstream of contemporary life. It was no coincidence that Meyer belonged in certain respects to the same tradition as August von Platen or that he moved away from musicality and popular forms. Popular composers did not put Meyer's lyrics to music so that they could be sung in middle-class drawing rooms and become an integral part of middle-class culture. Were this to become the dominant tradition, it would mark the end of any attempt to draw the less educated classes into a national cultural and ideological consensus.

---

67. Storm to Heyse, 7 July 1882, *Storm-Heyse* 3, p. 28; Storm to Schmidt, 5 February 1883, *Storm-Schmidt* 2, p. 73. Storm to Albert Nieß, 7 February 1882 and 20 January 1883, Brunswick City Library. See also *Storm-Heyse* 3, pp. 205f., note 15.

4

Prussia

4.1 The Potsdam Years: Adjusting to Reaction

Prussia in the 1850s was starkly repressive.[1] It is true that the Minister President, Otto von Manteuffel, distanced himself from the *camarilla*, an ultra-conservative group centered around the Gerlach Brothers, which wanted to abolish the constitution and revert to a pseudo-medieval state. Nevertheless key ministers like the Minister of the Interior and the Minister for Culture, Education, and Church Affairs were members of this group. The "imposed" (*oktroyiert*) Constitution of December 1848, which had retained democratic elements, had already been amended. The Junkers regained the privilege of entailing noble estates, recovered important policing powers on their estates, and fought off attempts to break their stranglehold over the old County and Provincial Diets (Kreistage and Provinziallandtage). While the principle of universal male adult suffrage was itself not tampered with, the introduction of a three-class franchise based on income weakened its democratic potential. This system was combined with an indirect voting system that had a similar effect. The Upper House, for its part, become a true *Herrenhaus*. The government intimidated or removed liberal and democratic civil servants. Judges could now be transferred or forcibly retired. A Disciplinary Law of 1852 heightened civil servants' dependence on the favor of the ministry. Promotion depended on exhibiting the "right attitude"; attendance at church was desirable. A complex system of surveillance was built up. Persecuted and demoralized, democrats did not take part in elections until 1855. If the powers and privileges of the nobility were

---

1. See W. Schmidt et al., *Die bürgerliche Umwälzung von 1780 bis 1871 (Deutsche Geschichte*, 4), East Berlin, 1984, pp. 275 ff. As good as any for capturing the flavor of these years is L.Pietsch, *Wie ich Schriftsteller geworden bin. Erinnerungen aus den Fünfziger Jahren*, vol. 1, Berlin, 1893. The legislation of these years is contained in P. Stoepel, *Preußisches Gesetz–Codex*, 2d ed., Frankfurt/O, 1862, vol. 3, *1849–56.*

strengthened, so too were those of the church whose influence over the educational system was extended. At elementary level, Ferdinand Stiehls's Regulations (1854) limited the syllabus in primary schools to the three Rs and put these schools under strict clerical supervision. In secondary schools and universities the liberal, humanist spirit of the Humboldt Reforms was attacked. Training colleges for teachers had to adhere to a restrictive syllabus.

Although the system of pre-publication censorship was not restored, the Press Law of 1851 introduced new repressive measures. All printers, booksellers, library owners and newspaper sellers now had to be officially authorized; copies of any but the most innocuous or official printed material had to be deposited with the police authorities before distribution or soon after it began; the editors of newspapers and magazines had to provide a security of up to 5000 talers; offending material could be confiscated and presses and plates impounded; depending on the court's findings, the copies already printed, like the plates, had to be destroyed entirely or the offending parts destroyed; printers stood to lose their livelihood. From 1854 onward serious press offences were no longer tried before a jury.[2] The Diet in Frankfurt consolidated these measures.

Writers who had been critical of the old system and often involved in revolutionary activities, had to make hard choices. Those who were civil servants or dependent on an official confirmation, privilege, or concession were often torn between their principles and fears of being victimized or disciplined. If they had lost their critical zeal or if literary activity was a leisure pursuit, they retired to the safer ground of cultured salons. In contrast, writers keen to retain the favor of their employer, the state, but also to achieve literary fame and financial success had various options. They could publicly recant, quietly abandon their previous principles, or try to elaborate strategies which would allow them to purvey at least some of their ideas without incurring official wrath. The state as employer and operator of the machinery of censorship and surveillance was one hurdle; the requirements of publishers and editors were another. Storm's

---

2. *Gesetz über die Presse*, 12 May 1851 in Stoepel, *Gesetz-Codex*, pp. 251ff; *Gesetz betreffend die Kompetenz der Gerichte zur Untersuchung und Entscheidung der politischen und der mittels der Presse verübten Vergehen*, March 1854, ibid., p. 419.

publisher Alexander Duncker, "bookseller by appointment to
the royal court," was an arch-conservative Prussian patriot with
a love of things military. His principles and his need to cater to
upper-class ladies able to buy expensive miniature, gold-leaf
editions meant that it was pointless submitting to him any overtly
radical works. In the early 1850s Paul Heyse, who had
recommended *Immensee* to Duncker, himself met with a frosty
reception from polite society when he attempted to present radical
political struggles and uphold the rights of "nature" in depictions of passion and adultery.[3]

In Potsdam and Berlin Storm also experienced the pressures
exerted by literary salons and societies. He encountered Berlin's
cultural and intellectual life in the so-called Tunnel über der Spree
and an offshoot, the Rütli.[4] Named after the first tunnel under
the Thames, the former, which met on Sundays in various cafes
and restaurants, comprised students, civil servants, professors,
doctors, business men, officers, artists and writers. Members
presented their creations, and a critical discussion followed. The
distinctions of rank in normal social life were blurred by bestow-
ing on all participants names like Tannhäuser (Storm) and
Immermann (Fontane). In theory the Tunnel proscribed politics
and religion; in practice, patriotic ballads about Prussian heroes
were not classed as *Tendenz* and enjoyed general favor. There
was even scope for political satires aimed solely at insiders. *Cher-
gal*, written by Wilhelm von Merckel about the Gerlachs, came
into that category. Radical, democratic views were another matter.
The same von Merckel – who took a strong liking to Storm –
coined the dictum "Gegen Demokraten helfen nur Soldaten."
Former 1848ers distanced themselves from their pasts. Thus Otto
Roquette wrote anodyne poetry, while the fastidious aesthete
Friedrich Eggers edited the *Deutsches Kunstblatt*. Feeling the
Tunnel to be insufficiently discriminating in aesthetic matters,
certain members set up a side-tunnel, the Rütli. Its leading light
was Franz Kugler, a professor in the history of art and a
high–ranking official in the Ministry of Culture, Education, and
Church Affairs. In 1848 he, too, had welcomed the revolution in
a collection of poems entitled *Deutsche Lieder*.

3. See M. Krausnick, *Paul Heyse und der Münchener Dichterkreis*, Bonn, 1974,
pp. 209f.
4. See T. Fontane, *Von Zwanzig bis Dreißig*, Berlin, 1898; H.Nürnberger, *Der
frühe Fontane, Politik-Poesie-Geschichte, 1840–1860*, Hamburg, 1967.

Storm, who was welcomed as a love poet (*Erotiker*) and writer of charming novellas, grasped this opportunity to present his poems and his theories on lyric poetry to a cultured audience. His lyric gifts were immediately recognized. Fontane, for example, despite having reservations about Storm the person and Storm the prose writer, did not waver in his praise of Storm the lyric poet. However, this circle encouraged only certain elements in Storm's repertoire, and he soon encountered opposition when he submitted to the group's magazine, *Argo*, his novella *Ein grünes Blatt* together with the poem "Ein Epilog." Fontane stressed that the editorial team could not risk publishing a poem that anticipated further spring storms, especially ones that would lead to a glorious, golden day! Storm was to give the poem a specifically Schleswig-Holstein slant and, by all means, emphasize the German-patriotic element: ". . . aber was nach der einigen, unteilbaren deutschen Republik schmeckt, könnte uns 'Beamteten' doch sehr verübelt werden. Sie fühlen dabei vielleicht: 'nette Kerle das,' aber das Märtyrertum, schon an für sich eine kitzliche Sache, kann unmöglich von Personen erwartet werden, die teils ausgesprochenermaaßen, teils unbewußt au fond du coeur die besten Preußen und Royalisten von der Welt sind."[5] Morally seditious pieces were also taboo. The poem "Geschwisterblut" with its theme of the incestuous love between brother and sister threw the group into consternation, and pressure was put on Storm to remove any suggestion that this was not some unnatural, ungodly perversion. Storm made changes.

His criticism of Prussia had to be confined to private letters and conversations with trusted confidants. Fear of the censor's prying eye and possible repercussions acted as a further brake. The isolated critical remarks in his letters to his parents were later often removed by Gertrud Storm. Thus she suppressed her father's indignation with a speech made at a dinner on the king's birthday by Seyfert, the vice-president of the audit office. Despite the fact that Frederich William IV was, Storm wrote, a demi-constitutional king after all, Seyfert applied to him the dictum so detested by Frederick II, *l'état, c'est moi*.[6] In conversations with

---

5. Fontane to Storm, 11 April 1853, *Storm-Fontane*, p. 28.
6. Storm to his parents, 7 October 1855. In 1862 Seyfert visisted Nordhausen and was keen to visit Storm in Heiligenstadt. Storm avoided the encounter: "Der Mann ist mir unheimlich." See Storm to his parents, 18 February 1862.

people like Theodor Fontane or Ludwig Pietsch, the artist, journalist and writer, Storm relentlessly criticized the Prussian system. He was particularly critical of the vast sums expended on the army.[7] This criticism of Prussia was given short shrift as long as German hagiography and literary criticism were dominated by "Borussian" categories. Storm was presented as an ill-informed provincial unable to do justice to Prussia and its world-historical role. Even afterward the fact that Fontane had denied his critical competence still counted against him. What was often forgotten was, first, that after 1848 Fontane's Prussian patriotism stiffened and, secondly, that financial and professional considerations made him court the authorities. Uncomfortable about these compromises, he was sensitive to Storm's outspoken, and no doubt often self-righteous, condemnation of those lacking the courage of their convictions. Storm's commendation of "goldne Rücksichtslosigkeiten," in the poem "Für meine Söhne" (LL 1, 66) continued to irritate him many years later. It is also often overlooked just how much Fontane, while criticizing Wilhelminian Germany, failed to see the link between this "new" Prussia-Germany and the "old" Prussia with which he identified.

The letters that Storm and Fontane exchanged in 1853 illustrated the two men's very different positions. Having praised the warmth of his reception, Storm referred to something he found antipathetic in the Berlin air:

> Es ist, meine ich, das, daß auch in den gebildeten Kreisen man den Schwerpunkt nicht in die Persönlichkeit, sondern in Rang, Titel, Orden und dergleichen Nipps legt, für deren auch nur verhältnismäßige Würdigung mir, wie wohl den meisten meiner Landleute, jedes Organ abgeht. Es scheint mir *im Ganzen* die "goldne Rücksichtslosigkeit" zu fehlen, die allein den Menschen innerlich frei macht und die nach meiner Ansicht das letzte und höchste Resultat jeder Bildung sein muß. Man scheint sich mir in Berlin mit der *Geschmacksbildung* zu begnügen, mit der Rücksichtnahme auf alle Factoren eines bequemen Lebens ungestört bestehen kann, während die Vollendung der sittlichen, der Gemüthsbildung in einer Zeit, wie die unsre, jeden Augenblick das Opfer aller Lebensverhältnisse und güter verlangen kann.[8]

---

7. Storm to Brinkmann, 18 December 1854, *Storm-Brinkmann*, p. 102.
8. Storm to Fontane, 27 March 1853, *Storm-Fontane*, p. 26.

In Fontane's view Storm was doing the people of Berlin an injustice. No other state, with perhaps the exception of France, was so close to achieving the "chimera of equality" as was Prussia:

> Die mannigfachen Kräfte unsres Staats wie unsres gesammten Lebens rivalisieren nicht untereinander und keiner drängt sich vor. Es giebt nirgends in der Welt, *auch in Frankreich nicht*, so wenig eine "exklusive Gesellschaft" wie hier bei uns. Geburt, Reichtum, Rang, Talent und Wissen vertragen sich hier in wunderbarer Weise und Graf Arnim, mit einem halben Fürstentum hinter sich, verkehrt mit dem Lokomotivenbauer Borsig oder mit Professor Dove völlig ebenso wie mit seines Gleichen. Ja, ich muß es bekennen, wie haben von diesem Nivellement zuviel und kranken an einer *Impietät*, die bereits der Ankergrund war und *wieder sein wird*, drauf die Revolution (bei uns ein reiner Einwanderer) ihren Haken auswirft.[9]

Storm replied that for him the yardstick with which to measure this alleged levelling was whether a count would marry his daughter to a locomotive builder or a professor. In his view, a young man should not frequent a house where he knew that he would not be considered a suitable match for any daughter. After that they let the matter drop. To the end of his life Fontane rejected Storm's position as philistinism.

In matters relating to love, behavior between the sexes and sex itself the two were poles apart. As we have seen, Storm drew a sharp distinction between the cult of love and sex in literary works and any discussion of intimate matters in company or even in private with a close friend. A man-of-the-world attitude to sex was alien to him. That, together with his obsession with "ladies' men" (*Courmacher*), meant that when Fontane talked to a third party about his, Fontane's, marital relations and addressed some *double-entendres* to Constanze, Storm accused him of "lacking seriousness."[10] A discussion about *pudeur*, decency, and chastity resulted. Forty years later this impugning of his moral character still rankled with Fontane. Free of Storm's prudishness at the level of social contacts, he was more inhibited at the literary level. In general he found Storm's depictions of love and passion overblown, unconvincing, and even somewhat lascivious.[11]

---

9. Fontane to Storm, 2 May 1853, ibid., p. 33.
10. Storm to Fontane, 24 July 1854, ibid., pp. 87f.

The works which Storm wrote in Potsdam reflect the constraints to which he was subject. *Im Sonnenschein* (1854) juxtaposes the old times with the new, contrasting the prospects of a modern young man and his bride with the fate of a great-aunt whose life is blighted by the prejudices of the urban patriciate against the aristocracy, by an authoritarian father and by an ethos which subordinates the demands of the heart to the interests of the family firm. It is the familiar Storm scenario of individuals betraying their true happiness by obeying class norms. Hero and heroine lack the values, the will, and the courage with which to challenge existing norms. Storm avoids any impression of wanting to criticize aristocratic exclusiveness. At a time when the least suspicion of democratic sentiments was taboo, he could only hope to maneuver his readers into feeling that love and the rights of the individual should prevail over class barriers and other interests if he proceeded discreetly. A Feuerbachian message could perhaps be conveyed by contrasting the two lovers' moment of happiness with the reminders of human mortality in the family vault and by juxtaposing the grandmother's long and fulfilled life and the happiness awaiting her grandson and his bride with Franziska's descent into illness and death.

In theory, a novella based on the early years of his marriage and his love for Doris Jensen could have enabled Storm to broach the issues of courtship, marriage, and monogamy. However, in 1855, the authorities would not have tolerated the trials and torments of adulterers or any questioning of monogamy. In the novella *Angelica* (1855) everything had to be cloaked, and unconvincing explanations found to explain why the lovers cannot marry. Analyzing the strains which destroy Angelica's integrity and produce a doppelgänger within her could have produced a fascinating study; but Storm's obsessions with women who betray their love and themselves by tolerating approaches from other males prevented that. With its clumsy, sultry climaxes and its mannered style and symbolism, *Angelica* represents Storm's writing at its worst.

---

11. See D. Lohmeier, "Theodor Fontane über den 'Eroticismus und die Husumerei' Storms: Fontanes Briefwechsel mit Hedwig Büchting," *STSG*, vol. 39, 1990, pp. 26–45.

4.2 Capitalism, National-Liberalism, and Poetic Realism

Reactionary though it was in political matters, the Prussian government encouraged the growth of a liberal, capitalist economy by extending the free trade area and introducing legal changes that made it easier to form joint-stock companies and raise capital with which to fund new ventures. Production and foreign trade more than doubled. The slump in 1857 only seemed to underline the need for German unity and a national market.[12] Publicists were confident that capitalism would shift the balance of power in favor of the middle classes by undermining the hegemony of the landed interest. The temporary vogue of Schopenhauerian pessimism passed, and abstract theories and airy utopias went out of fashion. The new slogans were "real," "actual," "practical," and "objective." Business men, scientists, empirical historians, and pragmatic politicians (*Realpolitiker*) acquired heightened appeal. The buoyant economy revived the hopes of those liberals advocating a united Germany organized on a monarchical, constitutional basis with a Prussian head and a restricted franchise. This *kleindeutsch* program was complemented by a body of aesthetic principles known as Ideal or True Realism and often loosely referred to as Poetic Realism.[13] In the *Grenzboten* Julian Schmidt and Gustav Freytag adapted older classical-idealist notions to the new socio-economic and political objectives. Instead of satirizing the status quo or sketching utopias, literature was to concentrate on "the true" (*das Wahre*), i.e. the positive essence underlying the present. The "actual" or "real" (*das Wirkliche*) was to be avoided: it might exhibit misleading superficial blemishes. If ideal and reality had not yet converged, they were on course to do so in the near future. During this period of transition, writers were to transfigure and poeticize the present. In this way they would contribute to the advent of the ideal – a unified, free Germany.

The great flagship of the movement, Gustav Freytag's novel *Soll und Haben* (1855) was well suited to purveying national-lib-

12. See T.S. Hamerow, *The Social Foundations of German Unification 1858–1871*, 2 vols., Princeton, 1969–72.

13 See H. Widhammer, *Realismus und klassizistische Tradition*, Tübingen, 1972; idem, *Die Literaturtheorie des deutschen Realismus (1848–1860)*, Stuttgart, 1977; H. Kinder, *Poesie als Synthese*, Frankfurt, 1973.

eral ideas to a wide audience blending as it did elements from Charles Dickens, Eugène Sue, Fenimore Cooper, romances and penny dreadfuls. The novel's professed goal was to convey the "poetry of work." Any criticism of capitalism is directed away from the hardworking, virtuous Schröter and his paternalist wholesaling firm and projected either on to the Jews with their shady ventures or on to cut-throat American capitalism with its speculative land and financial deals. In order to strengthen the middle classes' sense of their identity, the novel paints a critical picture of a Junker family, the von Rothsattels. With their lavish lifestyle they cannot hope to reverse their decline by engaging in agro-industrial ventures or mortgaging their estates to raise capital for dubious deals. On the other hand, if schooled in middle-class business practices, dynamic aristocrats can extend German influence over chaotic Slav elements by running estates based on innovative techniques in colonized territories. Despite the criticism of the Junkers one can discern here a potential future accommodation between them and the middle classes. The urban factory proletariat does not figure in the work at all. The manual workers who appear are depicted as childlike giants with idiosyncracies which would debar them from full political rights. They are loyal to their corporation and their employer; their sons proudly accept their subordinate position in firm, army, society, and state.

The novel stresses the need for the middle classes to overcome any fascination with the world of the aristocracy. The hero Anton Wohlfart thus recognizes that an aristocratic girl can never be a suitable bride for him. Sex and passion have no place in a middle-class marriage. The novel is racist, being both anti-Semitic and anti-Slav. A Jewish intellectual, Bernhard Ehrenthal, is condemned for refusing to acknowledge the poetry and drama inherent in middle-class business operations. He is interested only in the exotic and things past. Life finally overwhelms him.

Whereas Fontane commended the novel, Storm remained largely critical. In the coming years he would explore many of the same issues. But would he adopt Freytag's categorization of business activities? Would he depict the German middle class as enjoying a monopoly of ethical and intellectual qualities and immune to aristocratic norms? Would he suggest that the aristocracy's decline was inevitable and that an accommodation between sections of it and the middle classes might be desirable?

Would the state, society, family, and firm of the future be constructed on the same patriarchal lines? The novella *Auf dem Staatshof* (1858) provided the answers to some of these questions.

4.3   *Auf dem Staatshof*

Written over the period 1856–58, i.e. after Storm's move to Heiligenstadt but at a time there was still no end in sight to the Manteuffel Era, *Auf dem Staatshof* is one of Storm's major works. A fictional narrator, Marx, depicts the life and death of Anne Lene, the sole surviving member of a once proud and propertied patrician family. In a brief preface (LL 1, 392) he states that he can only relate what happened, not how it happened; that he does not know whether her end was a *eine Tat*, i.e. suicide, or *ein Ereignis*, i.e. an accident; and that he will relate events as they trickle into his memory. This preface has been interpreted as a statement of Storm's own aesthetic principles. He, like Marx, allegedly rejected a sharply focused, uncompromising analysis of reality since it would have promoted disillusionment.[14] I would argue that this is a questionable assumption and that, by identifying Storm with his narrator and privileging Marx's voice, it obscures the strategies employed to make the reader critical of Marx and his values. The *Schlesische Zeitung* rejected the story as "nicht spannend genug" (see LL 1, 1075), and the preface, which was added late in the day, may, with its suggestion of suspense and mystery, have been intended to whet the appetites of feuilleton readers. Its significance lies in the light it sheds on the values of this member of the educated, professional middle classes in the 1850s. Why does Marx retreat from analysis? Why does he claim to confine himself to unstructured reminiscences? Is his would-be objectivity not an illusion?

Throughout, the text underlines how Marx's behavior toward Anne Lene is rooted in middle-class norms and anti-patrician prejudices, according to which the middle classes – industrious, thrifty, healthy, and "moral" – must prosper while the improvident, foolhardy, effete patricians come to grief. Such providential

14. See D. Lohmeier, "Erzählprobleme des Poetischen Realismus. Am Beispiel von Storms Novelle Auf dem Staatshof." *STSG*, vol. 28, pp. 109–22.

arrangements should lead to an ideal, humane society. They manifestly do not. Indeed Marx is disillusioned by socio-economic trends. The middle classes are split into *Bildungsbürgertum* and *Bourgeoisie*. The latter's increasing influence on society has little to do with morality, humanity, truth, or justice. On the other hand, the text conveys Marx the *Bildungsbürger's* sense of being unable to shape reality. While continuing to practice as a doctor, he retires from an alienated reality to an equally alienating artificial paradise of beauty and culture.

In rejecting theory, abstractions and "ideals," Marx typifies a mood widespread in the 1850s. But here professional and commercial activities are not equated with morality and culture. Marx does not overcome a fascination with patrician culture and recognize work to be dramatic and poetic. His final position is the preface's "agnosticism" about causation and overall patterns of development. In fact, this champion of facts and sound practical principles espouses irrational categories like fate, presenting human beings as incapable of influencing their destiny and absolved of any personal guilt or responsibility for the course of events.

The text unmasks his "neutrality." Whatever he may say, his story is structured. Indeed the text suggests that he is impelled to write by a sense of guilt and a need to convince himself – and the reader – of his innocence. Storm maintains a constant tension between Marx's presentation and alternative categories and constructions. But because he does not employ a *raisonneur* or use an insistent, authorial voice, only attention to the contrary pointers in the text enables the reader to resist Marx's interpretations. Here I can only isolate key themes and sketch some of Storm's techniques.

Marx's account of a visit to the patrician farm as a small child (LL 1, 394f.) introduces the thematic complex of health, practicality and "realism," on the one hand, and their counterparts, degeneracy, impracticality, and "idealism," on the other. Marx annexes the former for himself and the middle classes, while projecting the latter on to Anne Lene and the patricians. His ambivalent attitude toward the patriciate emerges: he is torn between aesthetic, cultural fascination and moral disapproval. Thus he depicts Anne Lene as a fragile, rare being inhabiting an exquisite world, but one divorced from everyday reality. The text, in contrast, reveals an earthy, agrarian world where masters and men share the same roof as animals, implements, and hay and where elecampane is hung up to drive away midges. And while Marx is awed by the grandmother's cult of bearing and decorum, the sequence conveys how unresponsive he is to other more important human values like the warm affection for Anne Lene of the farmhand Marten and his wife Wieb.

In Marx's eyes the scene in the *Heubarg* (LL 1, 394f.) underlines Anne Lene's fascination with death. In fact, it underlines the importance for a small child of a sense of security and caring support. In a potentially threatening situation, the four-year-old boy's feeling of well-being depends on Wieb's presence, which is skillfully withheld until late in the scene. The episode also shows Anne Lene coming to terms with experiences like loneliness and bereavement of which Marx is unaware in his cosseted world.

For Marx the pavilion (LL 1, 396) symbolizes the fragility of the patrician world and is an omen of Anne Lene's later drowning here. What is really important escapes him – the significance, first, of his pleasure at seeing his mother take Anne Lene onto her lap and kiss her and, secondly, of the two children's feeling of total security as they play under the table. The reader alert to Storm's cues notices how the story is quietly stressing that human beings have a fundamental need for love and security. For a brief moment the orphaned Anne Lene enjoys them here. Much later (LL 1, 424) she still has a vague, warm memory of the incident.

In a finite, mortal world where aging, suffering, illness, and death play an important part, individuals' responses to other people's needs are crucial. Marx is repeatedly found wanting. All the certainties of his sheltered life are endangered as he looks into a deserted room after the death of Anne Lene's grandmother (LL 1, 401). He is on the brink of experiencing that "existential" sense of the loneliness of the isolated individual human being which underlies Storm's emphasis on the need for human love and support in a godless world without supernatural comforters. Yet he is disturbed before the potential revelation can make its full impact on him. The scene also brings out the inadequacy of his response to Anne Lene's grief. Instead of showing concern and affection, he savors the aesthetic effect of her pale face and golden hair against her black weeds. It is left to her to fling her arms round his neck and dissolve into tears. These details illustrate Storm's pictorial, "concrete" style at its most effective. The funeral with its pomp and ceremony only generates in Marx a pleasant *Feiertagsgefühl*. In his mind culture and love, death and beauty grow ever closer – in a realm divorced from everyday reality.

The novella captures Storm's fears about the educated middle classes' lack of an autonomous cultural identity. For Marx these Sunday flights to an artificial, exquisite world of "culture" divorced from the demands of workaday reality become part and parcel of his fractured response to life. Far from seeking a culture which emanates from the *Volksseele* or incarnates modern, democratic aspirations, he espouses *ancien régime* norms. The later sections of the novella conjure up the prospect of a society in which *Bildungsbürger* like Marx sever their social, cultural, and aesthetic, if not their professional, links with the new commercial and industrial bourgeoisie. But in opting to safeguard their fastidious standards, they condemn themselves to social irrelevance and leave the field open to others ready to humor the new paymasters.

Equally important in terms of Storm's ideals is the way in which the text presents emotional and sexual relations between the sexes. Marx's reification of Anne Lene into an exquisite, exotic object serves a real social function: a gracious porcelain figure (LL 1, 397) cannot command the commitment which a "real" woman might demand. Education and career are not affected. While Marx fantasizes, Anne Lene remains a lonely teenager starved of warmth and affection. Instead of being brought up to be kind and loving adults in a modern, humane society, middle-class males are initiated into feudal, chivalric patterns of social behavior. Ideas about relations between the sexes are fostered which make it impossible to show warm, spontaneous feeling and communicate naturally. The realization (LL 1, 404f.) that Anne Lene has grown into a young woman only heightens Marx's need to abstract from her real situation and turn her into a symbol of pure beauty tinged by death. He departs for the university without considering the effects on her of his absence and forgets her amid the "joys and sufferings" of university life (LL 1, 411).

The text also sheds light on Storm's assessment of German society's democratic potential. It is interesting to contrast the way in which Freytag, the liberal, depicts middle-class attitudes toward social inferiors with the manner in which Storm, the democrat, criticizes Marx's treatment of his boyhood "plebeian protégé," the cobbler's son Simon (LL 1, 399f.). Marx's attempt to portray

Anne Lene as guilty of caste-exclusiveness and blame his behavior on her obscures the fact that she moves away from caste prejudices (LL 1, 420), whereas he becomes further estranged from any artisan contacts. He dismisses the claims of the young beggar woman whom one of Anne Lene's ancestors cheated when she was his ward, and manhandles her out of Anne Lene's presence. She, in contrast, insists on Wieb telling her the truth about her family. Having digested the unpleasant revelations, she modifies her views and actions accordingly. She, not Marx, could become a citizen of a democratic society.

The novella also considers the educated middle classes' attitude to the aristocracy. Because Storm's own hostility comes through so strongly, it is easy to imagine that Marx and his father also share this unequivocal stance. Marx may present the *Kammerjunker* as a bird of prey and he is repelled by his tormenting of a fly; but he does not intervene. Nor does he act to prevent Anne Lene falling into his clutches. He neither questions the aristocratic principle nor challenges it. Further, nothing in the story suggests that the nobility's power is waning.

Storm's attitude toward the new commercial bourgeoisie is also not to be confused with Marx's. Claus Peters, the brewer's son, does emerge from Marx's account as brash and brutal and his behavior toward Drees does remind Marx of feudal robber barons; but it is Anne Lene who ends the disgraceful proceedings (LL 1, 417f). In fact, Marx consorts socially with Claus Peters and his set. It is he who gets them invited to the farm.

The later sections of the novella convey how bankrupt he is in human terms by highlighting his inability to register and respond to Anne Lene's needs. Yet the text does not present his alienation as total. Indeed it was vital for Storm to be able to postulate a core of involuntary needs and spontaneous impulses capable of surviving society's pressures:

In diese heimlichen Laute der Nacht drang plötzlich von der Gegend des Deiches her der gellende Ruf eines Seevogels, der hoch durch die Luft dahin fuhr. Da mein Ohr einmal geweckt war, so vernahm ich nun auch aus der Ferne das Branden der Wellen, die in der hellen Nacht sich draußen über der wüsten geheimnisvollen Tiefe wälzten und von der kommenden Flut dem Strande zugeworfen wurden. Ein Gefühl der Öde und Verlorenheit überfiel mich; fast ohne es zu wissen stieß ich Anne Lenes Namen hervor und streckte beide Arme nach ihr aus.

"Marx, was ist Dir? rief sie und wandte sich nach mir um. 'Hier bin ich ja!"

"Nichts, Anne Lene," sagte ich, "aber gib mir Deine Hand; ich hatte das Meer vergessen, da hörte ich es plötzlich!" (LL 1, 423)

But this "revelation" cannot triumph over his inhibitions and emotional disabilities. Having clasped her hand, he cannot do or say anything else. Storm skilfully uses gestures, expressions and words to convey this human *débâcle*. It confirms Anne Lene in her belief that this would-be knight errant and classical Orpheus cannot redeem her. To the end Marx does not give her any clear indication of love and does not commit himself to her. His ruminations about whether she slipped or committed suicide are diversions. The truth which he tries to repress is that he must bear the blame for much of her tragedy.

In the final paragraph he tells how Claus Peters, having become a prosperous beef exporter to Britain, tears down the old farm and builds in its place a modern, expensively furnished house, which he, Marx, never visited. He does not ask any of the questions posed by the text itself: Will such bourgeois be better or worse masters than the patricians? Will they challenge the aristocracy and struggle for a better, democratic future? Or will they be further feudalized and reach some accommodation with the aristocracy? If the educated professional classes retire from the economic, cultural, and ideological fray, who will articulate democratic aspirations? Storm would tackle these issues in the 1860s.

4.4 Heiligenstadt

In 1856 Storm was appointed to the County Court (*Kreisgericht*) in Heiligenstadt.[15] Like the whole Eichsfeld area, the town had belonged to the Bishopric of Mainz until it was transferred to Prussia in the early 1800s. It was staunchly Catholic. After an intermezzo in Napoleon's creation, the Kingdom of Westphalia,

15. For material on Heiligenstadt see G. Jaritz et al. (eds), *Theodor Storm und Heiligenstadt, Sonderausgabe der Eichsfelder Heimathefte*, Heiligenstadt, 1978; *Theodor Storm und Heiligenstadt. Beiträge zur Theodor–Storm-Ehrung 1988, Sonderausgabe der Eichsfelder Heimathefte*, Heiligenstadt, 1988.

it had in 1815 become a *Kreisstadt* in the Erfurt district or *Bezirk*, which itself formed part of the Prussian Province of Saxony. In 1858 it had under five thousand inhabitants, of whom four-fifths were Catholic. There was a small Jewish community. The town, which was not linked to the railway network and had to be reached by coach from Göttingen, was still ringed by town walls. Its three gates were closed each night, and a night-watchman blew the hours from a church tower. Street lighting was non-existent; in the main street water was drawn from the gulley flowing past the houses.

The administrative structure followed the standard Prussian pattern. The linchpin was the Landrat, the representative of central government at county level. The County Court had two divisions. Storm heard cases in the petty-sessions court, was a member of the court of assize, and sat on the panel of judges dealing with serious criminal cases. Petty sessions were also held in the surrounding villages. Heiligenstadt had a grammar school which, in Storm's view, was not "finsterlingisch,"[16] i.e. not a stronghold of dark superstition. There were the usual private schools, one of which his sons attended before moving to the grammar school. Confident that the atmosphere in the family home could neutralize any Catholic propaganda, Storm sent Lisbeth (b. 1855) to one run by an order of French sisters.

The area was economically backward. Storm learned from a maid how in the Eichsfeld villages all the members of a family worked on a farmer's land over the summer in return for the right to grow potatoes. At a time when butter cost six silver groschen per pound, the daily wage, if one was available, was two silver groschen. A pound of dripping was regarded as a luxury. This was hardship on a scale he had not dreamed of before.[17]

The role played by the Catholic church was also a novel experience. He saw the connection between the inhabitants' poverty and their piety: "Dabei ist das Mädchen von einer kindlichen gläubigen Naivität, und über all dem Elend schwebt der katholische Himmel mit seinen Weihrauchswolken, seinen Blumen– und Flitterkränzen und seinem Glockenläuten."[18] In 1862

16. Storm to his father, 8 October 1856, ibid., p. 9.
17. Ibid, p. 8.
18. Ibid, p. 8.

he would write to Theodor Mommsen of "der ganze katholische Schwindel."[19] The issue of whether Catholicism was compatible with enlightenment and modern ethical notions loomed large in his fiction during these years.

The social and cultural life which Heiligenstadt could offer was a far cry from what had been available in Potsdam and Berlin. The custom persisted of men, women and girls being invited out separately, the women and girls for tea or coffee, the men to dinners and for punch. Although Storm did not join a *Plauderklub* of teachers and civil-servants because he could not stand tobacco smoke, the Storms were members of a *Ressourcengesellschaft*, or leisure and entertainment circle, which was involved, among other things, in amateur dramatics. Constanze found the women of her class addicted to gossip and restricted in their interests.[20] Storm at last found the friend he sought in a seemingly strange quarter – in the Landrat, Alexander von Wussow. In the hope that he would be independent and dynamic enough to resist the Catholic clergy's ambitions, the Prussian authorities in 1857 appointed as Landrat a young Protestant aristocrat from outside the network of local noble families and married to a Protestant. Later Storm was to be equally attached to the Husum Landrat, Ludwig von Reventlow. Given his political views it may seem paradoxical that he should have had as his close friends two conservative aristocrats. In the case of Wussow the explanation – apart from the element of personal chemistry – lies in their shared passion for literature, art and music. Wussow, who had himself written a social novel, unabashedly poured out the feelings aroused by the novel *Maler Nolten* to its author Mörike. It also helped that Wussow's wife, a dyed-in-the-wool aristocrat, mothered the Storms and was very good to the children.

This friendship illustrates the hopes Storm attached to *Bildung*. It supposedly united people of all classes on a plane above and beyond class; the corpus of ideas and norms around which it was built would bring aristocrats to relinquish their prejudices. In psychological terms the notion of *Bildung* was invaluable to Storm and the *Bildungsbürgertum*. It both heightened resentment of aristocrat pretensions while at the same time making it easier

19. Storm to Mommsen, 15 April 1862, *Storm-Mommsen* p. 118.
20. Constanze to Charlotte Esmarch, 11 September 1857, SHLB; Constanze to E. Esmarch, 5 February 1857, SHLB.

to endure them in the short term. *Bildung* and *Humanität* would, it was confidently predicted, ultimately prevail. Storm forgot what he himself had recognized in Berlin, namely that in certain circles *Bildung* might well be an aesthetic, cultural goal but that this did not necessarily entail any commitment to democratic, humanitarian ideals. When, during Bismarck's first period of office, Wussow condemned the government's policies, *Bildung* seemed to be doing its quiet work. However, his support for Bismarck's policy in the Schleswig-Holstein crisis and a hardening of his conservatism soon disabused Storm. Relations cooled. Once both men had left Heiligenstadt, the old intensity was lost. In the late 1860s Storm could still not forgive the Prussians – and with them, Wussow – for their treatment of Schleswig-Holstein. There was occasional contact, but nothing more.

Storm attempted some minor social engineering, founding – as he had done in Husum – a mixed choral society open to all, in which he sought to transmit modern sensibility via the music of composers like Schumann and Mendelssohn. In an attempt to break away from established patterns of socializing and avoid the sumptuous entertaining which debarred the less well-off, some fifteen to twenty families formed a "Roman Evening," named after a similar venture which a participant had known in Italy. On Thursdays members met on an informal basis at one of their houses, with only tea and cake being provided. Activities included singing, reading, performing charades, and doing tableaux. In theory this arrangement could have helped bridge the cultural and educational gap separating the classes. In fact, its members were virtually all civil servants and their wives. The situation highlighted the wider problems facing middle-class democrats. In terms of education, life-style and professional outlook the great majority of them had more in common with the aristocrat civil servants, whose political opponents they were, than with the lower classes as whose champions they saw themselves.

Storm's experiences with his brother Otto typify these problems. After a chequered career the latter had bought a market garden in Heiligenstadt with capital provided by Storm senior. Despite having already failed once in Berlin, Storm renewed his efforts to integrate his brother into the world of educated notables since this was, in his view, a prerequisite for achieving the good and beautiful life. Indeed one cannot envisage him leading a social life revolving around artisans or workers – whatever the contrary noises in novellas like *Pole Poppenspäler*. Whereas Otto was sometimes rude to the high nobility,[21] Storm observed the forms. Feeling that he was only tolerated in the "Roman Evening" because of his brother ("Die Beamten, was die sich dünkten, er habe eben so viel oder mehr Bildung, als diese Kerls' etc."[22], Otto soon resigned. While ready to concede that some members might feel it beneath them to accept an invitation from a gardener, Storm denied that Otto's feelings were justified and spoke of "pathological arrogance." In fact, whatever Otto's oddities, it was Storm who had a blind spot in this area. He was conscious of being as educated as any member of this group; his status as a judge was secure; he was fêted as a poet; and he moved easily in these circles. Above all he was sustained by his conviction of the superiority and long-term prospects of middle-class *Intelligenz* and *Sittlichkeit*. And yet, as he himself admitted, even he could easily have felt offended when Wussow did not invite him to a dinner given for his father.[23] Otto lacked any of these breastplates and picked up the social prejudice toward him not just of aristocratic but also of middle-class members. His wife Wilhelmine came, as Constanze put it, from "simple circumstances." She found it difficult to relate to her sister-in-law and accept her notions of housekeeping and child rearing. In Constanze's eyes, the fact that she was always afraid of causing offense, was stiff in her movements and found all sorts of things unseemly[24] was proof that she did not belong to the educated classes. The two families avoided each other. Storm even thought of seeking a transfer.

He could not understand either Otto's apparent lack of any desire for an elegant, cultured ambiance or his resentment of those like himself who did. Later, on encountering similar traits in his own sons, he would regard them as inherited Storm traits. He himself had inherited Woldsen ones. Otto's behavior conflicted with Storm's notion of an innate "Drang nach schöner

---

21. Storm to Kreisgerichtsrat Schnee, 30 May 1858, SHLB.
22. Storm to his parents, 6 December 1861. Already, 30 September 1860, he had written to them: "Der Hochmuthsteufel frißt den armen Jungen noch völlig auf."
23. Storm to Contanze, 4 August 1858
24. Constanze to L. Brinkmann, 3 February 1862, SHLB, and to E. Esmarch, 13 January 1860, SHLB.

Gestaltung des Lebens" which underlies both *Späte Rosen* (1859) and *Auf der Universität* (1863). Whatever Storm may have written in the mid-1870s about Christoph, the hero of the novella *Drüben am Markt* (1860), being one of those gauche, helpless natures lacking the capacity to satisfy this aspiration,[25] the text largely attributes his tragedy to his socio-economic circumstances and the persistence of patrician social and cultural norms.

In the Heiligenstadt years the gap yawned wide between Storm's actual life-style and his ideal. In Husum his practice had prospered, and the Storms had no financial worries. Things changed dramatically when he entered the Prussian judiciary. Auskultatoren, Referendare and Assessore had to be content either with no salary at all or with a mere pittance. At the same time they were expected to maintain a fitting life-style from private means. Storm, who was granted Assessor status, at first received no salary at all, then a mere 25 talers. Temporarily it rose to 40. Even before he was appointed to Heiligenstadt, he was aware that he needed at least 1000 talers whereas his initial salary would be 500 or at most 600. One of the continuities of his life emerged: an unrelenting struggle to make ends meet. Particularly galling was the knowledge that the salaries of Prussian civil servants were depressed because of the large military expenditure: "Wenn nur die Soldaten nicht zu theuer wären."[26]

Although the cost of living was lower than in Potsdam, Storm continued to be dependent on his father. This lack of money affected all areas. Thus it initially prevented him approaching the Wussows and he had to make do without a piano until his father made him a gift of one. He felt himself to be on the brink of the proletariat.[27] Having to live from hand to mouth and to draw on his expectations from his father's will without being able to build up any capital of his own conflicted with ingrained class notions and his own psychological need for security. The itemized accounts presented to his father let one see exactly how the money was spent. Thus in 1858, with a quarterly salary of 147 talers, 22 silvergroschen, his outgoings were: 5 talers to Constanze as a supplement for "the last three difficult months"; 40 talers housekeeping money for April and 35 for May when the servant would be away; 10 talers for clothing for this quarter

25. Storm to K.T. Pyl, 7 April 1875, *Briefe* 2, p. 101.
26. Storm to his parents, 17 January 1861.
27. Storm to L. Pietsch, *Blätter der Freundschaft*, 9 July 1862, p. 82.

to Constanze; 10/20 talers for the two maids; 7 talers for a waistcoat, cloth and underpants for himself; 3 talers for school fees; 15 talers for civic taxes, poor-tax and charitable contributions; 9 talers to the maid for travel; 6 talers for miscellaneous items like postage, wages of seamstresses, medicine. The total came to 145 talers. But in addition a doctor's bill of 22 talers, 10 silvergroschen and one of 14 talers from the chemist had to be paid. For the quarter he still needed 35 talers housekeeping money for June and 22 talers for rent. He owed 6 talers for the transport of firewood and needed to buy another 15 talers worth – which would cost 6 talers to transport. Together with school fees and other outgoings it meant that, for the quarter, Storm needed 100 talers from his father by the end of the month. He found having to beg in this way an embarrassing and humiliating experience, the hardest part of the martyrdom of exile. And yet he and Constanze could not trim their budget any more without living like the family of a day laborer: "Aber wir sollen doch Wohnung und Kleidung haben, wir wollen alle essen und im Winter nicht frieren."[28] Cutting costs by heating a minimum of rooms and getting rid of a maid did not solve the problem; it did mean that Storm wrote works like *Im Schloß* cooped up in one room with his own and neighbors' children. If his father delayed a payment, further requests had to be made: "Da die Noth immer höher steigt – wir haben nichts mehr zu leben . . ."[29] His father-in-law also provided loans. Constanze complained of how difficult it was for a housewife with so many children: the cost of basic necessities was rising each week; the boys were eating more and more and yet the housekeeping money remained the same. To set an example, Storm did without sugar and butter in the mornings. But even here considerations of class and status interfered: they had to stop picking rosehips having been reminded that people of their class were expected to buy them from the locals.[30] One of the attractions of social visits to the Landrat's was that there the Storms enjoyed forbidden luxuries – tea and coffee. Storm's depictions of an affluent life-style in novellas like *Späte Rosen* (1859) and *Von jenseit des Meeres* (1865) have to be seen against this background.

28. Storm to his father, 12 April 1858, *Briefe* 1, pp. 341f.
29. Storm to his father, 26 November 1859
30. Constanze to Lucie Storm, 1 October 1861, SHLB.

Storm's frustrations were heightened by the consciousness that his judicial duties, while not enabling him to support his family, were preventing him from earning literary fees. His frustration at having to perform daily tasks where the sole interest was to get them out of the way[31] fueled his concern with alienation. In Potsdam he had spoken of "Menschenverbrauch" and "Menschenverkauf"[32] as well as of "Justizquälerei."[33]

He had complained of the "Arbeits-Hetzjagd" that prevented him having time or energy left for his real interests and his children: ". . . und ich gestehe gern, daß ich mein Leben nicht gering genug anschlage, um mich mit völliger Resignation als ein bloßes Rad in der Staatsmaschine anzusehen. Ich halte es vielmehr für Pflicht gegen die Meinen, und namentlich gegen mich selbst, wenn irgend möglich in andre Verhältnisse zu treten, in denen ich mein Pfund besser verwerthen kann."[34] Despite a much lighter workload, his sense of alienation remained: "Die verfl. Acten werden mich doch vor der Zeit tödten; wer den Drang zu einer individuellen Lebensarbeit in sich fühlt, der muß an dieser geistigen Tagelöhnerei über kurz oder lang zu Grunde gehen."[35] To Geibel he complained of water torture.[36] Later in life, as his creativity became more fitful, he appreciated more keenly the advantages of a steady income and warned younger writers against throwing themselves on the mercy of the market. But in the late 1850s and 1860s he often saw his duties as brakes on his productivity and throughout the 1860s and 1870s he dreamed of being able to afford to retire.

Storm's frustrations, besides helping him identify with other groups similarly thwarted in their aspirations, also shaped his retrospective view of conditions in Husum before 1848. Social discrimination and prejudice which had either escaped or not concerned him then, acquired a new significance. In *Abseits*(1864) the situation of Meta and Eberhard typifies the bleak prospects of maids and shop-assistants expected to live, unmarried, in their

31. Storm to F. Eggers, 8 July 1857, in H.W. Seidel, ed., *Storms Briefe an Friedrich Eggers*, Berlin, 1911, p. 52.
32. Storm to his parents, 7 May 1854, *Briefe* 1, p. 231.
33. Storm to his parents, 2 June 1856
34. Storm to E.and E. Esmarch, 22 December 1854, *Storm-Esmarch*, pp. 49f.
35. Storm to Amtsgerichtsrat Schnee, 30 March 1858, SHLB.
36. Storm to Geibel, 4 February 1858, in H. Schneider, "Storm und Geibel," *Die Heimat*, vol. 42, 1932, pp. 248.

employer's house. From his meagre earnings Eberhard cannot hope to acquire the means to set up his own business. When, after a windfall legacy, he and Meta sacrifice their hope of happiness in order to avert the bankruptcy of her brother, who has sacrificed everything for the Schleswig-Holstein cause, the text suggests that their action is as noble and as tragic as the sacrifices made by soldiers – and by Jesus Christ. Their joint, accumulated capital finally permits Meta's nephew to lead a full life.

4.5 Capitalist Expansion or Stagnation?

Storm glimpsed capitalism's potential for creating an unprecedented level of affluence which would benefit a growing number of people. At the same time his knowledge of towns like Husum and Heiligenstadt made him aware of the obstacles in the way of capitalist expansion. This tension is apparent in the works written at the turn of the decade, *Späte Rosen* (1859) and *Drüben am Markt* (1860). The former evokes an ideal situation in which the *Bourgeoisie* – in the person of a shipping magnate with a villa on the Baltic – shares the same values as the *Bildungsbürgertum* – represented by a scholar living in exile. Both men understand and respect each other's domain. The shipper reads the *Nibelungenlied*, Homer's *Odyssey* and Gottfried von Straßburg's *Tristan und Isolde*, while the scholar is conversant with double-entry bookkeeping. Capitalist enterprise is, however, not presented uncritically. For years competition compels Rudolph to devote all his energies to building up his business. He has no time for literature and the arts, and his sexual relations with his wife suffer. She, for her part, is preoccupied with bringing up two young daughters. Rudolph only overcomes his alienation when his business no longer demands all his energies. "Resurrection" comes on the morning of his fortieth birthday when the "revelation" afforded by a portrait of his wife as a young girl supplements the inspiration of *Tristan und Isolde*. This middle-aged couple make love in a summer house in the garden. Henceforth Rudolph's wife will ally the sexual intensity of an Isolde to the spiritual beauty and dignity of an Iphigenia.

If *Späte Rosen*, together with *Von jenseit des Meeres* (1865), is Storm's most optimistic evocation of capitalism's potential for creating a German Hellas in the north, *Drüben am Markt* conveys the backwardness of much of German society. It is true that an artisan's son may train as a doctor; encouraged by his mother, who nevertheless is still deferential toward social superiors, he may hope to marry the daughter of the Second Mayor, a prosperous businessman; indeed he may be friendly with an aspiring young civil servant at the castle and join in the music-making there; but ultimately, despite all his kindness and self-deprecating humor, his lack of social status combines with an absence of patrician elegance and breeding to rule him out as a possible suitor.

The novella also brings out how limited is the corpus of progressive ideas available to him in such a provincial town. It is little wonder that Christoph confuses his aspiration for a fuller, richer life with the lifestyle of the patricians. His notions of love are shaped by grammar school memories of Ovid, not by modern writers. His tiny library does contain a copy of the poems of G.A. Bürger, an eighteenth-century poet who experienced similar frustrations at the hands of polite society. But that is all. Otherwise woodcuts depicting scenes from Bernhardin de Saint-Pierre's Rousseauist novel *Paul et Virginie* are the only instances of social criticism which have made any impact on him. But one cannot adequately analyse contemporary society with such categories or formulate viable alternatives. Ironically, too, he glimpsed these scenes when delivering goods to a rich merchant's house as a boy. Naively he imagines that he can create a natural lovers' paradise on the first floor of his mother's cramped house. Having been rejected, he becomes an embittered, cynical loner, making fishing trips with his dog and finding human company and a consoling grog in the rough harbor pub. To the end he is torn between fascination and resentment, unable either to achieve any real insight into the make-up of society or to formulate a coherent alternative.

4.6 The Constitutional Struggle

The advent of the New Era in Prussia in 1858 encouraged liberals and democrats to hope for constitutional reforms and a strong national policy. Storm remained sceptical of the Prussian regent's talk of making "moral conquests" in Germany and critical of the particularism in the so-called "Preußenlied" ("ich bin ein Preuße, ich will ein Preuße sein")[37] Soon the timorousness of the new ministry and the so-called Old Liberals drove those wanting reforms to found a new party, the Progressives, in 1861. Conservative liberals like Julian Schmidt conjured up memories of democratic "excesses" in 1848/49.[38]

The Constitutional Struggle between the Prussian Lower House and the monarch/ministry centered on the issue of army reform and control of the army budget.[39] Wider questions like the respective power of monarch and parliament were at stake. The king was eager to weaken the role of the Landwehr and increase the size and importance of the regiments of the line. If the period of service there could be extended to three years, recruits could be better weaned away from civilian life and indoctrinated in the "right" spirit. In early 1862 the king dissolved parliament and dismissed all ministers suspected of liberal views. Gustav von Jagow became Minister for the Interior, and Heinrich von Mühler, Minister for Education, Culture, and Church Affairs. Storm referred to the latter as a pietist and spoke of him as "dieser unbedeutende Patron."[40] The appointment in the autumn of Bismarck as Prussian Prime Minister only inflamed the situation since he was firmly associated with the ultra-conservatives.

When a decree published by the Minister of Justice, Graf Leopold zur Lippe, in conjunction with von Jagow, sought to influence the way in which judges voted in the 1862 elections, Storm denounced this as an immoral attempt to destroy the moral integrity of the civil service. He tried to organize a plenary session of his colleagues in order that they could lodge an official

37. Storm to his parents, 23 March 1859, *Briefe* 1, p. 364.
38. See J. Heyderhoff, ed., *Die Sturmjahre der preußisch-deutschen Einigung 1859–70. Politische Briefe aus dem Nachlaß liberaler Parteiführer*, vol. 1, reprint, Osnabrück, 1967, p. 84.
39. See E.N. Anderson, *The Social and Political Conflict in Prussia, 1858–64*, Lincoln, 1954; K.H. Börner, *Die Krise der preußischen Monarchie von 1858 bis 1862*, East Berlin, 1976; M. Gugel, *Industrieller Aufstieg und bürgerliche Herrschaft. Sozialökonomische Interessen und politische Ziele des liberalen Bürgertums in Preußen zur Zeit des Verfassungskonflikts 1857–1867*, Cologne, 1975; H.A. Winkler, *Preußischer Liberalismus und deutscher Nationalstata*, Tübingen, 1964.
40. Storm to his parents, 10 April 1862; Storm to Brinkmann, 7 April 1863, *Storm-Brinkmann*, p. 125.

protest.[41] He regretted that for various reasons – indifference, cowardliness, career considerations – they were not prepared to match sentiments with actions. He also vainly urged Theodor Mommsen to ensure the publication in the *Vossische Zeitung* of a statement which he, Storm, had written condemning the decree. In Storm's view the *Intelligenz und Sittlichkeit* of North Germany were pitted against the *Beschränktheit und Unsittlichkeit* of the most rotten and corrupt Junkerism. At the time such sentiments were widespread.

During the Heiligenstadt years, while not being an avid newspaper reader, Storm subscribed to various newspapers: first, together with a Heiligenstadt lawyer, to the *Kölner Zeitung*, and then, with Otto, to the *Nordhauserzeitung*, which carried articles from the liberal *Nationalzeitung*. He sent his parents an extract from *Der Deutsche: Politische Zeitung für Stadt und Land* which appeared in Sonderhausen.[42] The conservative *Kreuzzeitung* was readily available, as was the local Heiligenstandt paper. He followed the proceedings in the Lower House, sending his father a cutting about the army debates which in his view epitomized the spirit of the officer class: "Man begreift kaum, wie bei der Höhe der nationalen Bildung in Deutschland eine solche mittelalterliche Rohheit bestehen kann. Und das ist die Kaste, die uns beherrschen will. Gott sie Dank, dieser Geist *kann* denn doch nicht siegen." He went on: "Aber ebenso gern würfe ich mein Kind in einen Zwinger voller wilder Bestien oder in ein Pestlazareth, als daß ich es unter dieße Bande thäte." Remarks made by a colonel about the abolition of the *Kadettenanstalten* elicited the comment:

Mit Recht hält gewiß unsre Zeitung die jetzige Krisis für im Grunde nichts andres als ein Zusammenprall dieses Geistes mit dem allgemeinen bürgerlichen Bewußtsein. Man versetze sich in den Geist, aus dem in vollem Ernst solche Worte fließen, wie "die Nation solle durch die Erziehung der Cadettenhäuser vor Entartung bewahrt werden" etc. Wie sieht ein solcher Mensch die Nation an? Welche Stellung nimmt er für sich und seine Standesgenossen in Anspruch den Millionen industriell und geistig thätigen andern Staatsbürgern

41. See G. Eversberg, "Storm Reaktion auf die Wahlbeeinflussungsversuche von 1862," *STSG*, vol. 39, 1990, pp. 69–74.

42. See Storm's letters to his parents, 29 March 1857, 4 May 1857, 1 December 1860.

gegenüber? – Und dieß ist ganz genau der Geist unsres Offizierßtandes. Ich sehe noch lange keine Hoffnung. Im Gegentheil da liegt die Krankheit unsrer innern Zustände. . . . aber nichts mehr davon."[43]

A young friend, Ludwig Löwe, the son of the local Jewish teacher, who had become a factory owner in Berlin and been elected to the city council, informed him about political developments there. A supporter of the Progressives (whom Storm consistently referred to as the Liberals), Löwe was in contact with Ferdinand Lassalle, who in May 1863 split from the Progressive Party and founded his *Allgemeiner Deutscher Arbeiterverein*. Harassment of oppositional civil servants and a tightening of the press laws heightened Storm's sense of outrage. In 1863 the government published an ordinance "concerning the prohibition of newspapers and periodicals." Any newspaper or periodical could be temporarily or permanently forbidden "wegen fortdauernder, die öffentliche Wohlfahrt gefährdender Haltung." The crucial factor was the overall attitude, not the content of individual articles. It was forbidden to undermine reverence for and loyalty to the king; to endanger the peace by exciting citizens against each other; to expose to hatred or scorn the institutions of the state, public authorities and their regulations by maliciously distorting the facts or defaming and ridiculing them; to incite people to disobey the laws and official orders; to undermine fear of God and morality; and to disparage the doctrines, institutions or customs of any of the Christian churches.[44]

Friction with Wussow and his circle grew. When Wussow stood as a candidate, Storm discreetly agitated against him. He described members of Wussow's circle as "pitch-black reactionaries" and complained again about the situation of Prussian civil servants: "Die Würde eines Preuß. Verwaltungsbeamten ist jetzt mit der eines selbständigen Mannes in der That nicht zu vereinen."[45] Wussow, for his part, branded both Storm and a visiting civil servant, Lepsius, democrats. Even before the Schleswig-Holstein crisis erupted, feelings were running high.

43. Storm to his parents, 24 September 1862.
44. *Verordnung, betreffend das Verbot von Zeitungen und Zeitschriften vom 1. Juni 1863*, in Stoepel, *Gesetz-Codex, Ergänzungsband 1: 1862–65*, Frankfurt, 1867, p. 30.
45. Storm to Constanze, 2–29 October 1863.

4.7 Religion and Politics in Literature

Confronted as he was in Heiligenstadt with the power of the Catholic church, it is perhaps not surprising that the novella *Veronica*(1861) focuses on religion. Treating such topics was not without risks, and as far as is known, Storm did not attempt to publish the story in a magazine or newspaper before book publication. It is typical of his enforced caution that he also insisted that an article entitled *Der Volksglaube* (or *Der Aberglaube) im katholischen Deutschland,* which Ernst Keil accepted for the magazine *Die Gartenlaube* in 1861, should appear anonymously. Keil in fact never published it (see p. 127).

A superficial reader could have read *Veronica* as a feuilleton story about an affair between a young wife and her husband's young cousin. After a moment of temptation in a dark mill she eventually confides in her understanding husband. A more discriminating reader would have recognized the weight attached to the critique of the Catholic sacrament of confession. As adulterous as any actual physical act, it represents an immoral intrusion into the privacy and sanctity of marital relations. True confession and communication can only take place between husband and wife.

But the novella is more ambitious than this. It questions the Christian scheme of sin and redemption and implicitly contrasts Veronica's development with Jesus Christ's agony and transfiguration in the Garden of Gethsemane, his crucifixion, resurrection and ascension. In a setting based on Heiligenstadt, she is shown emerging from the dark church into a springtime world. As she climbs the hill outside the town, she would in fact have passed the stations of the cross, including one depicting her Biblical counterpart. However, whereas the latter is remembered because her cloth received the imprint of Jesus Christ's features on his way to Calvary, Storm's heroine climbs to a hill top covered with thyme. There she experiences a natural, human revelation and transfiguration which transform her into an autonomous human being. In the manuscript version the text read: ". . . wuchs in ihr der schon lebendige Keim der Freiheit, des Bewußtseins, daß auch sie, wie Alles um sie her, ihren eignen Platz habe, nach dem sie Niemand fragen dürfe, auf dem sie durch sich selber stehen müsse oder fallen . . ." It went on: "Nicht mehr das Kind, das noch vor wenig Stunden verzagt und rathlos auf die Kirchenschwelle getreten war, das nicht das Gängelband zu lassen wagte, an dem man sie bisher geleitet hatte; sie war mündig geworden, sie ging aufrecht und mit festen Schritten."[46] Strong enough to dispense with the sacraments of the church, she recognizes the "divinity" of her relationship with her husband.

Christianity, in its Catholic form, is presented as a religion that employs all the resources of art and music to inculcate in the faithful terror of death and judgement in order to bring them to confess the sinful, fallen state of both human and physical nature. The text evokes the psychological impact of the great Easter Procession (which even today in Heiligenstadt involves the same larger than life figures). It is presented as part of the church's attempt to burden mankind with a barbaric crime committed in a past time and thereby keep individuals in its thrall. The novella helps explain how Storm could view Protestantism and Catholicism so differently. In his view, Catholicism, with its paternal, authoritarian tutelage, its collective pressure and its rituals and processions which overwhelmed the senses and the intellect, kept human beings at a childlike state of development. Protestantism, in contrast – at least in his typical nineteenth-century liberal view – was based on positive principles: the questioning of authority and the search for truth. Since the Reformation the latter had stripped away the dogmatic, irrational elements and laid bare Christianity's ethical essence. He was, however, convinced that further stages still had to be gone through on the road to a humanitarian culture. The draft version of the passage describing the position of Veronica's husband ran:

Der Justizrath gehörte zu der immer größer werdenden Gemeinde, welche schon jetzt die letzte Consequenz des Protestantismus ziehend in dem Auftreten des Christenthums nicht sowohl ein Wunder, als vielmehr nur ein natürliches Ergebniß aus der geistigen Entwicklung der Menschheit zu erblicken vermag. Sein scharfes Auge hatte überdieß sehr wohl erkannt, daß die Meisten derer, welche Gott den Herrn zu fürchten meinen, im Grunde nichts mehr fürchten als die Wahrheit; seine eigne Natur aber war eine zu tiefe, um sich in diesen Dingen, wie so Viele aus Bequemlichkeit, wenn nicht aus andern Rücksichten in einer bewußten Unklarheit gehen zu lassen, welche seinen Anforderungen an sich selbst auf anderen Gebieten des geistigen Lebens widersprochen hätte. Er ging deshalb in keine Kirche, weder in eine

46. Kladde, SHLB.

katholische, noch in die, welcher er durch seine Geburt angehörte. Seine Frau jedoch ließ er in der Gewöhnung ihrer Jugend und ihres elterlichen Hauses gewähren, vielleicht in Erwartung einer allmählichen selbständigen Befreiung, ein wenig auch vielleicht, weil er die Meinung mancher Männer namentlich aus den vorübergehenden Jahrzehnten theilte, daß die elementare Frauennatur der sinnlichen positiven Formel nicht entbehren könnte.[47]

In the final version the abrasive elements were removed.

Storm's rejection of Catholicism resurfaced around 1880 when his daughter Lucie was engaged to a young Catholic, Hermann Kirchner. The cluster of letters Storm wrote to friends and relatives after the engagement had been broken off revolve – in Feuerbachian fashion – around the distinction between the essence of Christianity and the cladding (*Gerüste*) constructed around it by human beings. This he defined as "the church." In his view, it separated human beings from other human beings. Only somebody with a free mind and able to stand above his/her particular church could be happy with a spouse brought up in a different religion. He feared that Kirchner's relatives and the local priest would put pressure on his daughter to convert and insist on the children being brought up as Catholics. Himself needing the church, Kirchner would be unable to protect her against these pressures. Lucie, in contrast, had been brought up in a house "wo freies selbstverantwortliches Denken als erste selbstverständliche Lebensbedingung gilt."[48] To his brother Otto he expressed his horror at the thought of having grandchildren who would be brought up as Catholics and referred to this "niedere, beschränkte Region."[49]

Perhaps the most striking expression of Storm's Feuerbachian atheism is a poem which he never completed and which he would have had difficult in publishing had he ever tried to do so. Here the coding has gone:

An deines Kreuzes Stamm o Jesu Christ
Hab ich mein sorgenschweres Haupt gelehnt;
Doch Trost und Kraft kam nicht von dir herab;

47. LL 1, 1106.
48. Storm to Hermann Kirchner, 6 March 1881, photocopy, SHLB.
49. Storm to Otto, 23 Septembe 1878, in private possession, copy in Storm Society Archive, Husum.

. . .

Du hattest weder Weib noch Kind, du warst
Ein halber Mensch nur; unseres Lebens Kern
Hast du nur halb erprobt; was uns die Welt,
Uns Lebenden, an Ungeheu'rem auflegt,
Du hast es nicht gekannt; dein Opfer war
Ein halbes nur. — Wärst du getreu befunden,
Wenn man dein Weib, dein Kind ans Kreuz geschlagen?
Die Antwort bliebst du schuldig. — Wohl mit Dank,
Mit Liebe blick ich zu dir ——

                            doch mich erlösen

Das kannst du nicht. — Einsamer Qualen voll
Neig ich das Haupt; da legt sich lebenswarm
Ans Herz mir eine vielgeliebte Last;
     —— und wie sie sich fassen,
Fühl ich den Ring des Lebens fest geschlossen
Gleich einer Mauer gegen Tod und Lüge.
Ich bin getröstet. — Komm geliebtes Weib
Wir müssen unser eigner Heiland sein.[50]

Veronica is silent on political matters. The novella *Im Schloß* (1862), in contrast, links religion and politics. In 1868, i.e. at a time when Bismarck's successes had destroyed many of his hopes, Storm could still write:

Wussow kannst Du auf seine großmütige Rede bestellen, daß, wenn meine Poesie überhaupt einen Wert hat, auch die darin enthaltene Demokratie ihren Wert und ihre Wirksamkeit haben wird. Habe ich keine Wirksamkeit auf die Gemüter, und in letzter Instanz auf die Taten der Menschen, so haben es Dichter und Denker überhaupt nicht; und das wird selbst der vernagelste Bürokrat oder Aristokrat nicht behaupten wollen. Es wäre doch sehr merkwürdig, wenn durch mein *Im Schloß*, das in der *Gartenlaube* von mehreren hundert Tausend Menschen gelesen, und mit Begeisterung gelesen ist . . . wenn dadurch nicht in vielen der Leser ein Nachdenken, eine Vorstellung, eine neue Einsicht oder ein schärferes Empfinden und Auffassen dieser

---

50. LL 1, p. 263. See D.A. Jackson, "Storm at the foot of the cross," *The Germanic Review*, vol. 59, 1984, pp. 82–89.

Verhältnisse des Lebens bewirkt worden wäre. Das widerspräche auch aller Erfahrung. Bin ich ein Dichter, so habe ich mit dem aus meinem Innersten Ausgeprägten auch eine Wirkung auf mein Volk. Freilich ist unsre Wirkung nicht so rasch und so handgreiflich, als wenn eine Armee gesiegt hat; aber daß die Wirkung da ist, das empfinden doch in unsrer Zeit die Gewalthaber deutlich genug.[51]

The theme of love between a middle-class tutor and an aristocratic girl was a familiar one. If presented with the usual middle-class bias, it was likely to appeal to the readership of a popular liberal/democratic magazine like *Die Gartenlaube*. However, Storm did not exploit the possibilities it offered in terms of contorted plot and dramatic suspense and avoided the torrid scenes and cheap lyrical climaxes popular with the writers of romances. In fact, the novella has a complicated structure and shifting perspectives, and the text skillfully generates a distance between the characters' self-awareness at the time when events occur and the heroine/narrator's retrospective viewpoint. Further, the tightly organized pattern of cues, leitmotifs and themes invites the reader to draw insights which escape her. Magazine readers unfamiliar with the codes and conventions of sophisticated literature were offered a broad, general entrance; less conspicuous points of access were made available to sophisticated readers. In this the work is typical of so much nineteenth-century fiction. Democratic writers like Storm had to adapt a demanding literary tradition to a rapidly expanding literary public with a wide range of expectations and reading skills. At the same time they did not want to debase the tradition.

Im Schloß tackles one of the most daunting challenges facing any Poetic-Realist writer reliant on concrete, visual "situations" rather than on abstract analysis, namely how to treat topics like the nature of religion, the moral and intellectual development of the human race, or the implications of the aristocratic principle. The novella sets out, first, to convey to magazine readers the suspect intellectual foundations and harmful consequences of the old orthodox, aristocratic ideology and then to evoke an alternative faith. Its analysis of religion reflects typical mid-nineteenth-

51. Storm to Hans, *Briefe* 1, pp. 522f. For a detailed study of the work see D.A. Jackson, "Storm's democratic humanitarianism. The novella *Im Schloß* in context," *Oxford German Studies*, vol. 17, 1988, pp. 10–50.

century liberal views before progressing beyond them and adopting a position close to Feuerbach's emphasis on nature and love. Religious beliefs are shown to reflect phylogenetic and ontogenetic developments. Thus the way in which the image of a kindly God-the-(grand)-father figure (LL 1, 492) satisfies Anna's emotional needs as a child corresponds to a pre-scientific, primitive stage in human culture. Her infatuation with a boy serf in an old portrait (LL 1, 495f.) and her adolescent fascination with a loving savior (LL 1, 508) correspond, in their turn, to the stage represented by Christianity's commendation of sympathy and suffering and its vision of a loving theist creator. Her reciting of a Protestant hymn provokes her scientific uncle to confront her with the internecine ferocity in the animal and insect kingdoms. According to him the notion of a loving god is simply the product of human beings' fear of being alone in a brutal world. In the original manuscript version Anna's dismay prompts him to concede: "Gott ist vielleicht die Liebe; nur ist das anders, als es dort in deinem Katechismus steht."[52] The uncle, a sceptical bachelor whose alienation is apparent in his "hard words" and "soft heart" (LL 1, 491), comes near to stating the Feuerbachian message that sympathy, compassion, and love are supreme values which alienated human beings have, however, projected on to a deity. But in terms of the uncle's characterization such insights would have been implausible. Storm amended the sequence, and his alternative only sowed confusion among later critics.

It falls to Arnold, the middle-class tutor, to replace Anna's theism with a new set of beliefs. Sparing her sensibilities – and those of *Gartenlaube* readers – he talks of seeking and finding "another God." The text goes on:

> Und nun begann er mit schonender Hand die Trümmer des Kinderwunders hinweg zu räumen, das über mir zusammengebrochen war; und indem er bald ein Geheimnis in einen geläufigen Begriff des Altertums auflöste, bald das höchste Sittengesetz mir in den Schriften desselben vorgezeichnet wies, lenkte er allmählich meinen Blick in die Tiefe. Ich sah den Baum des Menschengeschlechtes heraufsteigen, Trieb um Treib, in naturwüchsiger ruhiger Entfaltung, ohne ein anderes Wunder, als das der ungeheuern Weltschöpfung, in welchem seine Wurzeln lagen. (LL 1, 510)

52. Kladde, SHLB.

The imagery, concepts, and code would have posed no difficulty for Storm's educated readers. Jesus Christ takes his place beside the philosophers of classical antiquity in a natural scheme of ethical and intellectual development. The church, Arnold suggests, has abandoned the search for truth. In the final version the Biblical command, "Seek and ye shall find" is followed by the words: "Aber sie scheinen es nicht zu verstehen; sie begnügen sich mit dem, was jene vor Jahrtausenden gefunden oder zu finden glaubten." (LL 1, 520). In the manuscript this read: "Aber eben die, welche so gerne die Schrift im Munde führen, scheinen es am wenigsten zu verstehen; sie begnügen sich mit dem, was jene vor Jahrtausenden gefunden oder zu finden glaubten; sie reden von der Furcht des Herrn; aber sie fürchten in der That nichts als die Wahrheit."[53] Storm considered it wise to abandon such abrasive formulations. One of the great advantages of consulting manuscript versions of his stories is that one can sometimes see how self-censorship operates. One cannot of course judge the extent to which Storm censored himself before he ever put pen to paper.

It has been argued that the uncle represents a Darwinist viewpoint which is incompatible with Arnold's categories. Allegedly Storm himself was torn between Goethean, humanitarian categories and the ideas of scientific materialists like Büchner, Vogt and Moleschott. No evidence has, however, so far been adduced to support these claims. Nor is there any proof that Storm had by this time encountered Charles Darwin's *The Origin of the Species* (1859), whether in translation or in learned articles.[54] The Darwin furor first broke in Germany in 1863 after Ernst Haeckel's paper at the 38th Conference of German Scientists and Doctors in Stettin in September 1863. The juxtaposition of "nature red in tooth and claw" with the ethical standards operating in the human world is a familiar one. It is also worth noting that in an early draft Arnold himself went on to proclaim the gospel of science. While it is true that the scientist uncle emphasizes science's primary role in finding the other God, the text itself suggests that the role of the humanities and the arts is equally important.

The scene is described in tones befitting the enunciation of a new gospel. From *Veronica* onwards Storm builds up a new

53. Ibid.
54. See Jackson, "Storm's democratic humanitarianism," p. 69.

iconography to replace the Christian one. Indeed, part of the challenge facing promoters of a post-Christian world view was to create a body of images and symbols that would command the same devotion as their Christian counterparts. At the same time they had to destroy the awe attached to key Christian symbols and sacraments. This was a delicate operation. In *Renate* (1878) it is suggested that the sacrament of communion is a custom which the enlightened heroine finds repulsive.[55] In *Der Schimmelreiter* (1888) Jesus Christ's sacrificial death is linked to heathen notions of animal sacrifice. Here the uncle is presented as a modern St. Hieronymus. His mood one of reverential solemnity, he points to the works of natural scientists in the same way as saints and saintly persons point to the Bible in religious paintings. Arnold, too, is presented like a prophet transfigured by a divine revelation: his cheeks glow with enthusiasm, his eyes shine.

Had the intellectual and ethical odyssey of hero and heroine ended here, the novella would have fallen short of Feuerbachian positions since affirming brotherly love is by no means synonymous with recognizing the divinity of human love. But it does not end here. The tragedy which befalls Anna and Arnold springs from their failure to recognize the supremacy of human love. Despite having lost her faith, Anna still endorses the aristocratic notion of *noblesse oblige* and the ideal of self-sacrifice and self-denial. Anna "denies" her true savior by letting herself be married off to a gaunt, prematurely aged aristocrat. This marriage defiles and desecrates her body and soul. But even though Storm presented the issue discreetly, Ernst Keil still bowdlerized a key passage without any prior consultation and to Storm's lifelong mortification (LL 1, 1112f.). When Anna and Arnold meet again, neither is prepared to go beyond a purely spiritual and intellectual relationship. Indeed, when gossip threatens Anna's marriage, they stop seeing each other altogether. Her stoicism, after her husband has banished her to the castle and condemned her to a living death, is presented as futile, resting as it does on nothing but a pious hope that the situation will one day change. So great is her alienation that she even contemplates a reconciliation with her husband simply in order to prove to herself that nature and passion play no part in her love for Arnold (LL 1, 524). In terms of Storm's literary strategies the sequence provides a good

55. Ibid., p. 88.

example of how readers were to be maneuvered into feeling re-vulsion for norms and actions which hitherto would often have had positive associations for them.

Storm never endorsed the Christian stress on self-sacrifice and the ennobling power of suffering. Anna's spontaneous sense of release on receiving news of her husband's death (LL 1, 525) represents his verdict on her stoicism. The fact that such a *deus ex machina* is needed to end her agony and make marriage with Arnold possible may be a typical magazine-story ending: but, far from papering over the unresolved problems in society, it draws attention to them. Instead of encouraging belief in providence, it encourages readers to reflect on a system which allows such torture.

The final chapter, "Es wird Frühling" (LL 1, 524ff.), is part of the new iconography. The good tidings which reach Anna at Christmas, the news of her husband's death, usher in a process of natural, human resurrection that corresponds to the renais-sance of nature in spring. The tree burning in the sun's fire is no longer Jehovah appearing to Abraham: it symbolizes nature's divinity and the incandescence of love. It precedes the appear-ance of Anna's savior, Arnold. Their rapture as they embrace is the human essence behind the Christian notion of the beatific vision. The laying-on of hands is performed, not by a priest, but by the uncle and then by the grandmother. The final word be-longs to "der hohe, helle Tag."

Storm's critique of Christian categories is related to the second great thematic strand in the novella, the critique of the aristo-cratic principle. Here, too, the text focuses on the issue of aliena-tion. Storm declared to Anna von Wussow *à propos* of the novella that he was convinced that the nobility and the church were "die zwei wesentlichen Hemmnisse einer durchgreifenden sittlichen Entwicklung unsres sowie andrer Völker."[56] In 1864 he reiterated these sentiments to Hartmuth Brinkmann: "Du meintest einmal bei meinem letzten Besuch, Du könntest das Herunterreißen des Adels nicht haben; ich sage Dir, der Adel (wie die Kirche) ist das Gift in den Adern der Nation. Von welchen ihnen selbst als unwahr sehr wohl bewußten Voraussetzungen diese Leute ausge-hen, das ist ja ganz unglaublich."[57]

56. Storm to his parents, 9 December 1861, *Briefe* 1, p. 390.
57. Storm to Brinkmann, 18 January 1864, *Storm-Brinkmann*, p. 134.

The novella does not suggest that the nobility's power has been broken. While sections of the nobility like the Imperial Barons may have lost much of their power and property and while Anna's father, a baron and ex-diplomat, can buy but cannot maintain the hunting castle in its former splendor, the nobility still dominates at court and in the diplomatic service. Younger members like Anna's cousin, with their training in estate management, exploit the resources of large estates while remaining just as caste-exclusive as their elders. The novella concentrates instead on making the reader feel how unacceptable the aristocratic principle is in intellectual, ethical, and socio-political terms. Aristocratic caste-exclusiveness is shown to alienate and impoverish those who subscribe to it. Instead of relating to the local community and communicating with his children, the baron prefers solitary walks on which he dreams of receiving a portrait of the king; alternatively he communes with the silent company of aristocratic portraits acquired in the original sale. He is presented as uninterested in modern ideas, modern science, modern music, and popular literature. Christian orthodoxy is a far safer underwriter of the aristocracy's privileged role in society than either modern philosophy and science, and aristocrats interested in science are exceptions. In the jottings for the novella Storm wrote: "Stolz beruht wesentlich auf der *Schätzung* unser selbst. *Hochmuth* auf der *Geringschätzung* Andrer."[58] The text's harshest condemnation is, however, reserved for the aristocratic "lie," "Daß man mehr sei, als andere Menschen" (LL 1, 514). This belief is incompatible with the supreme moral law of brotherly love. It divides state and society. Storm attached great importance to the scene at the town hall (LL 1, 512f.) where the aristocrats show a total disregard for the feelings of middle-class folk. Given that his readers would be overwhelmingly non-aristocratic and would have had to endure similar humiliations in their daily lives, Storm could assume that such scenes would have a considerable impact on even unsophisticated readers. This was crucial since he was, after all, competing for the public's favor and editors' fees with writers like Friedrich Spielhagen, whose novel *Problematische Naturen*(1861) focused on many of the same issues. Furthermore, in 1861, Storm could afford to take greater risks. It was not until March 1862 that the king dismissed all his

---

58. Folio sheet with notes for *Veronica* and *Im Schloß*, SHLB.

Liberal ministers, and it was only after the autumn that Bismarck introduced stiff measures against both the press and liberal/ democratic civil servants.

Arnold symbolizes the ideal *Bildungsbürger*. His family's ascent from lowly serfs to freeholding farmers and urban professionals suggests the inroads already made into the aristocratic, feudal system. He studies philology and history, not law or theology. His interests are cosmopolitan: he is as well versed in Italian popular music and modern German composers as he is in philosophy and ethics. To all his intellectual gifts he allies warmth and richness of personality, kindness, and sensitivity. As a university professor he purveys the new ideas to enthusiastic public audiences. The whole presentation illustrates well how Poetic Realism has very little to do with "objectively" rendering contemporary reality and everything to do with constructing a particular vision of it designed to shape readers' perceptions – and actions.

The section (LL 1, 502ff.) which introduces Arnold's grandmother and the family farm reflects Storm's awareness that, for it to succeed, the democratic cause would have to be able to count on the support of a proud, independent peasantry free of any deferential subordination to "natural," god-given aristocratic masters. Bismarck, in contrast, would soon gamble on the conservatism of the rural classes and the hold of the church over them. His analysis was shrewder. Storm's picture of the grandmother and her behavior towards the baron is pure democratic propaganda, as is the evocation of the civic community with its pride in its traditions and its developing self-identity. One can here speak of democratic iconography.

The novella's great strength, its concentration on ethical issues, is also its great weakness. In this it anticipates the essential weakness of the democratic cause when confronted with the successes of Bismarck's *Realpolitik*. The appeal to ethical values and long-term trends encouraged a tendency to self-deception. In their own way, democratic ideas were often as rigid as the conservative, Christian ideology against which they were pitted. Bismarck would exhibit a greater flexibility than the champions of either view.

4.8 Democratic Social Criticism

Auf der Universität(1863) describes the career of Lore, a French émigré tailor's daughter, who grows up in a provincial town modelled on Husum, moves to a university town and commits suicide after being involved with an aristocratic student. As in *Auf dem Staatshof* Storm employs a fictional narrator from the educated middle class, and here too the text invites the reader to question the latter's categories. The assumption underlying the novella is the by now familiar one that all human beings have an innate urge to achieve a good and beautiful life. The question is whether this aspiration can be fulfilled in contemporary society. On the strength of a glimpse of the life of small-town aristocrats and notables and of her father's accounts of life at the French court in Versailles, Lore, like Christoph in *Drüben am Markt,* identifies the good life with the lifestyle of her social superiors. Like him she is torn between two worlds. Acceptance of her lot and fear of striking out for new shores coexist with frustration at the prospects of women of her class. Fascination with a forbidden world is offset by hostility toward those who either ostracize her as a social inferior or, alternatively, use and then discard her. Working as a seamstress in a university town, she enters the houses of the well-to-do and sees the outwardly glamorous student world. Her experiences further alienate her from the life awaiting her as an artisan's or master's wife. Once her fiancé's apparent jilting of her provides her with the pretext and impulse to overcome her inhibitions, she becomes an easy prey for an aristocratic student. The text could have attributed her suicide to a pregnancy, to fears of scandal, to grief at losing her aristocratic lover, or desperation at having destroyed any hope of becoming a respectable artisan's wife. In fact, Storm attributed it to her consciousness that she has besmirched her innate ideal. Her "transfiguration" at the end was intended to ensure that this lower-class Ophelia emerged from the dark waters of the Styx pure and beautiful in the soul of the reader (LL 1, 1151). Her suicide, like that of the lovers in Gottfried Keller's *Romeo und Julia auf dem Dorfe* is not evidence of any growing corruption in the lower classes: it reflects Storm's belief in an innate notion of morality and human dignity.

The issue of class is to the fore; indeed its influence is all-pervasive. Thus the Amtmann's daughter is addressed as "gnädiges Fräulein" by the dancing master; Philipp, for his part, can expect "Herr Philipp"; Lore has to make do with an an albeit affectionate "Kleine Beauregard." The dancing class (LL 1, 533ff.) is restricted to those of suitable rank. Lore is only tolerated as a stop-gap, and the only girl to have anything to do with her is the Postmaster's daughter, herself someone barely acceptable. Lore's mother is allowed to attend functions only as a waitress. It is all too easy to miss Storm's irony when the mayoress comments as she measures Lore and the Amtmann's daughter: "Ihr scheint mir ziemlich egal zu sein" (LL 1, 533). It is equally ironic that the mayoress warns her: "Du bist sonst immer die Meisterin gewesen; nimm Dich in Acht, daß die Dir nicht den Rang abläuft" (LL 1, 534). Although Philipp tries to present the community as united, the divisions between the classes dominate the scene on the mill-pond, and all his Homeric, classical language cannot disguise this. If as a boy Philipp was friendly with the family joiner and even began to learn manual skills, this soon petered out because of social and educational segregation. His friendship with Christoph, the joiner's son, is marked by tensions throughout. The artisans and the grammar-school boys form quite separate factions, and these social tensions continue in the university town. Philipp's attitude, however, is one of prim, superior incomprehension (LL 1, 530).

The novella again paints a critical picture of university life. Philipp is presented as typical of those students who immerse themselves in their studies and are blind to what is going on around them. But the harshest criticism is reserved for the fraternity students whose aristocratic ringleader reminds even Philipp of the days of *Faustrecht*. Storm's revulsion for the custom of duelling comes through as strongly as does his rejection both of the students' delight in humiliating and degrading lower-class girls and also of their treatment of "menials" like waiters (LL 1, 574ff.). It is symptomatic of the feudalization of students that Fritz, the mayor's son, imagines that he can avenge Lore by duelling with the aristocrat.

The text again examines society's regulation of relations between the sexes and the effect of this on the emotional development of middle-class males. Educated in single-sex grammar schools – an arrangement which Philipp finds "monastic" (LL 1, 562) – the sons of the well-to-do meet their female social peers in highly formal situations. The system of dancing classes and balls, based as it is on feudal, chivalric notions, does not encourage natural relations and natural communication. Sex is taboo. On the other hand, Philipp's involvement with Lore is marked by self-indulgent fantasies. This beautiful Cinderella, his protégée and property, is expected to satisfy his notions of beauty regardless of whether she might be sensitive about his largesse and about having to wear a dress made up out of another woman's notorious cast-off. In general he lacks any awareness of her objective position in this society and of her subjective feelings. His classical education also influences his behavior toward her. He imagines himself a classical hero abducting his Helen. When she protests, he threatens violence. The scene on the frozen mill pond (LL 1, 542ff.) suggests both impotence and repressed sexual urges. As the serpent-like fronds of the aquatic plant writhe up to its undersurface, he both fears and longs for the virgin ice to break. The fact remains that he is incapable of establishing any real relationship with Lore. The symbol of ballroom-like ice with dark, murky waters beneath it and the later contrast between sparkling ice and the stagnant waters of the Styx clearly have a wider social application in the story.

By the time Philipp is a sixth-former, the division of women into inaccessible ones and lower-class, sexually available ones is established. But while his classmates hang round the Ratskeller, ogling and dancing with exotic, Asiatic harpists, he prefers solitary walks in search of butterflies. The symbolism is transparent: instead of hunting for a rare specimen, he should be seeking to win the love of Lore, a rare, exquisite human being. During his search he experiences one of those revelations which are a hallmark of Storm's novellas. The episode is prefaced by verses evoking a life of natural harmony and fulfillment, i.e. one that contrasts sharply with the social division and unnaturalness prominent in earlier and later chapters. The actual sequence (LL 1, 550ff.) is constructed around a leitmotif which runs through Storm's works and which originated in a picture entitled *Seuls sur la terre* that he saw in Husum at the Michaelmas market. Henceforth it symbolized for him perfect oneness and love. Fusing Biblical and classical elements in order to suggest the divinity of life, the text depicts an isolated, slender tree standing by dark waters, bathed in sunlight and covered with delicate white blossoms, with bees humming in its foliage like Aeolian harps:

Ich gedachte eines Bildes, das ich vor Kurzem gesehen hatte. In einer Gegend, weit und unbegrenzt wie diese, stand auf seinen Stab gelehnt ein junger Hirte, wie wir uns die Menschen nach den ersten Tagen der Weltschöpfung zu denken gewohnt sind, ein rauhes Ziegenfell als Schurz um seine Hüften; zu seinen Füßen saß – er sah auf sie herab – eine schöne Mädchengestalt; ihre großen dunkeln Augen blickten in seliger Gelassenheit in die morgenhelle Einsamkeit hinaus. – "Allein auf der Welt" stand darunter. – Ich schloß die Augen; mir war, als müsse aus dem leeren Raum dies zweite Wesen zu mir treten, mit dem selbander jedes Bedürfnis aufhöre, alle keimende Sehnsucht gestillt sei . . . (LL 1, 554)

Butterfly catching is abandoned. However, the scenes at the fairground and in the castle gardens underline how far removed contemporary society is from this ideal. The arcadian paradise yields to a fairground world of illusion in which a seamstress like Lore acts out fantasies of being a proud lady on a fine horse. The impotence theme returns: her appearance as Diana the huntress turns Philipp to stone. He suffers from all the inhibitions and repressions which characterize many of Storm's heroes. After a furtive kiss the two drive themselves out of their troubled paradise. Henceforth serious interest on his part in Lore disappears.

Storm may affirm Lore's human dignity, but he does not engineer a happy ending that papers over social tensions and divisions. Once again his strategy was to work on his readers' *Gemüt* and maneuver them into feeling the inhumanity of existing arrangements. But he was treading on thin ice with his critique of student life. Hartmuth Brinkmann, himself an ex-student and member of a fraternity, denied that student life was coarse and brutal (see LL 1, 1148f.). Equally risky was the suggestion that his middle-class female readers' respectability was bought at the price of other women's degradation. It was a bold step to attempt to enlist their sympathies for Lore and bring them, at least at the level of feeling, to question the automatic rightness of existing arrangements. In terms of Storm's hopes for the democratic cause, *Auf der Universität* is not encouraging. Philipp and the students do not show any commitment to democratic values. Indeed the novella reflects Storm's fears that, instead of articulating the frustration of the artisans and lower classes and combining with them to struggle for a democratic society, the educated middle-class could become further estranged from them, further feudalized.

4.9 Sex, Love, and Marriage: Life and Art

After his affair with Doris Jensen, Storm never allayed fears that, deep down, Constanze was estranged from him and that ultimately he was therefore alone. We do not know whether he kept these ruminations at bay when they were together, or whether, like his obsession with the thought of her remarrying after his death[59,] they gave rise to painful exchanges. In her absence they engulfed him.[60] Constanze's sexual responses became a gauge of the intensity and permanence of her love.[61] Any hint of coldness or indifference provoked existential doubts. Because Storm practiced no sort of birth-control and had long since declared Constanze's body his exclusive property, her married life was one long list of pregnancies and miscarriages. Although seven children survived, she lost at least the same number through miscarriages. Dogged by gynecological disorders, she aged prematurely. In 1863 her brother-in-law, Dr. Ernst Stolle, diagnosed a collapse of one wall of the vagina. Too weak to stand the treatment, she collapsed. But soon she was pregnant again. She died of puerperal fever in 1865 after the birth of Gertrud.

None of this found its way into Storm's depictions of love, sex, and marriage, at least not directly. One of the cornerstones of his Poetic-Realist aesthetic was the conviction that in marriage human beings could, given the right preconditions, achieve happiness and fulfillment. Art's brief was not to reflect all the warts and blemishes of reality; it was to hold up an idealizing picture which would stimulate emulation. Ideal scenarios were living proof that aspirations could be fulfilled. A work like *Im Schloß* echoes verbatim sentiments and language first used in the letters Storm wrote to his fiancée and then repeated in letters to her after rereading the letters in the late 1850s and early 1860s. Arnold's song (LL 1, 513f.), for example, is a poetic rendering of sentiments expressed in a letter to Constanze on 23 July 1859.

59. Storm to Constanze, 31 May 1856.
60. Storm to Constanze, 28 June–4 July 1862, *Briefe* 1, pp. 401ff.
61. Storm to Constanze, 24 November 1853, *Briefe* 1, pp. 215f.

Precisely because love was so all-important, it had to be conveyed in an elevated, ritualized manner. The closing scenes of *Im
Schloß* or *Veronica* provide perfect examples. Elements of reality
which could not be transfigured or poeticized were edited out.
In *Späte Rosen* Rudolph and his wife, unlike the Storms, enjoy an
affluent lifestyle; instead of a large family, they have two very
undemanding daughters. The problem of whether renewed sexual
passion will revive their old problems by leading to more babies
is sidestepped. The reality of art had to underwrite the actual
feasibility of the ideal.

A writer intent on stressing the importance in marriage of
shared sexual passion faced difficult problems of presentation.
Yet, paradoxically, art was more permissive than actual social
life. Storm prohibited himself and Constanze from ever discuss-
ing intimate, sexual matters with any third party. In June 1862,
having listened to Wussow elaborating his idea that monogamy
was the only possible option and that one had to sacrifice the
lesser good (passion) to preserve a higher one (ethical behavior),
Storm remained silent: "Ich hätte unsern Freund ja wohl belehren
können, wenn mir Andern gegenüber über so heilige Dinge nicht
der Mund verschlossen wäre."[62] It would have been unthinkable
to raise such matters in polite society. Literature, in contrast,
provided a forum for articulating them. Whereas rigid taboos
were maintained in life, in art one enjoyed freedom to explore
sensitive, even shocking topics provided that one respected certain
taboos and conventions. Classical, exotic and historical subjects
allowed one to broach topics that were dangerous to treat in a
contemporary, German setting. If one chose such a setting and
depicted characters and situations with which people could easily
identify, one entered the danger zone. In a complicated way art
both upheld and questioned social and moral taboos. It was the
safety-valve which ensured that the repressive pressures could
be maintained. The more authors wanted to incorporate taboo
content from contemporary reality, the more they had to push
the formal presentation in the direction of idealization and
poeticization. In this way, suspect topics could elude the readers'
moral censor and collude with their unfulfilled longings without
bringing them into conscious conflict with moral notions. Often
it was a self-defeating strategy in that this poeticization neutral-

62. Storm to Constanze, 8 June 1862.

ized the force of the original criticism. But that, too, may have been part of the implicit understanding between writers, readers and authorities. Ultimately few writers wanted to have social opprobrium heaped upon them or to be hauled before the courts.

This relationship between fears and aspirations, life and art is illustrated by letters Storm wrote to Constanze while she was in Segeberg in 1863 being examined by her brother-in-law Ernst Stolle. He was concerned that continence, even for limited periods, would be like passing a sentence of death on him:

> Denn die beständige Aufregung, in der ich mich unvermeidlich während der verbotnen Zeit befinden würde, würde mich mit Sicherheit einer jener Abnehmungskrankheiten überliefern. Schon jetzt leide ich in Folge dieser Tage am fortwährenden Drang zum P-n und Schmerzen im Unterleibe. Und ich darf ja doch noch lange nicht sterben, und mag es auch nicht, so lange ich so irdisch stark zu lieben vermag. Was sollte denn auch aus all den kleinen Mäusen werden? Es würde ein humoristischer Streich von der Natur, wenn sie mich an deiner Krankheit sterben ließe.[63]

He could not drive away thoughts about the actual examination:

> Mir ist – ich kann nicht anders sagen – als wenn du geschändet wärest. – Wie jene fabelhaften Vögel mit Menschenköpfen, die den Gefährten des Ulyßes Alles, was sie zum Munde führten, verunreinigten und besudelten, so setzt sich auf jeden Gedanken an dich dieß entsetzliche Bild. Am schlimmsten ist diese Folter, wenn ich mich nachmittags, um zu schlafen, auf mein Bett lege; an Schlaf ist nicht zu denken, in der Einsamkeit beginnt eine Jagd von immer verabscheuungswürdigeren Bildern und Gedanken. "Jetzt, jetzt" denke ich, "ist vielleicht der Augenblick, wo es geschieht – und es wird —— wer kann den Arzt controliren!" – bis ich es am Ende nicht länger aushalte, aufspringe, mich anziehe und zu den Kindern hinauf gehe . . .[64]

His remedy was to read the idyllic love episode between Heinrich Lee and Anna in Gottfried Keller's novel *Der grüne Heinrich*. It helped him drive away his fancies, and he suggested to Constanze that they should read it together on her return.[65]

---

63. Storm to Constanze, 13 October 1863.
64. Storm to Constanze, 10 October 1863.
65. Storm to Constanze, 12 October 1862.

4.10   Children and Education

Studies of Storm have dwelt far less than studies of Keller or
Stifter on the question of children, child development and child
education. This is surprising because the area is just as central to
his work as it was to theirs. Indeed any writer concerned with
anticipating the "new times" could hardly avoid considering these
questions. The belief that human nature was good had profound
implications for the organization of child-rearing, education, and
general socialization.

Storm was torn between ideal aspirations and recalcitrant
reality. Ideally, the revolutions of 1848 should have brought about
a new state and a new society with a reformed, secularized
educational system. In fact, the government and the church tightened their control over education. The Stiehl Regulations were
the expression of this. Storm was faced by a dilemma: on the one
hand he wanted to bring up his children in a non-authoritarian
manner and encourage them to develop their full human potential; on the other he had to pilot them through the education
system toward future careers. Everything hinged on whether this
could be done without having to sacrifice or pervert basic human
needs. In his opinion, it was. He was confident that, given the
goodness of human nature and the power of the home environment, his children could develop into happy, fulfilled adults. In
an atmosphere where love and affection would be freely expressed, children would be partners, able and eager to communicate with their parents. In short, the family would be a micro-
cosm of human fulfillment until such time as society and state at
large corresponded to the ideal.

A "passionate father,"[66] Storm was fascinated by the magical
nature of a child's world. He wrote fairy tales and poems for
his children, read them fairy stories, old and new, and later
supplemented this fare with the works of the great children's
writers of the Enlightenment, Campe, Pestalozzi, and Weiße. His
delight in passing on to friends his children's theories about God
and the world reflected his interest in human development. As
heir to the Enlightenment tradition, he believed in a general
timetable of child development (see also p. 109) The underlying

66. Storm to Mörike, 2 December 1855, *Storm-Mörike*, p. 53.

Rousseauistic assumption was that all would be well if one nurtured nature's growth. He had no time for the brutal corporal punishment still thought acceptable at the time, and in general visitors were struck by the "child-friendly" atmosphere in the Storm-household.[67] More conservative friends were disconcerted by the Storms' principles and surprised, for instance, that he did not chastise one of this sons when he took a bite out of Wilhelm von Merckel's calf under the table.

From the start this ambitious project contained within it the seeds of its own undoing. His belief in the goodness and potential of human nature was still linked to expectations of academic success.[68] Whatever his criticism of grammar school education in his fictions, Storm could not envisage his sons either failing to get on to the educational ladder to middle-class respectability – or falling off it. Fears that they might, made him behave in ways that worked against his vision of communication and partnership. Having assumed the role of teacher, he found himself locked in battles of will with his sons. They, for their part, reacted to his impatience and frustration with resentment and psychosomatic illnesses. Their shortcomings, disorders, and ailments then produced in him a mixture of anxious mollycoddling and disciplinarian rigidity. Convinced that his "thoroughness" would triumph,[69] he was not beyond punishing Karl, his third son, by making him copy out pages from the *Preußisches Gesetzbuch*.[70]

Hans' failure to be ready to attend the Heiligenstadt grammar school in 1857 and his asthma and chest troubles fueled anxieties. Without any concern for the psychological consequences of this step, his parents sent him north to his grandparents in order to build up his health. Although at Michaelmas 1859 he at last entered the quarta with Ernst, he soon had to be withdrawn. Neither Storm nor Constanze showed any great insight into puberty and adolescence. Hans, who was tormenting his younger brothers and sisters and was as unpopular with them as with his classmates, was again sent to his grandparents. Anxious to build up his own health, Storm joined him there and conveyed all his anxieties in a letter home to Constanze. Gertrud Storm omitted

67. E.g. Pietsch, *Wie ich Schriftsteller*, vol. 2, p. 95.
68. Storm to his parents, 19 October 1860.
69. Storm to his parents, 6 April 1860.
70. Storm to his parents, 3 July 1863.

it from her edition. Yet this is the experience which Storm repeatedly alluded to in later years. He wrote:

Ich wurde in Husum in den ersten Tagen von einer Sorge heimgesucht, die mich – *vergiß das nicht!* jetzt verlassen hat, und *die dich daher nicht mehr beunruhigen darf* – Als ich neulich ankam, traten mir sofort und bald darauf die Schrullen unsres kleinen Hans so scharf und hartnäckig entgegen, seine sonderbare Eitelkeit, sein Hochmuth, sein Mißtrauen gegen die Menschen und sein Hang sich allein zu beschäftigen, daß mir der entsetzliche Gedanke kam: Liegen denn in dem Kinde vielleicht auch die Keime zu dem fürchterlichen Erdübel, was hie und da in der Familie aufgetaucht ist; – denn diese Sonderbarkeiten sind die Factoren des Wahnsinns. Ich sprach mit Aemil und Lotte. Sie hatten gegen einander denselben Gedanken ausgetauscht. Denk dir, wie ich den Abend nach Hause kam, – ich war bei Aemil – wie ich unsern Jungen mit seinem kleinen zarten Gesicht so friedlich auf seinem Kissen schlummern sah; und wie ich nun grübelnd davor stand, und mir die vergebliche Frage vorlegte, ob denn das Entsetzliche in meinem armen unschuldigen Kinde sein stilles, unsichtbares Wachsthum begonnen habe. Ich verbrachte traurige Nächte, nicht grade schlaflos, aber wie in bleiernen Tod verzerrt, und die Tage in der aufreibendsten Aufregung; denn ich hatte das Kind, so viel ich konnte, um mich und studirte ihn, und ging den Quellen dieser krankhaften Gemüthsrichtung nach, und suchte sie zu beseitigen. – Ich habe mich nach und nach darüber beruhigt; es ist mir Alles erklärlich geworden, das Kind hat sich mir zutraulich erschloßen, und meine Gegenwart hat ihm wohl getan. Ich lasse ihn auch ruhig dort; denn er findet dort nur Freundlichkeit und Liebe. Sein Gemüth bedarf aber geradezu der *Zärtlichkeit*; darum bet ich dich auch, schreib ihm; er fragt jedesmal nach einem Brief für sich. So heilbringend nun auch meine Gegenwart für ihn gewesen, so sehr habe ich darunter gelitten. Ich war so herunter, daß ich 8 Tage hindurch jede Nacht gegen 2 U in einem fieberhaften Zustand erwachte, und dann nur wenig und zerbrochen mehr zu schlafen vermochte.[71]

For the first time he voices the fear that hereditary factors outside people's control could determine their lives. He expressed similar fears about physical handicaps preventing people developing their potential when faced by Ernst's emotional instability in puberty. Ernst, who had inherited all his father's hypochondria and complained like him of heart defects, heart cramps, and nerves, was also dispatched to Husum. The letter is typical of the

71. Storm to Constanze, 18 September 1860.

neurotic anxieties in the Storm family. The insanity of Storm's sister Cäcilie was both a symptom and a cause of such anxieties. She had become pregnant in the course of a relationship with a young Danish trainee lawyer in the early 1850s. Although the couple had been forced into marriage, neither the child nor the marriage had survived. Finally Cäcilie had to be interned in the mental asylum in Schleswig. It never seems to have occurred either to Storm or to his doctor brother Aemil that it might have been unwise for them both to have married sisters, their blood cousins. Yet many of the disorders in the Storm family undoubtedly sprang from this.

Although after 1870 Storm criticized the Prussian education system, in the early 1860s such notes were rare. Hans was put back into school and had to endure the humiliation of being unable to cope even in a class of younger boys. The nearest Storm ever came to accepting an alternative career for Hans was when he was so impressed by Ludwig Löwe that he contemplated letting him work for the local locksmith for two years, go to the Provincial Technical School for two years and finally study for three years at the Polytechnical Academy in Karlsruhe. If he was to pursue this alternative route to status and respectability, steps would have to be taken to ensure that his general *Bildung* continued. After a brief trial period the idea petered out. When Hans later contemplated becoming a market-gardener like his uncle Otto, Storm feared that because such a job was held in low social esteem, he might be denied the social and cultural contacts with educated people to which he, Storm, attached such importance.[72]

4.11   Finances and Fees

It is often assumed that by dovetailing his literary and judicial activities. Storm was spared the financial worries and temptations of full-time writers. In fact, he was no less dependent on literary fees than they were, and many of his dilemmas as a writer can be attributed to this. The greater his need to maximize his earnings, the greater was the pressure to write stories that met the expectations of publishers and editors. He could not afford to disregard financial matters. Although *Immensee* had become a

72. Storm to Esmarch, 18 June 1865, *Storm-Esmarch,* pp. 106f.

best seller, the terms negotiated with Duncker were unfavorable. When Duncker refused to raise his fees, Storm looked for alternative publishers: "Den Verleger habe ich lediglich wegen des Honorars gewechselt . . . Weßhalb, wenn die poetische Arbeit einmal da ist, soll man den reellen Nutzen gradezu bloß dem Händler lassen?"[73] Since his expenses were outstripping his income, it was vital that any work should first appear in the feuilleton section of a large newspaper or in one of the popular new magazines before being published in book form. If it could be published in various formats – miniature, octavo, even quarto – and in illustrated editions or collections, it could also match seasonal needs and meet the requirements of the lending libraries.

Family magazines like Ernst Keil's *Gartenlaube* represented a great new opportunity. Founded in 1853, it already had over 100,000 subscribers by 1861. It was complemented by other magazines like *Der Bazar, Illustrirte Damen- und Modezeitung; Der Salon für Litteratur, Kunst und Gesellschaft; Victoria. Illustrirte Muster- und Mode-Zeitung;* and *Über Land und Meer. Allgemeine Illustrirte Zeitung.* Any would-be contributor had to provide the product which editors and readers demanded. Works had to be tailored to specific requirements as regards length or designed so that they could be serialized. The *Schlesische Zeitung* rejected *Auf dem Staatshof* as insufficiently exciting for newspaper readers. Although *Drüben am Markt* was accepted by *Über Land und Meer* and *Am Kamin,* a collection of ghost stories, by *Victoria,* Storm's breakthrough came with Keil's acceptance of *Im Schloß.* The *Bazar* had approached Storm and offered him ninety talers for a work of the same length as *Immensee.* On that basis he asked Keil for 120 for a work a third longer. Keil, whose top rate was seventy-two talers per sheet, was only prepared to offer him sixty-four, i.e. well below what he was demanding. Storm's reply stressed both the quality of the work and the time spent on it. Eventually he proposed a compromise solution of 100 talers, hoping that he could recoup the loss by boosted book sales.

The new outlets brought with them new constraints. While ready to accept his article on popular belief/superstition in Catholic Germany (see p. 104), Keil insisted on his right to change sentences in the introduction, which was critical of the Catholic

---

73. Storm to H. and L. Brinkmann, 29 September 1855, *Storm-Brinkmann,* p. 108.

church. His magazine was, he wrote, read by too many Catholics for him – "bei allem Festhalten des Princips" – not to show some consideration.[74] The article never appeared. The editor of the *Bazar*, Oskar Loebel, showed little interest in ghost stories. Instead he hoped for a little reflective article in prose on a theme like winter flowers.[75] He made acceptance of any ghost stories conditional on further stories having a more pleasant background and addressing a quite different subject matter. He had, he stressed, to think of his young female readers.[76] In a subsequent letter he returned to the issue: "Zusagen wird uns Ihre Dichtung gewiß, da diesselbe sich innerhalb der engen Grenzlinien bewegen wird, welche die Rücksichtnahme auf die *jungen* Leserinnen des 'Bazar' gebieterisch ziehen; ebenso sind Religion und Politik verbotene Gebiete."[77] Editors had to humor the susceptibilities of a wide readership. Market considerations were now as important as not incurring official wrath. Indeed the new breed of editors and publishers were largely commercial animals, for whom the deciding factor was whether a book would sell or not. Writers had to adjust.

The expansion of the literary market proved restrictive in terms of content and form. Having to cater for the consumer had far-reaching implications for writers keen to promote positions which conflicted with the views of substantial numbers of readers or at least ran the risk of doing so. For the moment Storm felt himself attuned to the will, real or potential, of the *Volk*. It was therefore a question of manipulating people's sensibilities so that they would follow him down the road to humanitarianism. Problems would occur when he lost this sense. The more his readers adopted views hostile to his own, the more he had to redouble his efforts to maneuver them in unfamiliar directions without, in the process, alerting their ideological sensors. The pressure to earn large fees and the will to promote change had to strike shifting compromises.

Judging the market was not always easy. His appetite whetted by Keil's fee, Storm had negotiated a good price for the book form of his next work, *Auf der Universität*, before finding a magazine to take it. To his dismay, first one and then another rejected

74. Keil to Storm, 1 October 1861, SHLB.
75. Loebel to Storm, 14 October 1861, SHLB.
76. Loebel to Storm, 18 October 1861, SHLB.
77. Loebel to Storm, 8 November 1861, SHLB.

his demands. Although he kept on cutting the price, he was still left with the story on his hands. Eventually he had to settle for book publication only. When, in October 1862, J.J.Weber, the editor of the *Leipziger Illustrirte Zeitung*, approached him about a Christmas contribution, Storm pointed out that he could not write to order and that he spent five or sixth months working on any story. He still accepted, promising to do his best to supply something by the end of November.[78] Weber was delighted with *Unter dem Tannenbaum*, paid Storm 100 talers, and ordered a similar story for the following Christmas. Having to work at such short notice and produce "seasonal goods" did not necessarily mean that Storm turned out shoddy goods. In this case he grasped the opportunity to bring the Schleswig-Holstein cause back to the forefront of people's minds. But it has to be said that large sections of the work lack substance and artistic organization. The pattern would be repeated in the 1870s and 1880s.

78. Storm to Weber, 28 October 1862, SHLB.

5

Prussianization

5.1 The Schleswig-Holstein Crisis

In March 1863, in contravention of the international treaties of 1851/52 the Danish king proclaimed the constitutional separation of Schleswig from Holstein. For many this was the prelude to the total incorporation of Schleswig into Denmark. Storm, who was already committed to providing a Christmas contribution to the *Leipziger Illustrirte Zeitung*, used *Abseits* to revive memories of the 1848 Rising. It evokes the grim plight and heroic determination of the Schleswig-Holsteiners under Danish rule, and conjures up the vision of a future united Germany. But even after the Federal Diet had at last voted for Federal Execution against Denmark in October, its continuing inaction encouraged the Eiderdanes to pass a joint Basic Law for Denmark and Schleswig in November.[1]

In November the Danish king died without heirs. In accordance with the London Protocol of 1852 Prince Christian of Schleswig-Holstein-Sonderburg-Glücksburg succeeded in Denmark, Schleswig, Holstein and Lauenburg. However, many towns in the duchies, including Husum, refused either to send the customary deputation to the funeral or to dispatch the usual addresses of dutiful homage to the new king. The great majority of officials refused to swear the oath of allegiance. A new claimant to the duchies had appeared on the scene: Prince Friedrich of

---

1. Post-1870 Prusso-German historians offer only thin and extremely tendentious presentations of the period. A pro-Augustenburg version is provided by K. Jansen, *Schleswig-Holsteins Befreiung*, ed. K. Samwer, Wiesbaden, 1897. On the other hand, the SHLB possesses a wealth of contemporary pamphlets. See also H. Hagenah, "1863. Die Nationale Bewegung in Schleswig-Holstein," *ZSHG*, vol. 56, 1927, pp. 271–396; J.V. Olshausen, ed., "Briefe aus der Zeit der Befreiung Schleswig-Holsteins," *ZSHG*, vol. 69, 1941, pp. 132–290; L.D. Steefel, *The Schleswig-Holstein Question*, London, 1932; C.v.Tiedemann, *Aus sieben Jahrzehnten*, 2 vols., Leipzig, 1905, vol. 1, *Schleswig-Holsteinische Erinnerungen*. I have explored the specific question of Storm's return in "Theodor Storms Heimkehr im Jahre 1864," *STSG*, vol. 33, 1984, pp. 19–44.

Schleswig-Holstein-Sonderburg-Augustenburg. In a move designed to win the support of liberals and democrats, he declared his acceptance of the September Constitution of 1848. Influential members of the Ritterschaft, who had hitherto supported the Nationalverein, a Germany-wide pressure group founded in the late 1850s to promote the Prussian, *kleindeutsch* cause, were so disillusioned by Prussian policy that they too rallied to Friedrich. This group included Ludwig von Reventlow, an aristocrat with democratic sympathies in 1848, who later became Amtmann in Husum and Storm's good friend. But although the rulers and parliaments of many medium and small German states recognized Friedrich's claims, the Federal Diet did not, and Prussia and Austria insisted that any action could only be on the basis of Denmark's violation of the 1851/52 treaties. In contrast, German Schleswig-Holsteiners and the German national movement wanted total separation of the duchies from Denmark.

Storm deemed the time ripe for political poetry. Choosing the outlet which promised maximum publicity and effect, he sent the poem "Schleswig-holsteinische Gräber" (later entitled "Gräber in Schleswig," LL 1, 83) to the *Gartenlaube*. It revives his hope of a popular war to liberate the duchies ("Die Erde dröhnt; von Deutschland weht es her,/ Mir ist, ich hör ein Lied im Winde klingen,/ Es kommt heran schon wie ein brausend Meer,/ Um endlich alle Schande zu verschlingen.") But this mood is dispelled: the "Germans" persist in sticking to the "London paper." Before the poem could reach its intended readers, Bismarck had banned the *Gartenlaube* in Prussia.

At a time when national concerns had replaced social ones in many people's minds, Storm wrote to Brinkmann: "Der Herzog ist, wie alle Gekrönten, meinem demokratischen Herzen eine sehr gleichgültige Person."[2] The poem "Schleswig-holsteinische Hoffnungen," which appeared long after his death, runs:

> Und haben wir unser Herzoglein
> Nur erst im Lande drinnen,
> Dann wird, mir kribbelt schon die Faust,
> Ein ander Stück beginnen.

---

2. Storm to his parents, 21 December 1863, *Briefe* 1, pp. 435f.

Der Junker muß lernen den schweren Satz,
Daß der Adel in unsern Zeiten
Zwar ebenfalls ein Privatpläsier,
Doch sonst nichts hat zu bedeuten.

Vor allem muß lernen Hinz und Kunz
– Und das ist ein Stück, ein hartes –
Daß diese hochhinschauenden Herrn
Sind keineswegs was Apartes.

Denn nur so lang, als man sie glaubt,
So lang nur gibt's Gespenster.
Drum schaffet Licht und aber Licht,
Und öffnet Tür und Fenster!
(LL 1, 264)

Given the fanatically pro-Augustenburg mood in the duchies it would have been unwise to try to publish it. This poem in the vein of Heine helps put into context another written in January:

Wir können auch die Trompete blasen
Und schmettern weithin durch das Land;
Doch schreiten wir lieber in Maientagen,
Wenn die Primeln blühen und die Drosseln schlagen,
Still sinnend an des Baches Rand.
(LL 1, 85)

In the face of the surge of political poetry, it was advisable, were the fourth edition of Storm's poems to have any chance at all of selling, to remind readers that he could also write political poems – even if the great majority of poems in the volume treated other topics. Ironically, it was his lyric antipode, Emanuel Geibel, who, having been court poet in Munich, now discovered his Prussian heart and would soon be acclaimed for his monarchist, conservative poems.

On 23 and 24 December Saxon and Hanoverian troops at last effected the Federal Execution in Holstein. The Danes withdrew to Schleswig. At the end of the month Friedrich landed in Kiel. Deputations from every town and village flocked there to pay homage to him. However, Austria and Prussia delivered an ultimatum to Denmark in mid-January declaring that they would occupy Schleswig as a security for the fulfillment of the 1851/52 treaties and that they reserved the right to regulate the future position of the duchies in the event of hostilities. When their troops invaded Holstein and ousted Confederation troops from key strategic positions, Storm's indignation brimmed over. Whereas Brinkmann deemed the aristocracy indispensable, he pronounced it, together with the church, the poison in the veins of the German nation.[3] The poem "Es gibt eine Sorte" (LL 1, 85) stresses the need to purge the body politic of such foreign bodies. But despite all Ludwig Löwe's efforts, nobody in Berlin was prepared to publish it.

Storm viewed the impending struggle as a rerun of the 1848 revolutions: "Es ist mir sehr wohl bewußt, daß der überall unausbleibliche Kampf zwischen der alten und neuen Zeit bei uns ein sehr hartnäckiger werden muß. Diesen sozialen Kampf in meiner Heimat noch zu erleben und rüstig durch das begeisterte Wort mitkämpfen zu können, ist in bezug auf das äußere Leben mein allerheißester Wunsch."[4] As Friedrich would, in Storm's view, stand by his Junkers, a fierce struggle was inevitable in which he hoped to be the "Tyrtaeus of democracy" (see p. 52).

Having hitherto made no overtures to the Augustenburg camp, Storm feared that he ran a real risk, should Friedrich become duke, of finding all the posts in the civil service occupied by those who had registered with a bureau set up in Gotha. At the end of January he dedicated the forthcoming edition of his poems to Friedrich as duke. Despite the reluctance of his Berlin publisher, the dedication was typeset. Storm suppressed it only when he was already installed as Landvogt in Husum. Had the Prussian authorities seen in him an Augustenburg supporter, he may not have been confirmed as Landvogt.[5]

On 1 February Austrian and Prussian troops invaded Schleswig and rapidly proved superior to the Danish forces. Storm was torn between hopes of an independent Schleswig-Holstein and fears that the Austrians and Prussians would restore the status quo ante. When a telegram arrived from Husum offering him the post of Landvogt, he took leave in order to seek further informa-

---

3. Storm to Brinkmann, 18 January 1864, *Storm-Brinkmann*, p. 134.
4. Ibid., p. 135.
5. Jackson, "Heimkehr," p. 33. See also LL 4, p. 408.

tion. In Husum he learned that he had been elected at a public
meeting of the citizenry. However, in view of the confused situation, he felt unable to accept before first seeking an interview in
Berlin with the Minister of Justice, Leopold Graf zur Lippe, with
a view to being granted temporary leave or guaranteed the right,
should worst come to worst, of re-entering the Prussian judiciary
without any loss of seniority. The audience confirmed him in his
revulsion for the present régime. The minister ruled out either
prospect. Knowing that he was committing himself and his family
to an uncertain future but with the satisfaction that he had obeyed
the categorical imperative, Storm tendered his resignation. On 12
March he set out for Husum with Hans and on 17 March began
his duties as Landvogt. By early May he was already so desperate about the position that he wrote in terms echoing Dante's
Inferno that his sole literary ambition was to create a sulphurous
hell "Um, die sich Mensch nennt, diese Kreatur,/ In die ver-
fluchten Kreise einzureihen."[6]

For one brief moment that spring, when Austria and Prussia
announced at the London Conference that they favored separating the duchies from Denmark and fusing them in a single
state under Duke Friedrich, it seemed that the will of the *Volk*
had, after all, triumphed over particularist, dynastic machinations. Storm immediately wrote the poem "1864":

> Ein Murren erst, ein deutlich Reden;
> Von allen Seiten kam's herbei,
> Des Volkes Mund ward laut und lauter,
> Die Luft schlug Wellen von Geschrei.
>
> Und die sich stets entgegenstemmen
> Dem Geist, der größer ist als sie,
> Sie waren in den Kampf gerisssen
> Und wußten selber kaum noch wie.
>
> Sie standen an den deutschen Marken
> Dem Feind entgegen unverwandt,
> Und waren, eh sie es bedachten,
> Das Schwert in ihres Volkes Hand.[7]

---

6. Storm to Tiedemann, 2 May 1864, *Briefe* 1, p. 458.
7. *Murren* was later changed to *Raunen* for the final version. See LL 1, 84.

The proposals disappeared from the table, and the war against Denmark resumed. In July Denmark was forced to sign an armistice and in Vienna renounced all claims to the duchies and Lauenburg in favor of Prussia and Austria. Having first set up a condominium in both duchies, Prussia and Austria agreed in Gastein in 1865 that Prussia should administer Schleswig and Austria Holstein. The arrangement held till the Austro-Prussian War of 1866.

5.2   Eurocentricity

Von jenseit des Meeres (1865) is a paean to North German civilization and culture. It was on the basis of such *Sittlichkeit, Intelligenz,* and *Bildung* that Storm justified the duchies' claim to be an independent state. The novella also reiterates his conviction that the "religion" of the modern age must be a cult of love centered on marital and family relationships. As in *Späte Rosen* a material framework is sketched in which an innate, European aspiration for a full and beautiful life can be satisfied. The notion of a mature European civilization capable of fully assimilating and humanizing sex and passion is at the core of the novella.

Capitalism and colonialism play crucial roles. While the profession of the hero Alfred's father is left undefined, the reader is told that the deserted factory-building adjacent to the house dates from the time of his grandfather. In the case of the Woldsen family it was a sugar-beet factory which had gone bankrupt in the face of competition from plantations in the Danish colony of St. Croix in the Antilles like the one referred to here. The father of the heroine Jenni leaves the duchies as an impecunious businessman and becomes a wealthy plantation-owner there. Yet he insists on his daughter being brought up and educated in Europe and builds himself a splendid villa in Pyrmont for his retirement. It is significant that in a text written so close to the American Civil War there is no mention of slavery nor any hint that colonialism may be exploitative. It is shown to benefit both the plantation owners and the Europe to which they return with their profits, while providing the "colored" population with a comparatively affluent, contented lifestyle commensurate with their primitive cultural and moral standards.

As a generator of the good life in Europe, colonialism is a means to an end rather than an end in itself. Neither Alfred nor his brother is involved in commerce or industry: Arnold is an architect, while his brother trains at an agricultural college before buying and running a former aristocratic estate. In this respect the novel is close to Adalbert Stifter's *Nachsommer* (1857). In middle-class hands North Germany can retain its pre-industrial beauty and aristocratic elegance provided that primary wealth is produced in the third world. Storm's vision of preserving eighteenth-century patrician values in a democratic modern world returns. In the New World, in contrast, the struggle for economic survival is not humanized and softened by European family and social arrangements. The plantation owner has no loving spouse to return to. Without such a family matrix *Bildung* and *Sittlichkeit* cannot develop. "Colored" women, for their part, can only be concubines, and love for them only sensual fascination since they lack the cultural and moral qualities of middle-class German womankind. An authoritarian economic system on the plantations promotes similar behavior in the private sphere. Indeed the text suggests that many of the problems in the novella could have been avoided had Jenni's father communicated with her.

The North German middle class, on the other hand, is shown to blend the poetic and the practical, the ideal and the real. Thus Alfred designs basilicas *and* farm buildings. Its members have a deep emotional and spiritual life; but it is especially in their family life that they excel. Here any harshness bred in the economic world disappears. The ideal German family is a supportive community where individuals can satisfy all their needs for security and love. Members of this family meet to discuss their plans and problems; they consider each other's needs and tend for each other in sickness. Although Alfred's authoritarian father may still be poor at relating to children, his mother embodies the ideal of the caring, loving parent. In this she contrasts with Jenni's negress mother who is capable only of wild, elemental maternal love.

This North German world has accumulated the positive elements of developing European civilization: the pagan, classical cult of beauty and the senses, Christian spirituality, German inwardness, French classical rococo beauty, the English garden style and modern scientific, technical, agricultural and commercial techniques. Its culture is strong enough to channel into acceptable forms the negro elements in Jenni's make-up. Her wildness, her tomboy-like delight in climbing trees and her malicious mischievousness can be restrained, even if her litheness

and physical vitality which smack of the jungle ("die Ursprüngli-
chkeit der Wildnis," LL 1, 669) only heighten her sexual attractiveness for Alfred. However, in public places and social intercourse this vitality expresses itself in decorous games of shuttle-
cock on Sunday afternoons when connoisseur male eyes savor
such non-European athleticism (LL 1, 668f.). Since North German *Bildung* is equated with *Humanität*, Jenni must acquire it at
a German boarding-school. Here she acquires an advanced
European sensibility with regard to relations between parents
and children and filial duties. She becomes, in the text's terms, a
true human being.

The novella stresses that in North Germany love is not mere
sexual infatuation: it grows over a long period and satisfies a
range of needs. Communication and companionship are at the
heart of Alfred and Jenni's relationship when they are children;
they enjoy a feeling of cosy security together. Gradually "an
unconscious sense of belonging together and of being mutually
responsible for each other" (LL 1, 658f.) develops. This does not,
however, exclude the supreme moment when the "blue flower,"
that symbol of ineffable romantic love, blossoms. The labored
symbolism of the Venus statues in the park underlines Storm's
thesis that a modern, marital Venus is neither a sensual pagan
beauty without modesty and pudeur nor the demonic seductress
painted by Christian poets like Eichendorff. Symbolically standing by the empty pedestal, Jenni declares herself to be a poor
human being in need of help (LL 1, 674). Venus is brought out
of enchanted moon-lit solitude into a respectable nineteenth-
century middle-class family. The true "holy family" can flourish
in this "paradise" (LL 1, 662) where there is no suggestion of
domestic drudgery, cramped circumstances, financial worries, or
alienated work.

The novella may not endorse the view of the black *femme fatale*
purveyed in Charles Sealsfield's novel *Die Farbigen* where
"coloured" women are presented as less than fully human,
seductive creatures, the evil geniuses of male European immi-
grants (LL 1, 666); but it does present them as children whose
primitive language corresponds to their primitive human needs:
"Aber man durfte sie nicht reden hören; der schöne Mund
stümperte in der gebrochenen Sprache der Neger; es war das
Geplapper eines Kindes" (LL 1, 681). Negro blood can, it suggests, at best inject a certain new vitality into the racial and genetic

stock. Jenni can only be rescued and put on the road to *Bildung* because of her European blood. In contrast, those without European blood and those of mixed race living in the West Indies in the "colored" community simply lack the positive moral qualities and needs of middle-class Europeans living in North Germany. Jenni's mother feels no need for the privacy and intimacy of a true home and keeps a lodging-house. Lacking any *pudeur*, she does not conceal her past; indeed she is grateful to Jenni's father for setting her up like this. She tolerates familiarities from a mulatto, who bares his teeth like a dog, and is even prepared to marry her daughter to him. According to Jenni, the voices of the dock workers are more like the howling and cries of animals than of human beings (LL 1, 690). They inspire terror. She recognizes that her notions of the distress felt by a mother whose child is torn from her do not apply to this "base region where no such noble suffering can thrive" (LL 1, 691).

Storm would have considered the work progressive in suggesting that the daughter of a negro concubine could be accepted into respectable white European society. But Jenni is acceptable only because the sole signs of her negro blood are the half-moons on her nails. The novella is silent on the problem of what will happen if Alfred and Jenni have a dark-skinned child with negroid features. Magazine editors like Rodenberg who did not dare present their readers with an illegitimate heroine would not have printed such a story.

5.3 Annexation and Tyranny

During the years in exile return to Schleswig-Holstein had been a tantalizing hope. Storm had now returned, not only to his native town, but to the esteemed post of Landvogt. For a brief moment it seemed that, liberated from Danish rule and constituted as a separate state, Schleswig-Holstein might become a democratic model for the other German states. Its position within a future united liberal/democratic Germany could be defined later. The events of the coming years destroyed these hopes.[8]

---

8. For this period see: W. Franz, "Einführung und erste Jahre der preußischen Verwaltung in Schleswig-Holstein," *ZSGH*, vol. 82, 1958, pp. 163–215, and vol. 83, 1959, pp. 117–242; O. Hauser, *Preußische Staatsräson und nationaler Gedanke*,

After the *débâcle* of 1848–51, Storm consoled himself with the
thought that the restoration of the *ancien régime* was only a stay
of execution. Neither the high moral ground nor the overall vision
of history had been ceded. Developments within the Prussian
middle classes now threatened this prospect. In 1866 the latter
finalized the accommodation with the aristocracy which had
slowly been materializing and had only been disguised by the
parliamentary furors of Bismarck's first period of office. The
latter's brand of conservatism had stolen the liberals' clothes.
Conservative apologists had hitherto underwritten the old system with legitimist, feudal arguments. In their view, national
unity would bring down both the international, dynastic framework and also the pyramid of powers and privileges in the
individual monarchies, principalities and duchies. Bismarck had
recognized that the Prussian ruling class could only preserve its
pre-eminence in a world of capitalist nation states if it satisfied
certain middle-class national and economic aspirations. To this
end he was ready to incur the enmity of his old conservative
backers. Eloquent propagandists like the ex-liberal Treitschke set
out to fashion a new ideological consensus. After the Prussian
victory over Austria in 1866 professors and publicists systemati-
cally questioned key tenets of liberal, enlightened thought as
they sought to legitimate the new arrangements and cement them
in a wider historical scheme. It was against them that any
democratic writer had to compete in an unequal struggle for the
public mind.

In 1863/64 Prussian policy toward the duchies was denounced
in and outside Schleswig-Holstein; but after the Prussian victories at Düppel and Alsen a shift in middle-class liberal opinion
in Prussia was perceptible. Both liberals and democrats had no

Neumünster, 1960; idem., *Provinz im Königreich Preußen* (Geschichte Schleswig-
Holsteins, 8/1), Neumünster, 1966, reissued as *Staatliche Einheit und regionale
Vielfalt in Preußen. Der Aufbau der Verwaltung in Schleswig-Holstein nach 1867*,
Neumünster, 1967; P.v.Heedemann-Heespen, *Die Herzogtümer Schleswig-Holstein
und die Neuzeit*, Kiel, 1926, pp. 723ff.; K. Jürgensen, "Die Eingliederung der Her-
zogtümer Schleswig, Holstein und Lauenburg in das Preußische Königreich," in
P. Baumgart, ed., *Expansion und Integration. Zur Eingliederung neugewonnener Gebiete
in den preußischen Staat*, Cologne and Vienna, 1984, pp. 327–56; *Schleswig-Holstein
und die Annexion von einem Schleswig-Holsteiner* (Karl Lorentzen), Freiburg, 1867;
M. Liepmann, *Briefe Kieler Professoren*, Stuttgart and Berlin, 1916; G. Reinhardt,
Preußen im Spiegel der öffentlichen Meinung Schleswig-Holsteins, Neumünster, 1954.

wish for Austria to have a permanent presence in North West Germany; nor did they wish to see the duchies or any part of them returned to Denmark. They were prepared to abandon the principle of self-determination if upholding it in Schleswig-Holstein meant the creation of another particularist duchy and the loss, in Kiel, of a potential naval base. Support for the idea of a Prussian annexation grew. In 1866 the Progressives joined in the universal condemnation of Prussian policy for allying with France and waging war on Austria and her allies, Baden, Württemberg, Bavaria, Saxony, the Hesses, and Hanover. The mood changed dramatically, however, after Prussia's rapid victory. Liberals distanced themselves from their previous positions, and the passing of the Indemnity Bill sealed the reconciliation of the majority of them with Bismarck. The National Liberal Party was founded. The appetite for national power had triumphed over concern to achieve it in tandem with a parliamentary constitutional monarchy on the British model. Demands for parliamentary control over the monarchy in key areas were scaled down. Liberals were, however, confident that in the debates about the North German Confederation and in the coming years they could shape the state in their own image.

Though signed and sealed by January 1867, the Annexation Patent regarding the duchies did not come into effect until 1 October 1867. In the interim the Prussian monarch assumed all legislative functions, and the hated Oberpräsident Baron Scheel-Plessen ruled by decree. It is true that the Patent affirmed the monarch's intent to preserve the laws and institutions of the duchies as far as they were the expression of "justified peculiarities" and as far as this did not affect the unity of the state or its interests; but although some concessions were made to old territorial and institutional arrangements, the administrative reforms represented a radical break with the past. The duchies' fate was typical of the other territories annexed in 1866, all of which were assimilated as speedily as possible into the structures of the Prussian monarchy. For those outside the National-Liberal, pro-Bismarck lobby these were difficult times. They saw themselves as powerless, disenfranchised victims of an alien invader. Their identity, their historical traditions were being violated.

In the duchies the Prussian Kreis system replaced the old patchwork of administrative units and jurisdictions. The Amtmann or Oberbeamter was replaced by the Landrat. Unlike in the old Prussian provinces he was neither elected by the members of the Kreistag nor from among them: he was a royal appointee. The Kreistag itself enjoyed only limited powers, and elections to it were conducted according to the principle of three separate estates, i.e. the large estate owners, the towns, and the rural communities. The wealthiest landowners still enjoyed the right to their own personal vote or *Virilstimme*.

In the Prussian system the next highest representative body, the Provinziallandtag, was relatively unimportant compared with both the Kreistag and the Prussian Landtag in Berlin. Although elected directly – and not, as the Prussian government originally wanted, from within the members of the Kreistage – it, too, was based on the estates principle. To their disappointment many Schleswig-Holsteiners had to recognize that such a body could not become a democratic version of the old Ständeversammlung, i.e. a regional assembly with real powers. The duchies' concerns had now to be voiced in the Prussian Landtag or the Reichstag, where their elected members constituted only a tiny fraction. Since elections to the Landtag were conducted on the three-class-franchise and on an indirect system of voting, more wealthy, conservative members tended to be returned to it than to the Reichstag, elections to which were based on universal, adult male suffrage.

Only in the area of municipal reform did the Prussian government make major concessions to local democracy and self-government when it largely accepted the proposals of Albert Hänel, a law professor in Kiel and a Liberal politician.[9] The Städteordnung of 1868 resulted in more progressive arrangements than in the old Prussian provinces. Citizens elected the Magistrat. They also elected the mayor from a list of three. The person elected had then to be confirmed by the king. The principle was also affirmed that the two "colleges," the Magistrat and the councillors, should deliberate in joint sessions. Policing was split between the centrally organized police responsible for security matters and the so-called "welfare police" which was left in local control. On the other hand, citizenship was restricted to those

---

9. See J. Jacobsen, "Das Husumer Lokalstatut von 1869," *Nordfriesisches Jahrbuch*, new series, vol. 7, 1971, pp. 73–89; idem, "Landesregierung und städtische Verwaltung in Schleswig-Holstein am Ende der dänischen und Beginn der preußischen Zeit, dargestellt am Beispiel der Stadt Husum," ibid., vol. 10, 1974, pp. 143–57.

owning a dwelling, plying a trade, or paying a certain amount in class-tax.

Storm's verdict, first on the Prussian-Austrian occupation and condominium and then on the Prussian annexation did not waver: they violated the basic human right of self-determination. Supposed liberators had become oppressors. His public position – one designed to protect him against Prussian disfavor – was to distinguish between Prussia *per se* and its government. In fact, given his conviction that the latter would remain in power for his lifetime, the distinction did not amount to much.[10] He would, he declared, have been prepared to accept annexation if it had been the will of the elected Schleswig-Holstein Estates. As it was, Prussian policy remained "Räuberpolitik," Caesarism, terrorism.[11] He spoke of "freche Junkerherrschaft" and referred to "die verfluchte Junkerbrut." Might and brutal force had triumphed over right; naked Prussian *raison d'état* over the justified wishes of the people.[12]

The period during which Austria and Prussia and then the Prussians ruled by decree, appointed and sacked people at will, closed down newspapers, forbade any oppositional activity or demonstrations, and threatened those found guilty of very minor political offences with long sentences in a convict prison, encouraged the feeling that one was at the mercy of naked force and chance.[13] In January 1868 Storm wrote to Brinkmann: "Ich komme über die Vergewaltigung meines Heimathlandes nicht weg, nie mehr. Die Preuß. Regierung – Junker u. Korporäle – hat dadurch, daß sie die Existenz von Menschen in dem Lande Schleswig Holstein ignorirte, wieder bekundet, daß sie trotz ihrer königl Constitution von einer berechtigten Nation nichts wissen, daß in Pr. überhaupt nur der Recht hat, der die Gewalt hat."[14] To Turgenjev he wrote: "Die Regierung hat auch bei uns gezeigt, daß sie kein Recht der Nation respektirt als das, wozu sie auf

10. Storm to Pietsch, 10 December 1865, *Blätter der Freundschaft*, p. 158.
11. Storm to Pietsch, 27 December 1864, ibid., p. 141; Storm to Hans, 13 February 1867, *Briefe* 1, p. 499; Storm to Pietsch, *Blätter der Freundschaft*, 12 May 1866, p. 163
12. Storm to Pietsch, ibid., 27 December 1864, p. 141; Storm to Pietsch, Whitsun, 1864, ibid., p. 21; Storm to Eggers, 16 August 1867, *Storm-Eggers*, pp. 64f.
13. Storm to Pietsch, *Blätter der Freundschaft*, 12 March 1867, p. 174.
14. Storm to H. and L. Brinkmann, 21 January 1868, *Storm-Brinkmann*, pp. 153f.

den Barrikaden gezwungen wird."[15]

Whereas the new opinion-makers greeted the changes as necessary steps toward the creation of a strong, united Germany and many National-Liberals would have preferred an even more unitary, centralized system than that imposed on the North German Confederation, Storm condemned this abolishing of Schleswig-Holstein's institutions without any consultation and the "imposing" (*oktroyieren*) of others at the Prussians' pleasure.[15] It was not simply a case of bemoaning the loss of cherished idiosyncracies or a reflection of his belief that the emergence of large states entailed the loss of one of the finest things in life – *Heimatgefühl*.[16] What was so distressing was the feeling that an organic tradition with great potential was being destroyed. Storm's evocations after 1870 of the Schleswig-Holstein past would attempt to keep alive the memory of this past and its values. Even the autocratic paternalism of royal officials in his youth was preferable to the new system.[17] If in the 1870s and 1880s he was, according to Ferdinand Tönnies, an "ethical democrat," attaching more importance to the spirit in which power was exercised rather than to political structures,[18] this has much to do with the disillusionment of these years.

The reform of the judicial system compounded his sense of humiliation. The common Schleswig-Holstein practice of combining judicial, administrative, and policing functions in one post and one person was incompatible with the Prussian system. Civil servants were therefore required to opt either for a judicial or an administrative career. Since all civil servants in the duchies were legally trained, those not assigned to one area for political reasons, could themselves make the choice. Storm was conscious that as Landvogt things might be demanded of him in his policing role which he could not do; yet he also knew that if he stood by his principles, that could also cost him his job.[19] Since as a senior administrator he would probably have to implement measures which he could not endorse and since he was anxious

15. Storm to Turgenev, 30 May 1868, in K.-E. Laage, *Theodor Storm und Iwan Turgenjew. Persönliche und literarische Beziehungen*, Heide, 1967, p. 104.

16. Storm to K.T. Pyl, 20 April 1875, *Briefe* 2, p. 103.

17. See LL 4, 431f.

18. F. Tönnies, *Gedenkblätter. Theodor Storm zum 14. September 1917*, Berlin 1917, p. 61.

19. Storm to Pietsch, 12 March 1867, *Blätter der Freundschaft*, p. 174.

to stay in Husum, he settled for the modest post of Amtsrichter, one of two such posts created for the town. It was a bitter blow. His fears persisted:

> Wer der Gewalt genübersteht
> In Sorgen für der Liebsten Leben
> Der wird zuletzt von seinem Ich
> Ein Theil und noch ein Theilchen geben,
> Und athmet er nach reinster Luft,
> Er wird zuletzt ein halber Schuft. (LL 1, 266)

When the Prussian Penal Code replaced all other codes, he complained that the Schleswig-Holsteiners were being treated like a conquered tribe: their law was being abolished and the conquerors were dictating their own in its stead. He found particular laws abominable and considered certain paragraphs far more dangerous for honest people than rogues.[20] Particularly unpopular at the time, though Storm does not mention them specifically, were paragraphs 101 and 102, the so-called "Haß- und Verachtungsparagraph" and the one outlawing any insulting or slandering of public authorities and officials.[21] Storm regarded capital punishment as a practice from a darker age (see p. 190), and the Minister for Justice's performance during the debates in the North German Reichstag on the question of returning press offenses to jury courts made him want to spit.[22] In contrast, he praised Virchow, Lasker and Schulze-Delitzsch for their stance. Although Storm is silent about them, other reforms were progressive. To this category belong the abolition of patrimonial jurisdiction and of the legal exemption of the knights and privileged large estate-owners, the introduction of jury courts and the conducting of legal proceedings in public and orally.

The introduction of the Prussian bureaucratic system and the influx of Prussian civil servants, judges and state prosecutors generated great friction in the duchies. The government had decreed that there should be an exchange of civil servants between the old provinces and the new. In addition, it was found that because of the separation of criminal investigation, prosecution

20. Storm to Pietsch, 16 August 1867, ibid., p. 176.
21. See Reinhardt, *Preußen im Spiegel*, pp. 95f.
22. Storm to Ernst, 2 November 1869.

and sentencing, thirty-eight percent of the requisite judges and state prosecutors had to be recruited from officials in the old Prussian provinces. Storm found the behavior of these senior Prussian officials obnoxious. Thus, when Privy Councillor Krüger was sent from Berlin to inspect the system of justice in the duchies and outline the reforms, Storm complained that he was typical of all those behaving as if they had conquered the duchies in person, had superior wisdom to impart and were bent on teaching Prussian obedience: "Auf diese Weise einigt man Deutschland nicht."[23] What made this all the more galling was that, in his view, the duchies had contributed to the intellectual life of the nation a contingent scarcely matched by any comparable part of Prussia. In Storm's eyes it was symptomatic of the new climate that a Privy Councillor had complained that a train had not been kept waiting for him and had not come back after he had telegraphed. Storm classed the new officials as "subalterns," i.e. very subordinate officials in the old Schleswig-Holstein system. They were a cross between schoolmasters and corporals, treating their colleagues as subordinates and with a supercilious peremptoriness or a patronizing condescension which made one feel like a schoolboy or a silly boy.[24] As a servant of such a government and in such a *Gewalt-Staat*, one could not be a true *Staatsbeamter*.[25]

In the old duchies local officials had enjoyed considerable independence and discretionary powers as well as maintaining close ties with the local community. Storm found his own post as Landvogt congenial in these respects. In place of this system the Prussians installed a centralized, bureaucratic one in which the collegiate principle was replaced by a hierarchical chain of command. Civil servants became cogs in a machine, mere puppets (see p. 185). Storm was not alone in being appalled by the tide of new regulations and the massive growth in paperwork. The poem "Der Bureaukrat" (later entitled "Fortschritt" and finally "Der Beamte") runs:

> Er reibt sich die Hände: "Wir kriegen's jetzt!
> Auch der frechste Bursche spüret
> Schon bis hinab in die Fingerspitz,"

23. Storm to Eggers, 16 August 1867, *Storm-Eggers*, pp. 64ff.
24. Storm to Pietsch, 30 January 1867, *Blätter der Freundschaft*, p. 173.
25. Storm to H. and L. Brinkmann, 21 January 1868, *Storm-Brinkmann*, p. 154.

Daß von oben er wird regieret.

Bei jeder Geburt ist künftig sofort
Die Bitte zu formulieren,
Daß die hohe Behörde dem lieben Kind
Gestatte zu existieren!

"Antrag" later replaced "Bitte" – to good effect (LL 1, 85).

The restructuring of the educational system also aroused his misgivings since he was, of course, familiar with the Prussian system. The adoption in elementary schools of the spirit enshrined in the Stiehl Regulations was for him synonymous with intellectual oppression.[26] Teachers themselves voiced their disquiet at ministerial statements which defined the function of such schools as to inculcate fear of God and loyalty to king and fatherland and to educate youth for the army. What, they asked, was to become of broader definitions of *Bildung* and of notions of *Humanität* if education were made to serve party-political purposes in a strictly regulated, uniform system?[27] Concern extended far beyond the elementary level. As early as 1864 high-ranking officials from the Prussian Kultusministerium visited Schleswig to report on the state of grammar school education. Friedrich Lübker, who had once taught in Husum, and Ludwig Wiese both visited the town in these years and were instrumental in the decision to restore the grammar school.[28] After 1866 the educational authorities' concern was to maximize uniformity of curricula and levels of achievement in equivalent educational establishments in the old and new provinces. Until now grammar school pupils in the duchies had not needed to pass any formal Maturitätsexamen or Abitur before entering the university. Further, now that all males were liable to three years service in the army and it was no longer possible to pay for substitutes, there was every incentive to qualify for the one-year period of service as a volunteer providing one's own equipment, an option only available to those who had attained a certain educational level. Foreseeing these

26. Storm to Rodenberg, 27 May 1868, *STSG*, vol. 22, 1973, p. 39.
27. See *Bericht über die Versammlung des allgemeinen schleswig-holsteinischen Lehrer-Vereins in Schleswig den 29.30 u.31 Juli 1867*, Kiel, 1867, pp. 49ff.
28. See W. Weimar, *Geschichte des Gymnasiums in Schleswig-Holstein*, Rendsburg, 1987. See also L. Wiese, *Das höhere Schulwesen in Preußen. Historisch-statistische Darstellung*, 3 vols., Berlin, 1864–74.

developments, Storm had enrolled Hans in Kiel in 1866; later he was to have problems with the regulations in the case of his third son, Karl.

A Provinzialschulkollegium was set up, and sweeping powers invested in a Schulrat. The authority's brief was to supervise the whole system and ensure that the "harmonization of educational goals" was achieved. Even those like the future headmaster of Husum's grammar school, Heinrich Keck, who were converts to the Prussian cause, questioned the rigidity and monotonous uniformity of the syllabus. He criticized the introduction of rote learning and NCO-type drill ("das unteroffiziersmäßige Drillen"), the imparting of mere factual knowledge and the concentration on narrow examination targets in order to impress school inspectors. Schools and teachers had, he complained, suffered a loss of autonomy and individuality.[29] In other respects, however, Keck embodied the new ethos. Schools were there, he declared, to teach obedience and subordination; they had to be run in accordance with a military-like régime.[30] At the consecration of the reopened grammar school, which Storm attended, the new headmaster, Gideonsen, criticized Germans for excessive cosmopolitanism and impracticality in the past; now they had returned from the land of their dreams and possessed a German Fatherland. A statesman, Bismarck, had replaced a poet, Goethe. The school, he declared, had to teach its pupils the need to overcome an egoistic life of pleasure and enjoyment and instill a sense of the need to make sacrifices for the commonweal. It would emphasize German, national history. The victory at Düppel had decided the future of Germany in a Prussian, i.e. a national sense.[31] The Provost closed with a thanksgiving to God and the king. Storm could not have been greatly edified. When a teacher complained about Karl's disobedience, he allegedly retorted: "Gehorsam verlange ich nicht von meinen Kindern. Gehorsam ist eine Hundetugend."[32] I shall deal with his general reaction later (p. 188).

29. K.H. Keck, *Das Leben des General-Feldmarschalls Edwin von Manteuffel*, Bielefeld and Leipzig, 1890, pp. 137ff, 161ff.
30. Idem, *Ueber das Wesen der Bildung und den Anteil des Gymnasiums an demselben. Eine Schulrede*, Schleswig, 1867.
31. *Programm der königlichen Gelehrtenschule zu Husum*, Easter 1868, new series, no. 4, p. 13.
32. L. Bäte, *Aus Theodor Storms Lebensgarten. Ein Bild seiner Tochter Gertrud*, Rothenfelde, 1921, p. 40.

Registering private dissent was one thing; articulating it in public and in literary works was another. In 1852 Storm had been prepared to go into exile for his principles; after 1864 he knew that physically he could not stand another period of exile. He may have dreamed of fleeing with his family to some primeval forest; but he was well aware that, with so many mouths to feed, he could not afford to be dismissed like either the Husum Amtmann or the Amtsverwalter, Franz Rehder. Although contemptuous of opportunists and those who fawned on "Pasha Manteuffel," the Prussian ex-Governor of Schleswig, and bestowed honorary citizenship on him,[33] he could not afford to get caught up in incidents like that involving Rehder and the new Landrat, Ludwig von Reventlow, at the consecration of the reopened grammar school. An incensed Reventlow had struck Rehder with his stick. Impotent hatred and bitter silence were the order of the day: "Wie zur Dänenzeit kann ich nur stumm die Faust geballt den Schrei des Zorns in meiner Brust ersticken."[34]

The news in late 1866 that his salary as Landvogt was to be cut from 6000 to 4200 marks, i.e. a salary-cut of almost thirty percent, threw him into consternation since this would take him and his family back to their lifestyle in Heiligenstadt. Again they would have to eat rolls without butter and drink tea without sugar,[35] and he would continue to depend on his father. Apart from having to finance his sons' education, he had to pay back a loan taken out to buy a house in the Wasserreihe (the present Storm House) which he wanted to modernize and extend. Even before the rumored cut he was 1000 marks adrift on a salary of 6000 marks, and although his remonstrations brought an increase of 500 marks, he still had to rent out the ground floor and move with his family to the first floor. In terms of status and self-esteem it was a terrible blow. His fears about leading a proletarian, hand-to-mouth life returned.[36] Even though his salary as an Amtsrichter was adjusted to reflect his salary as Landvogt, Storm henceforth knew that he could only keep his head above water if he increased his literary earnings. His bitterness was heightened by the reorganization of the tax system. By introducing

33. Storm to Pietsch, 12 March 1867, *Blätter der Freundschaft*, p. 174.
34. Storm to H. and L. Brinkmann, 21 January 1868, *Storm-Brinkmann*, p. 153.
35. Storm to Hans, 27 November 1866.
36. Storm to Pietsch, *Blätter der Freundschaft*, 30 January 1867, pp. 172f.

income tax, a class tax, and a business tax while at the same time reducing the percentage derived from the tax on landed property, the Prussian government hit middle-class professionals like Storm and benefited noble landowners.

If he could not afford to antagonize his employers, he also did not dare risk alienating his readers. Prior to 1864 he had been able to count on editors and readers eager to see Schleswig-Holstein depicted as an oppressed German outpost longing to be liberated and welcomed into the national fold. After 1866, on the other hand, if any depiction of the Schleswig-Holstein struggle was to be palatable to the North German, National-Liberal middle classes, it had to praise the exploits of the Prussian forces against the Danes. Any suggestion that Prussia had betrayed Schleswig-Holstein and that the annexation was a rerun of Danish rule had to be avoided. Insistence on their right to self-determination was liable to be denounced as parochialism, a selfish refusal to recognize the sacrifices made by Prussian soldiers in the national cause. Outlets for critical material shrank. Bismarck's intimidation, manipulation and "buying" of the North German press had its intended effect.

Storm could not be as outspoken in his novellas as he was in his private letters to trusted confidants. Self-censorship became necessary. The original opening scene of the novella *Eine Malerarbeit* (1867) was highly critical of the system whereby young artisans were presumed to be suspect characters, forbidden to deviate from the route prescribed in their passes and required to report at successive police stations. The assembled company find this an affront to human dignity – all, that is, except a supercilious Assessor who mocks at such notions (and also shows no regard for the human dignity of the hero, the deformed painter Edde Brunken):

> "Das sind ja demokratische Träume . . . diese Leute müßen fühlen, daß sie controlirt werden . . ."
>
> "Demokratisch, Herr Assessor?" erwiderte der Maler." Ich habe noch nie drei beisammen gesehen, wovon auch nur zwei über dieß gemißhandelte Wort miteinander im klaren gewesen. Mich kümmert das nicht; aber mich empört die Kränkung der Menschenwürde, die in dieser angemaßten Bevormundung eines ganzen Standes liegt."
>
> ". . . halten Sie so viel auf Menschenwürde?"
>
> "Herr Assessor . . . ich kenne kein armseligeres Vergnügen, als sich für etwas Apartes zu halten . . ."[37]

The scene was toned down. One suspects that self-censorship increasingly took place so early that "dangerous" ideas were filtered out before ever finding their way onto paper.

To his dismay Storm found that there was no market for the products he had available. *Märchen* were only in demand as anodyne Christmas reading. Thus *Bulemanns Haus* was rejected by seven editors before it was accepted, and Rodenberg only printed *Der Spiegel des Cyprianus* in his *Bazar* after removing any hint of the heroine's apparent infertility and eventual pregnancy. The more Storm depended on literary fees to supplement his income, the more he was vulnerable to the pressures of publishers and editors and the more he had to heed the tolerance thresholds of his readers. Rodenberg, for example, rejected *Von jenseit des Meeres* because the heroine was illegitimate. Storm's creative periods were now fitful and unpredictable. After having completed *In St Jürgen* and *Eine Malerarbeit* in the first half of 1867, he dried up. Even though Rodenberg offered him a handsome fee if his name graced the first issue of his *Salon*, he could not oblige. His hopes turned to persuading a new publisher, Hermann Heiberg, in Schleswig, to bring out a collection of novellas in octavo format rather than in the miniature form in which they had previously appeared. In this format, they had, he hoped, a chance of breaking into the lending-library market. Feeling his career at an end, he then switched his hopes of being able to fund his sons' studies with a possible edition of his collected works. He approached Georg Westermann to be the "executor of his will,"[38] although fearing that the price Westermann could charge would be depressed by the ending of copyright on the German classics. He suggested to Westermann morally and legally suspect means of guaranteeing sales. Thus, instead of providing a gratis specimen, Westermann was to circulate a paper-covered part-volume which could break off, for example, in the middle of *Auf dem Staatshof*; on the cover it would carry a statement that anyone cutting the pages was committed to buying the entire collected works. He asked Westermann to check the legality of this proposal.[39] In August 1869 he had to

37. See K.-E. Laage, *Theodor Storm. Studien zu seinem Leben und Werk*, 2d ed., Berlin, 1988, p. 22.

38. Storm to G. Westermann, 28 June 1868, *Briefe* 1, p. 530.

39. Storm to Westermann, 22 July 1868. See M. Ebert, *"Storm und seiner Verleger Paetel und Westermann."* M.A. thesis, Kiel, 1989, p. 68.

borrow another 1000 marks without knowing how he would pay the interest. Fortunately his father agreed to pay the interest on his house loan. He described his situation in terms of Jeremias Gotthelf's story *Die schwarze Spinne*:

> ... die Nahrungssorge sitzt wie eine schwarze Spinne auf meinem Gehirn; wenn nicht eine Erleichterung eintritt, so weiß ich nicht, wie es werden soll und – wie ich's ertragen soll, ohne krank zu werden ... Die Ausgaben sind ungeheuer, und mein armer Kopf ist krank, ich kann außeramtlich nichts mehr erwerben.[40]

Even his brother Aemil had to provide a loan. By now the idea of editing an anthology of lyric poetry had moved to the fore as a potential source of income. However, having at last found a small Hamburg publisher, Mauke, Storm refused to include any poems by the influential critic Rudolf Gottschall, who had himself edited a rival anthology. Gottschall, the "oracle of the retail book sellers," took immediate revenge (see LL 4, 881f.). By August 1870 Storm was facing the prospect that he could not afford to pay for three sons to study: "Ich rufe mir dann meinen alten Satz zu: "Das Nächste thun! was für mich so viel heißt als ein Buch schreiben, und der alte Kopf will immer nicht mehr."[41]

5.4 Storm's Second Marriage

After Constanze's death in 1865 Storm could not cope either in emotional, sexual, or practical terms. He was very much a man of his time in that, despite criticism of this ethos in *Marthe und ihre Uhr*, his ideal solution would have been to entrust care of the household to an elder daughter. But Lisbeth was only a child. Nor did Constanze have unmarried sisters who could, in conventional fashion, have filled the gap. Rumor has it that he thought of marrying a younger woman, the musically talented Pauline Petersen with whom he worked in his choral society.[42] The depiction of the hero's affection for the young Eveline in *Eine Halligfahrt* may owe something to these feelings, and in the

---

40. Storm to Ernst, 10 December 1869.
41. Storm to Hans, 10 August 1870, *Stargard*, p. 27.
42. See A. Petersen, "Vor sechzig Jahren. Auch eine Theodor Storm Erinnerung," *Hamburger Nachrichten*, no. 240, 26 May 1925.

manuscript version more space is devoted to Eveline's own inner conflicts. Storm continued to be attracted to young women. Thus he was flattered by the attentions of the young writer Hermione von Preuschen and aroused by a photograph of her in a low-cut dress.[43] The depiction in *Waldwinkel* (1874) of an older man's affair with a teenager may also relate to fantasies about marrying a younger woman and being cuckolded.

In 1865 his sexual drive was still strong, and one of the many, conflicting desires behind his decision to marry his former lover, Doris Jensen, was the hope that they could rediscover their former sexual *rapport*. This could rejuvenate him and revive his poetic powers. His calculations went awry. His remarriage, barely a year after Constanze's death, met with disapproval from his sisters-in-law and plunged him into feelings of guilt. This was predictable given his cult of monogamous love and his obsession with surviving partners who betray their dead spouses. Once disillusionment set in, his cult of Constanze's memory assumed pathological proportions. He saw Doris as a stop-gap and re-placement mother, referred to her as *Stiefmütterchen* and for-bade the children to address her as mother. Overwhelmed by his moods and obsessions and by having to run a large household and cope with difficult, resentful teenagers, Doris became so depressed that Storm feared she could become permanently mentally ill. He himself sank into morbid depression and moods of panic and despair. His hypochondria intensified, as did his psychosomatic complaints. A sense of the transience of all things haunted him.

Sexual problems compounded the difficulties. In her late 30s, after years of spinsterhood, Doris was expected to become a passionate Isolde. Storm had to make a painful readjustment, which affected his view of sex and his own sexuality. This "mid-life crisis" fed into the novella *Eine Malerarbeit* (1867). In this version of the story of *Beauty and the Beast*, the Beast is a mis-shapen, dwarfish painter who vainly longs for beauty and love. Symbolically he has to remove himself from the foreground of the picture and take satisfaction in the loves of the younger generation. Venus is a goddess for the young. In this *conte moral* (LL 2, 9) the moral is simple: one must cut one's coat according

---

43. See Storm to H.v. Preuschen, 20 September 1877, *STSG*, vol. 22, 1973, p. 77.

to one's cloth. The fairy tale is replaced by Campe's tale of the pug which barked at the moon. The advice given to a husband who "seemed almost willfully intent on destroying his family life because he was displeased with his wife even though he had freely chosen her" is simple: "Man muß sein Leben aus dem Holze schnitzen, das man hat . . . und damit basta" (LL 2, 9). He must "plane her smooth"! The sister of Brunken's protégé is to do the same to her drunkard of a husband.

The most revealing comments Storm made about his second marriage are contained in letters written in the later 1870s to a correspondent in Brunswick, Alfred Niess, who himself had lost his first wife and married again very quickly. Storm questioned this haste, suspecting that "longing for a woman, a woman as such," had proved overpowering:

> Aber seien Sie geduldig, gerecht und von nimmer müder Güte. Hat die erste Frau uns getragen, die zweite müßen wir tragen, bis sie sich stark genug in unserem Hause fühlt. Und verlangen Sie von ihr nicht mehr Gefühl für ihre Stiefkinder, als das einer wohlwollenden Freundin, und verlangen Sie von den Kindern nicht, daß sie die Freundin Mutter nennen.[44]
>
> Gewiß, eine zweite Ehe, die Vaterschaft zu Kindern einer Lebenden und einer Todten bleibt immer ein Verhältniß, zu dessen glücklicher Beherrschung die stete und aufmerksame Anwendung unserer besten Kräfte nöthig ist. Auch mir ist es nicht leicht geworden, und ich habe manchmal das, was recht und noth war, nicht gethan; aber seit Jahren schon darf ich sagen, es ist gut, es ist für uns Alle ein Glück, wie es jetzt ist.[45]
>
> Aber Sie sind, gleich mir, ein Mensch, der nicht die Ruhe hat, die Göttin Gelegenheit bei ihrem goldblonden Schopf zu fassen; solche Leute wie wir greifen zu früh zu, und wenn sie dann wirklich vorüber kommt, so haben wir schon die Hände voll; aber was wir ergriffen, es ist uns selten das Rechte. Nun – man muß zufrieden sein.[46]

The birth of a daughter Friedericke in 1868 did not solve the problems. Storm referred to the baby as "unsere kleine, süße Mißgeburt,"[47] and when Doris had a miscarriage in 1871, he expressed his relief that, given their financial straits, the boy had

---

44. Storm to A. Nieß, 2 January 1879, Brunswick City Archive.
45. 4 December 1879.
46. 8 January 1881.
47. Storm to Hans, 23 August 1869, *Stargard*, p. 17.

not survived.[48] The novella *Viola tricolor* (1874) may paint a rosy picture of how the problems of a second marriage are resolved; but one should guard against confusing it with reality.

5.5 Masters, Artisans, and Servants

In St. Jürgen (1868) revolves around issues familiar from the works of the early 1860s. It questions the values inspiring its model, *Charakterbilder aus dem vorigen Jahrhundert. (Nach den Erzählungen einer 70jährigen Frau mitgetheilt): 3.: Das Heimweh,* which had appeared in the 1849 number of Biernatzki's *Volksbuch.* Here a saddler journeyman, having got engaged to a girl in Schleswig, obeys his father and goes on his *Wanderung.* In Dresden his mortally ill master, whose business has suffered during his illness, obtains from him a promise to look after his wife and children. Once the saddler has partially restored the family's fortune, his widow implores him not to abandon the family, and he eventually marries her. More than fifty years elapse before he can satisfy his longing to see his Gretchen again. He returns home, only to find that she died many years ago. But his mood is not one of despair and emptiness: "Jetzt ist Dresden meine irdische Heimath. Das andere Heimweh ist gestillt. Aber wenn ich zu Haus bin, dann werde ich bald sterben, – dann wird der himmlische Vater aus Gnaden mich armen müden Pilger und Fremdling zu sich nehmen in sein Vaterhaus und mich da auch *Die* finden lassen, die ich hier so treu liebte und bis an mein Ende lieben werde" (LL 1, 1210). The moral is clear: true love and true homesickness must be directed to the hereafter since only a heavenly father in his grace can satisfy all the needs of poor mortal pilgrims. For Storm the challenge was to restructure the text so as to bring out his ideal of human love and substantiate his thesis that belief in an after-life is an illusion. The text suggests that those who sacrifice human love whether for reasons of ambition or for "noble," "moral" motives like sympathy, concern or filial love nevertheless forfeit their true salvation.

The text employs a fictional narrator. Like the framework narrator in *Aquis submersus* and the schoolmaster in *Der Schimmelreiter,* he is somewhere along the road leading from orthodox

48. Storm to Ernst, 19 January 1871.

Protestantism to a more liberal variety. But his position still falls far short of Storm's own humanitarianism, and the text generates a distance between his value-judgements and those which the reader is invited to make. A world is depicted that is steeped in values which originated in the Reformation and which reflect the norms of a hierarchical, pre-industrial society. The almshouse – modelled on the St. Jürgen Foundation in Husum – bears continuing witness, with its cells, its chapel and its graveyard, to the world view of the Reformers who preached under its huge lime trees (LL 1, 694). Echoing the pattern of significances in *Veronica* and anticipating that of *Aquis submersus*, the framework juxtaposes the dark, stony world of the chapel with the natural world of flowers and sunlight outside. As a child, the fictional narrator, may still attend divine service, but the sermon makes little impact on him. He is fascinated instead by the portrait of an old pastor whose melancholy black eyes look out from the "dumpfen Welt des Wunder- und Hexenglaubens in die neue Zeit" (LL 1, 698). It remains to be seen whether he will be critical of more subtle manifestations of Christian values.

A key structural device is the contrast between the spontaneous, natural behavior of swallows and the alienated behavior of human beings. The former build their nests and raise their families; they may migrate but, with unerring instinct, they again return. If they are petrified by fear of a bird of prey, they soon recover once they are again given the freedom of the sky (LL 1, 696). Human beings, in contrast, sacrifice their instincts and potential natural happiness for other concerns; their vitality is destroyed by worries and obsessions; they seek resurrection in a Christian after-life. Agnes Hansen, the heroine, a master's daughter, may show great understanding of swallows and defend their nests, but she herself never makes her own love nest. Instead she spends her adult life caring for her father, and then working as a servant for the narrator's grandmother. Her maternal instincts have to be catered for by looking after other people's children and playing with them. Yet, far from ever realizing that she has forfeited her unique opportunity to achieve full mortal happiness, she believes to the end in Christian hopes of another life. She also firmly believes that she was right to endorse her lover Harre's decision to leave rather than try to persuade him to stay. She could at last win her father's affection by tending him in his distress. Altruism and self-denial, it is suggested, are not without an element of egoism.

Agnes never doubts the sense of devoting her life both to trying to restore her father's reputation and to building up again the inheritance of his ward Harre, which her father squandered in his hunt for buried treasure. In her view, only then could she be a fit wife for the master craftsman she hopes Harre will be on his return. She has no wish, the text suggests, to marry a mere artisan. Indeed, so trapped is she in notions of rank and status that she looks back with affection to a past world when society was divided into notables, masters, and people in "honorable" professions and into mere servants and those in "dishonorable" professions (LL 1, 699). Ironically, it is this world with its stress on status and honor that is the cause of her misfortunes. Her God-fearing father is prepared to indulge in what he regards as sinful, superstitious practices rather than go bankrupt and forfeit his reputation in the difficult times of the Continental Blockade.

The text conveys the tribulations of masters and artisans, not only during that period but also in later decades. In fact, the liberalization of trades and abolition of guild regulations pushed through by the North German Reichstag only compounded the problems of many artisans and masters and fueled their hostility to mechanization and large-scale capitalism. Whereas both liberals and socialists had little sympathy for such artisans, Storm never lost his concern for their plight. The text compellingly conveys these masters' nightmares as they struggle to stave off bankruptcy. Harre himself is typical of the many journeymen desperately striving to achieve master status. Perhaps more than any other Storm work until *Carsten Curator* (1878) or *Schweigen* (1883), *In St. Jürgen* abounds in instances of angst and terror. Such moods contrast with the Storm leitmotif of the earthly paradise: "Mir war plötzlich, als sähe ich über allen Dunst der Sorge hinweg in eine sonnige Zukunft; als brauchte ich nur den Fuß hineinzusetzen. . . . Ich dachte auch an Harre und zuletzt, glaub ich, nur an ihn" (LL 1, 702). However, Harre's "annunciation" in the garden is no gospel of love. Social ambitions override.

Harre's tragedy is that of a talented young man, who, having been orphaned, cannot pursue his studies at the grammar school. Instead, he adopts his father's trade as a joiner. Having, on his

travels, discovered his talent for fine work, he would have settled
elsewhere in order to develop these skills but for his love for
Agnes. His hope is that, with his parents' legacy, he can still set
up as a master in the town. The tensions between social ambitions
and the demands of love are here presented in an artisan context.
Once Agnes's father squanders his legacy, Harre's calculations
collapse. It is suggested that, whatever the "moral" reasons he
adduces for leaving the town without seeing Agnes' father again,
it is his ambition which blinds him to his human duty to stay
and help Agnes and her bankrupt father in their distress. His
ambition may reflect a valid aspiration to achieve a fuller life,
but he fails to recognize that love must be at the heart of this life.
In contrast, his readiness to stay and help his master's wife and
family is related to the fact that he can thus both indulge his love
of children, books and learning and also acquire new skills. His
altruism is not beyond question. Further, there is a suspicion that
he would never have married the widow had marriage not been
the means of finally becoming a master. His true feelings toward
her are made clear the moment this ambition has been achieved:
they are those of hatred (LL 1, 728). In Harre's self-righteous
world it needs God to lead him into temptation and help him
overcome it before he can settle down and live a life which, by
normal standards, is contented and happy (LL 1, 729f.). Harre's
account of his life is an *oratio pro domo*, an attempt to get the
narrator to endorse his decisions. But the pointers in the text
enable the reader to remain critical. Harre's hope is that after
fifty years he can still return, find Agnes, and obtain her forgiveness. This hope in such a convenient providence and such convenient grace and forgiveness proves misplaced. The transience
of all human life, "der drohende Ernst des Todes" (LL 1, 734)
and the recognition that he has betrayed both Agnes' and his
own sole chance of human happiness – these are the realities.

5.6   The Franco-Prussian War

War between France and Prussia broke out in July 1870. Bismarck succeeded in presenting the French to the world as the
vainglorious aggressors. Storm rejected a suggestion that Austria
should ally with France against Prussia:

Niemand kann das spezifisch preußische Wesen mehr hassen als ich,
denn ich halte es für den Feind aller Humanität; aber es gibt Dinge,
die selbstverständlich sind, wie das Atmen zum Leben; dazu gehört
bei dem Angriff einer fremden Nation das Zusammenstehn aller
Stämme der eignen. Ich meine, so weit sollten wir jetzt doch sein.
Was liegt an Österreich, was an Preußen? *Deutschen* Herd und deutsche
Gesittung haben wir jetzt zu verteidigen gegen die Romanen.[49]

However, by early August he was already suspecting diplomatic
ambiguity and a possible lust for conquest on the German side,
too. He referred to the injustice done by Bismarck to the Danes
in North Schleswig by witholding the right granted them in the
Treaty of Prague (1866) to decide in a plebiscite whether to remain
in Prussia or join Denmark. In the face of this the talk of holy
national wars rang hollow: "Hinten den Nachbar heimlich im
Genick gefaßt und vorne schöne Reden gehalten. Die Nation selbst
allerdings steht für ihren Herd. Trotzdem habe ich keine Begeisterung, sondern nur das Bewußtsein von der Notwendigkeit der
Abwehr."[50] The German victories made him fear that the "solid"
German nation might itself acquire a taste for *gloire*.[51] He declined to contribute a patriotic prologue for a performance of
Schiller's *Wallenstein*: ". . . ich finde vor lauter Ehrfurcht und staun-
ender Bewunderung dessen, was Alldeutschlands schwertgewal-
tige Söhne auf Frankreichs Boden jetzt vollbringen, kein
Wörtchen."[52] A report in the *Volkszeitung* of thirty fatalities caused
by army drill elicited the response:

Das dämpft denn meine Begeisterung für diese Erfolge nach außen.
die der größte Teil nur erringen hilft, weil er kommandiert wird.
Solange wir uns dergleichen von unsern eignen Gewalthabern gefallen lassen, wogegen die Behandlung der Neger in den Zuckerplan-
tagen noch eine milde ist, so lange sind wir doch nur noch ein Volk
von Knechten.

Hat erst der Sieg über fremde Gewalt
Die Gewalt im Innern besiegt,
Dann will ich rufen: Das Land ist frei!
Bis dahin spar ich den Jubelschrei.[53]

49. Storm to Ada Christen, n.d., *Briefe* 2, p. 17.
50. Storm to Ernst, 3 August 1870, ibid., pp. 18f.
51. Storm to G. Westermann, 2 September 1870, *Briefe* 2, p. 24.
52. Storm an Heinemann, 30 September 1870, ibid., pp. 24f.
53. Storm to Ernst, 8 August 1870, ibid., p. 22.

He had, he wrote, more enthusiasm for the struggle within the
state than for the struggle for its borders.[54] Freytag was soon to
write that never had a struggle been fought for a greater ideal,
that never perhaps had Nemesis struck down the guilty so vio-
lently, and never perhaps had any army had such warmth, such
inspiration, and such a deep poetic sense of the fact that the
dreadful work of the battlefields served a higher ethical purpose.[55] Storm in contrast saw war in bleak Malthusian terms:

> Was mich hauptsächlich beherrscht – und das verschlingt alles an-
> dere – das ist der Ekel, einer Gesellschaft von Kreaturen anzugehören,
> die außer den übrigen ihnen von der Natur auferlegten Funktionen
> des Futtersuchens, der Fortpflanzung etc. auch die mit elementaris-
> cher Stumpfheit befolgt, sich von Zeit zu Zeit gegenseitig zu ver-
> tilgen. Das Bestehen der Welt beruht darauf, daß alles sich gegenseitig
> frißt, oder vielmehr das Mächtigere immer das Schwächere; den
> Menschen als den Mächtigsten vermag keines zu fressen; also frißt er
> sich selbst, und zwar im Urzustande buchstäblich. Dies ist die
> eigentliche *Ursache* der Kriege, die andern sog. Ursachen sind nur die
> Veranlassung. Keine Zivilisation wird, ja *darf* das je überwinden. Aber
> niederdrückend ist der Gedanke; es ist so einer, bei dem man verrückt
> werden könnte . . . Ist der Gedanke richtig, so ist schon der Umstand,
> daß man ihn fassen konnte, doch wieder ein Beweis, daß wenigstens
> der einzelne sich über diesen Zustand erheben kann.[56]

He would echo these sentiments in the first version of the novella
Eine Halligfahrt (see p. 186).

---

54. Storm to K.T. Pyl, 14 November 1870, ibid., p. 29.
55. See G.A. Craig, *Germany 1866–1945*, Oxford, 1978, pp. 34f.
56. Storm to Ernst, 3 August 1870, *Briefe* 2, p. 19.

6

A Democrat in the Second Empire

6.1 The Bismarckian Settlement

In older studies of German history, literary as well as political, 1871 became *the* crucial caesura.[1] At the time the sense of achievement felt by National-Liberals was matched by confidence that they would be able to influence the exercise of political power and shape institutions in ways congenial to themselves. Whatever their reservations, they could live with the Imperial constitution, which represented Bismarck's attempt "to create the institutions of a national state that would be able to compete effectively with the most powerful of its neighbors, without, however, sacrificing, or even limiting, the aristocratic-monarchial order of the pre-national period."[2] Contemptuous of notions of popular sovereignty, he held the Reich to be the creation of Germany's dynastic houses; this gift from above could be withdrawn at any time. Indeed in later years he toyed with the idea of a *coup d'état*.

Unlike its predecessor of 1848, the constitution contained neither a bill of rights nor a declaration of fundamental liberties. The democratic elements in the system, e.g. universal male suffrage and the secret ballot, were designed to undermine the influence of the Liberal middle classes and allow the government to profit from the supposed Conservativism of the lower classes, especially the rural population. As the towns and cities grew, so too did the bias in favor of rural constituencies. Key areas of government were still the prerogative of the hereditary emperor, who was also automatically king of Prussia. He controlled foreign policy; he declared war and concluded peace; he was commander-in-chief of all German forces in time of war; and he alone appointed and dismissed the chancellor and all other officials of

1. A perfect instance is H.v. Sybel, *Die Begründung des Deutschen Reiches durch Wilhelm I*, 7 vols., Munich, 1889–94. See also Böhme, *Die Reichsgründung*.
2. G.A. Craig, *Germany 1866–1945*, Oxford, 1978, p. 39.

the federal government. Thus he controlled the administrative, military and diplomatic institutions and personnel of both Prussia and the Empire. In firm control of the executive and judiciary, the monarch also enjoyed extensive legislative rights. The emperor was empowered to summon, prorogue and close the Reichstag, whereas the latter had few powers of initiative. If government draft legislation found no majority in the Reichstag, elections did not automatically have to be called. Indeed, conscious of their lack of popular support and the effectiveness of the government's propaganda machine, the Liberals were often reluctant to provoke a dissolution. Governments were not formed from the strongest party or coalition of parties, and ministers could not be members of the Reichstag. The chancellor, although the "responsible minister," was not responsible to the Reichstag, which had no legal control over him. He depended solely on the monarch's favor. The Reichstag further weakened its powers when in 1874 it passed a law restricting to seven-year intervals its right to discuss the army budget, i.e. the main item of expenditure. Although the individual states enjoyed considerable autonomy in fields like education and although sovereignty technically lay with the Bundesrat, in practice the will of the Prussian government prevailed.

From a democratic point of view this depressing picture was further heightened by the failure – despite some successes on paper – to democratize and extend the scope of local government at town/city, Kreis, and provincial level. In rural areas the aristocracy's dominance persisted. Its social and economic power, boosted by boom years in agriculture and by the kudos won in war, would soon be maintained at the expense of urban consumers and taxpayers by subsidies and duties on cereal imports.[3]

Not that the picture was totally bleak. During the National-Liberal ascendancy, other liberal gains apart from the legal and economic ones were made. The educational reforms of Adalbert Falk, the Kultusminister, replaced the Stiehl Regulations. They were linked to the so-called *Kulturkampf*, the attempt, albeit by often illiberal means, to assert state control over the Catholic church both in civil matters like education or marriage and also in matters of internal organization. The principle of a state

3. See H.-U. Wehler, *Das deutsche Kaiserreich 1871–1918*, Göttingen, 1973, pp. 41ff. (Transl. as *The German Empire, 1871–1918*, Leamington Spa, 1985.)

education free from clerical control was established, and in 1875/ 76 civil marriage was introduced. Finally, the Press Law of 1874, while still stipulating that copies of publications had to be deposited with the police authorities, was liberal in spirit and continued to underly legislation after 1918.

Yet overall, judged in terms of his democratic hopes in 1848 and in the 1860s, the Bismarckian settlement was a cruel disappointment to Storm. Neither a republican nor a monarchical state based on popular sovereignty had been set up; real power in this semi-absolutist, pseudo-parliamentary system still lay with the old order; the abolition of aristocratic privilege anticipated in 1847/48 and 1863/64 was still outstanding; the elective principle had made no inroads in the state administration, the higher echelons of which were still the preserve of the aristocracy; the prestige of an undemocratic, largely autonomous army had been heightened; in local government, especially in annexed provinces like Schleswig-Holstein, the power of the appointed state-bureaucracy headed by aristocrats had grown.

The Protestant church had been neither democratized nor disestablished – although it, like the Catholic church, was losing its hold over the urban proletariat. Indeed it remained a major conservative force in the state. Some of its more adventurous members soon began to venture into state or monarchical socialism. Anti-semitism made inroads from the later 1870s onward. In the case of the Catholic church, the government's attacks on it only confirmed it in its hostility to liberalism and modern thinking.

In the economic field the hopes attached to laissez-faire capitalism dimmed. The often purely speculative floating of new companies in the early 1870s, followed as it was by the crash of 1873, shook confidence in the ability of the uncontrolled market to generate sustained growth. Storm's hope that entrepreneurs would cooperate with democratically minded members of the *Bildungsbürgertum* had evaporated. In the later 1870s heavy industry and the agrarian interest moved even closer together as both demanded protective tariffs. Few believed that Germany's socio-economic problems could be solved without some sort of state intervention.

In the ideological field, developments after 1870 were no more encouraging for a democrat. The opinion-makers in higher education and the media continued their work of fashioning for the new state traditions, ideals, and norms that would legitimate it. In- and out-groups were defined, scapegoats created. "Negative integration" became a prime means of fashioning a sense of national identity. Hanoverians, Catholics, Poles, inhabitants of Alsace-Lorraine, defenders of particularist identities like Schleswig-Holsteiners, Democrats, and Socialists were all liable to be denounced as *Reichsfeinde*.[4]

In this task of forging a new ideological consensus, annexation of Germany's past became almost as crucial as territorial conquests. The laws of history had to be shown to operate to the greater glory of Bismarck and Prussia. It was no coincidence that Gustav Freytag had turned to the German and Germanic past in *Bilder aus deutscher Vergangenheit* (1859–67). He now followed it with *Die Ahnen* (1872–80). The new nation was fitted out with an ethnic-national identity traceable through the centuries. Historical dramas, novels and stories served to disseminate in popularized form the "truths" of historians, philosophers, and publicists. They reinforced the official view of historical development and causation, of the central role of ethnic and national struggles and of the respective importance of individual, state, and community. They presented the part played in Germany's past and path to greatness of various dynasties, emperors, and kings, while, more generally, providing social and political models for relations between kings, nobles, "burghers" and "peasants." Past socio-political scenarios like the struggles between medieval emperors and popes were ideal vehicles for treating contemporary issues such as the *Kulturkampf*.

Before 1864 Storm had been confident that his views were shared by broad sections of the middle classes. After 1870 the rump of the Progressive Party shrank even further; factory-workers and artisans joined the socialist parties in increasing numbers, while Storm's "natural allies" in the *Bildungsbürgertum* continued to drift to the National Liberals or further to the right. His vision of a democratic body politic had depended on unity among all the non-aristocratic classes and groups. Now the divide between the middle classes and the proletariat grew.

The mere presence of socialist parties played a crucial role in redrawing literary boundaries since it lowered the tolerance

4. Ibid., pp. 105ff.

thresholds of middle-class readers faced by criticism of the Bismarckian settlement and of middle-class mores and culture. Criticism that formerly could have been interpreted as strengthening the identity of the middle classes, was now seen as undermining their position. The greater the threat from the left was felt to be, the more the middle classes demanded of their literary purveyors endorsement of their norms and lifestyle. Even when working from within a bourgeois, capitalist framework of values, a writer who drew attention to social problems and tensions could only do so if the solutions envisaged were idealistic, ethical, or Christian, charitable ones. Any concrete measures proposed had to be ones instituted from above. Even then one could easily move beyond the pale. Topics affecting the organization of social and family life, sex and morality were equally suspect because they, too, could play into socialist hands.

6.2   Retreat From Political Commitment?

His hopes dashed by 1870/71, Storm could have fallen silent. One can imagine him resignedly working out the remaining years to his retirement and immersing himself in his family, his choral society, and a sheltered, private world of literature, poetry, and music. That did not happen.

But awkward questions have to be answered. Having reconnoitered the lie of the new imperial lands, did he not perhaps adapt his fictions to the prejudices of publishers, editors, and readers? Accepting that he who pays the piper calls the tune, was it not prudent to humor the customer? Was he not perhaps so disillusioned with events that he concentrated on personal and family issues instead of addressing wider socio-political ones? Did not the mere fact of living in Husum and – after his retirement – in Hademarschen-Hanerau prevent him fully registering the problems facing Germany in the 1870s and 1880s?

At first sight it would seem reasonable to expect that anyone seriously concerned about such problems would have left as many comments in his letters on developments in the 1870s and 1880s as he had done on trends in the 1860s. Yet references to political issues are few and far-between. On the other hand, one must not forget that he had lost the one great recipient of his outbursts in the 1860s, Ludwig Pietsch, after Pietsch had become a member of the new establishment. His contact with Brinkmann had virtually ceased, while other correspondents like Paul Heyse or Erich Schmidt were literary rather than political animals whose importance for Storm lay in the literary stimulus and advice they afforded. Unfortunately we have little information on the topics discussed in his Husum circle, especially with the Landrat, Ludwig von Reventlow, or with relatives and friends in Hademarschen-Hanerau. Reventlow was an anti-semite, but it is only by chance that we know of the anti-semitism in Hademarschen-Hanerau after 1880. Yet that mood affected Storm. For example, he referred to Otto Brahm as "das kluge Jüdchen" and as "ein gescheites Jüdchen." Having once again praised Heine, he added: ". . . ich kann nichts dafür, daß er ein Jude war." Jews and Jewishness become an issue in the correspondence with Erich Schmidt.[5] We know that Reventlow continued to see in Storm a "Fortschrittler" and that Tönnies, who discussed socialism with him, classed him as "an ethical democrat."[6] The gap separating him from the Socialists remained. The attempts on the emperor's life in 1878 had, Storm wrote to Keller, the effect of turning natural sympathy into revulsion for such riff-raff (*Dutzendgesindel*).[7] But visitors' accounts of his religious views are not matched by statements on social and political matters. Storm was not going to bare his chest to any but trusted confidants, especially if this could harm him in the eyes of the Imperial public.

On the face of it one might surely have also expected an author interested in contemporary issues to have tackled topics like the fever of speculation which gripped the middle classes in the so-called *Gründerjahre* before 1873, the *Kulturkampf*, the rise of socialism, and "the social problem." Would he not have sought to capture the great technological and scientific revolution taking place as Germany entered the age of the electrical and chemical industries? Would he not have broached issues like emigration, the great immigration into the cities or the disintegration of traditional lifestyles and customs? And, in terms of his own previous concerns, would not the growing militarization and feudalization of society and the emergence of a new breed of

5. G. Haase to Storm, 13 December 1880, SHLB; Storm to Schmidt, 13 December 1883, 22 December 1884, 24 August 1884, *Storm-Schmidt* 2, pp. 85, 105, 98.
6. Storm to Hans Speckter, 12 September 1882, Krakau; for Tönnies, see Chap. 5, note 18.
7. Storm to Keller, 29 August 1878, *Briefe* 2, p. 164.

civil servant have presented themselves as ideal subjects?

It is, of course, crude to think that what constitutes the social writer is a wish to be some sort of political commentator chasing the topical matters of the day. But the issues mentioned above profoundly affected the lives of people living during these decades; many were inimical to democratic, humanitarian standards. Was Storm so conscious of his position as a Prussian judge and as a commercial writer that he simply avoided sensitive issues? Or are at least some of these issues perhaps present in his later work, even if not in the "social realist" guise familiar from British and French nineteenth-century fiction?

It has to be conceded, as we shall see, that after 1870 Storm was preoccupied with family problems; but the reasons for his apparent neglect or avoidance of contemporary socio-political issues lie deeper. The loss of a forward-looking perspective did profoundly affect Storm's writing. The historical, cultural process in which he had believed had ground to a sharp halt. During the pre-1865 period many liberals and democrats had not concerned themselves with the practical details of politics. Excluded from decision-making, they had been sustained by the conviction that the unfolding *Idee* was the motor of progress and that nothing could withstand it. It was also assumed that the middle classes were the agents of this process, more by dint of their culture, ethics, and work than because of any political expertise or popular power-base. Having seen so many of his allies melt away, Storm had to recognize that, at least in the foreseeable future, the *Idee* was not going to shape political developments. He was left with no march route, no plan of operations. The more he felt himself part of a dwindling band of believers, the more indeterminate the future became. On the other hand, he was not prepared – at least with few exceptions – to indulge in self-indulgent make-believe.

A further factor which has to be given full weight in assessing his later work is the effect of his classical-idealist aesthetic (see also pp. 228ff.). Indeed in terms of his understanding of the nature and function of art, the absence of overt political and ideological subject matter should come as no surprise. In contrast to the social and political criticism of the Storm and Stress, Weimar classicism had retreated from direct, "realist" engagement in contemporary affairs as the means of purveying progressive ideas and effecting change. It sought to create a sphere outside church and castle where one could muster one's intellectual and emotional forces and then gradually invade ever wider areas of sensibility and thought until eventually art's quiet revolution was complete. Once ideas and feelings had been molded, actions would follow. The rationale of art was built around this idealist view of its operation and effect, not on an abdication of political interest and responsibility. Politics might still be the preserve of kings, princes, and their advisers; but art eluded their control. It constituted a superior, "classless" realm of freedom open to those ready to renounce caste-exclusive, feudal, orthodox categories. Even though it was politic to claim that art and politics were distinct spheres, this insistence on separateness in no way denoted lack of interest in the future shape of society and state. Indeed, because of the pre-established harmonies between physical, natural, moral, and human spheres, such compartmentalization was impossible.

Storm's position reflected this tradition. Bismarck might dominate the political world; but this did not mean that he also controlled the sphere of art. Yet if one were to challenge his sway, one had to utilize all art's specific resources. Had Storm moved nearer to political journalism or *Tendenz*, he would have regarded that as playing into the hands of his opponents. By robbing art of its unique powers and trespassing into the concepts and language of politics or other social sciences, he would have capitulated to the politicians. Enlightenment and humanitarianism would have lost their best ally at a time when lesser allies like philosophy and history were deserting the cause.

Because of the obvious dissimilarities, it is tempting to assume that German Poetic-Realist literature was intrinsically different from its "realist" counterparts in France or Great Britain with their overt concern to capture social reality and socio-economic trends and convey a sense of history in the making.[8] One should not, however, fail to recognize common denominators. Late Fontane may have evolved a type of social novel that, despite its affinities with the Poetic-Realist tradition, is closer to the western tradition. But social issues can be presented in more than one form. Indeed it would have been strange had very different aesthetic and ideological traditions and divergent social, politi-

8. The most influential formulation of this claim was by E. Auerbach in his *Mimesis. Dargestellte Wirklichkeit in der abendländischen Literatur*, Berne, 1946.

cal, and economic constellations produced works identical in form and content.

The German cult of art and *Dichtung* was, however, a mixed blessing. It provided Storm with a refuge at a time when other certainties were crumbling all around him. But it also brought with it disadvantages. In fact it is remarkable that he extracted so much by way of social analysis from an aesthetic which in its Poetic-Realist variant emphasized concreteness and pictorial "objectivity" – in the sense of *Gegenständlichkeit* – at the expense of analytic techniques. Certain features made it unsuited to rendering the complexities of modern social existence: its tendency to assess problems in absolute, ethical terms and *ideal* categories rather than in socio-economic, structural ones; its proneness, even when stressing period- and class-specific factors, to emphasize timeless, universal human qualities; its high level of abstraction from the world of politics, economic activity and institutional organization; its emphasis on individuals; its reliance on configurations from older societies and earlier literary presentations; its corresponding lack of resources for sketching the role in modern society of bureaucracies, corporate institutions, trade unions, pressure groups and political parties or impersonal, abstract trends, and ideological shifts; and finally the limits imposed by its linguistic conventions and its avoidance of all specialist and scientific language.

6.3   Prodigal Sons?

After Constanze's death Storm projected his emotional needs on to his sons. His hope was that the principles that he and Constanze had tried to apply in bringing up the children would now bear fruit. One of the great tragedies of his life was that for a long time it looked as if he was estranged from all three sons and as if all three were bent on self-destruction. Their behavior imperilled the prospects of his wife and daughters.

In 1866, even though Hans had been unable to complete his grammar school education and was a teenager with severe behavioral problems, Storm, in consultation with the Husum headmaster and his brother Aemil, decided to send him to Kiel University to study medicine before the new regulations requiring a school-leaving certificate came into force. His concern was Hans's asthma and possible tuberculosis. Hans was given a generous allowance so that he could enjoy the cultural and polite social life that Storm himself had been denied as a student. Letters of recommendation smoothed his way into the salons of academics and professional people, where he was to acquire the *Bildung* so central to Storm's definition of *Humanität* and which as a medical student he would not directly encounter in his studies. He, like his brothers later, was sent money so that he could attend operas and dramas that Storm considered part of the cultural canon.

Storm failed to see that such social contacts could not satisfy all his son's needs, especially his emotional and sexual ones. He was not prudish in his dealings with his children or in his choice of literature for them.[9] In fact, he railed against prudery in schooleditions,[10] and was frank about the dangers of contracting syphilis through casual sex like their uncles, Otto Storm and Ernst Esmarch.[11] But apart from stimulating a dread of possible fearful consequences and trusting in their moral fiber and attachment to nobler notions of love, he had little to offer by way of practical solutions. His sons were expected to implement the same repression and deferral of basic human needs that he had criticized in his novellas as alienating manifestations of an alienated society.

His refusal to be a distant, authoritarian father and his hope that family members could provide each other with mutual support had questionable consequences. His need for a confidant imposed great strains on Hans, the child with whom he shared the most memories of Constanze. He burdened him with all his poignant nostalgia, his sense of transience, his fears of creative

---

9. See G. Eckermann, "Zu Gast bei Theodor Storm," *Rheinische Landeszeitung*, 25 February 1944.
10. See Ernst's comments in a letter of his father to Georg Scherer, 12 February 1873. Quoted in Jackson, "Storms Stellung," pp. 76f.
11. See Storm to Karl, 15 April 1877. He wrote to Ernst (3 April 1872): "Laß Dich, mein alter lieber Junge, nur nicht zur Liederlichkeit verführen; das würde dich bei deinen körperlichen Verhältnissen zerstören; zumal auch jetzt nach dem großen Kriege jene Orte mehr als je die Brutnester der furchtbaren Krankheit sind, die ungesehen kommt, und in vielen Fällen das ganze Leben des Menschen in jahrelanger stiller Arbeit untergräbt." To Karl he wrote (16 March 1874): "Hüte dich vor dergleichen, mein Junge! Onkel O. in Hlgstdt hat es auch gehabt; jetzt wird sein ältester Junge von Ausschlag befallen; und ich fürchte sehr einen innern Zusammenhang. Es ist bei dieser Krankheit für das ganze künftige Leben eine Furcht; die Jugendblüthe ist mit ihr zerstört. Onkel Aemil sagte damals: 'Wär ich O., ich würde mir eine Kugel vor den Kopf schießen!' Und durch die Kriege ist jetzt die Krankheit so furchtbar verbreitet."

sterility, and his professional and financial worries. Hans – and after him Ernst and Karl – was given accounts of his illnesses and his fears of imminent death. He made his continued survival dependent on his sons being industrious and frugal, completing their studies, and not causing him the least worry or excitement. Few young people would have been able to bear this burden and respond in the manner Storm expected.

Already as a sixth-former Ernst had kicked over the traces. As a student he joined a duelling fraternity and spent time in the student prison. His riotous behavior impelled Storm to indulge in somber warnings about syphilis. A chronic hypochondriac like his father, Ernst would subsequently be beset by fears that his excesses had impaired his spinal fluid and that he could be overtaken by paralysis or insanity. His heavy drinking and amorous adventures continued throughout the 1870s, and at the time of his marriage he still had large debts. Although he ultimately settled down, Storm's disillusionment in the late 1860s and 1870s was all the more bitter because he regarded him as his *alter ego*.

Storm had encouraged Hans to think of himself as the son of a man of means. Once his circumstances worsened, he attempted to rein him in. Although Hans moved restlessly from university to university, Storm was slow to grasp how serious his situation was becoming. On the other hand, there was no mistaking his own financial plight. By 1870, with his literary career seemingly over and Karl almost ready to start studying, he despaired of being able to finance his sons' studies. His behavior toward his sons changed. The tone he adopted destroyed his hopes of frank communication and trust – and thus compounded his troubles. His notions of *Bildung* contributed to the disaster. Thus he was often angry, rude, and reproachful if he judged letters short or superficial, if they were written in student jargon, or dwelt on things which he regarded as unimportant. Pedantically he drew his sons' attention to orthography. The more irregular and unsatisfactory, in Storm's eyes, Hans' letters became, the more he commanded and upbraided – and the more he drove his son into silence. The same pattern was repeated with Ernst and Karl. As his estrangement from his sons deepened, so too did Storm's frustration and despair; but by the time he regretted outbursts of rage and bitter denunciations, the damage had been done. Although he oscillated between authoritarian behavior and pleading assurances of support, his sons' disregard for regularity and orderly communications and his own fear that money was being squandered invariably proved so frustrating that he reverted to threats and lectures and denounced them as good-for-nothings.

By 1871 he had to accept that he was estranged from his eldest son: "Ich habe nun zwei Briefe an dich geschrieben; aber das Tiefste und Eigentliche habe ich noch nicht ausgesprochen. Die Nahrungssorge ist nur ein ordinäres Leid; die Entfremdung von meinem Kinde ist es, die mich ganz zu Boden drückt."[12] His ideal of a non-authoritarian upbringing and his emphasis on communication and mutual support had been expected to solve the problem of individual loneliness. Yet now a sense of utter isolation overcame him. His sons had become expensive strangers. In March 1872 he had not seen either Hans or Ernst for eighteen months. When Hans did at last come home, there was no mistaking his drinking problem. He drank late into the night in the Ratskeller with Adolf Möller, a teacher and prominent member of Storm's choral society, who was himself an alcoholic. Not only was he in danger of forfeiting his own reputation; the reputation of the family and the marriage prospects of his sisters were at stake, too.

If worries about his two eldest sons were not enough, Karl also soon gave rise for concern.[13] Thinking that he had musical talent, Storm sent him as an immature boy to the Conservatory in Leipzig. Having found pornographic material in his bedroom after his departure, he feared that this self-styled Carolus Tempestas (= Karl Storm) with his passionate interest in the opposite sex would be at risk. He repeated his warnings about syphilis. Determined not to repeat the mistakes made with his elder sons, he kept Karl on a shorter rein. The usual exhortations to be hard-working and frugal abounded. Karl managed to conceal his failure to cope with his teachers' demands, and it was only by chance that Storm discovered that they knew nothing of his existence. Bitter accusations and dire predictions ensued. When debts came to light, the reins were tightened even further. What Storm did

12. Storm to Hans, 2 December 1871, *Stargard*, p. 50.
13. See D.A. Jackson, "The Sound of Silence." Theodor Storm's Son Karl and the Novelle *Schweigen, German Life and Letters*, 45, 1992, pp. 33–49.

not know was that Karl had contracted syphilis and, in all likelihood, had received no proper treatment.

In September 1872, unable to finance the studies of three student sons away from home, Storm summoned Ernst back to Husum. There was no mistaking Hans's condition, and after he had been examined by his uncle Ernst Stolle, Storm wrote to Karl in March 1873: "Es steht traurig um deinen Bruder. Außer dem unsäglichen Kummer, muß ich mich wieder in noch größere Schulden stürzen, um, wenn es nicht zu spät ist, ihn noch zu retten."[14] The letter was to be burned so that nobody should know about the family's shame. Storm's faith in many of the certainties underpinning his humanitarian ideal faltered. He had to face the possibility that his belief in the goodness and potential of human nature was an illusion: "Trifft mich dabei eine Schuld, so ist es nur die, daß ich die menschliche Natur überhaupt zu hoch geschätzt habe."[15] While in his dealings with his sons it was politic to stress will-power, hard work, and conscience, he increasingly asked himself whether factors outside their control were determining their conduct. The possibility that innate, inherited characteristics could prevent individuals achieving happiness and behaving in ethical, enlightened ways emerged from the wings and for a time threatened to take over the stage entirely. His sons' misfortunes also stimulated ruminations about his own "guilt" in all this. The emphases of Storm's humanitarianism had to be adjusted, the grand expectations scaled down.

6.4   The Hidden Biography: Financial Pressures, Publishers

By the early 1870s Storm was in a state of crisis on all fronts. The situation did not markedly improve in the years that followed, and the impression created by older Storm critics that his last eighteen years, in Husum and then, after his retirement, in Hademarschen, were years of fulfillment during which he experienced a sustained surge of creative energy and produced works superior to those of earlier decades is misleading. Before looking at individual works from the period between 1870 and 1875, I

14. Storm to Karl, 28 March 1873.
15. Storm to Karl, February 1873.

should therefore like to intercalate a section covering the whole period up to 1888. It continues where Chapter 4.11 broke off in its remarks on Storm's dealings with editors and publishers and will, I hope, convey something of the biographical background of these years and its implications for the quantity and quality of Storm's works. It should also provide a framework within which to locate the issues discussed in subsequent chapters.

Storm's later novellas were squeezed out of him by financial pressures, amid complaints of artistic decline or even bankruptcy and amid chronic worries and psychosomatic ailments. Unable to live on his salary, he was as much at the mercy of the market as a full-time writer like Paul Heyse who had to produce work after work in order to maintain his fairly grand lifestyle. Being part of a system where literature was a commodity like any other and in which price was determined by the laws of supply and demand, he became a hard-headed, sometimes devious market-operator.[16] Dismissing any talk of writers' associations, the furthest he was prepared to go by way of collective action was to contact other top earners like Keller and Heyse to ensure that they agreed on the fees they could and should demand of editors and publishers. In justifying his high fees, he continued to cite the time spent on works and their high artistic quality compared with the average product. He expected this superior quality to be reflected in editors' fees. But essentially he accepted that the overriding criterion in fee-fixing was the price that editors and publishers set on his value as a contributor.

From the start he was uneasy about *Eine Halligfahrt*, a new departure in artistic terms (see 6.4):

> ... es ist nicht so wie es sein sollte ... Entsinnst du dich noch, wie du als Knabe unter hervorspringenden Thränen mich fragtest: 'Ums *Geld*, Vater? Ums Geld?' Nun, damals hatte es nichts zu sagen, wenn es auch ums Geld war; denn wenn ich ein M.S. absandte, so hatte ich stets das Bewußtsein, das ist gut, keiner macht eben dies dir nach, du kannst darauf pochen. Nun habe ich vorigen Donnerstag (heute ist Dienstg) trotzdem (die Andern drängten mich) das M.S. an Rodenberg für den Salon abgeschickt. Du glaubst nicht wie mich das diese Tage bedrückt hat ... Jedenfalls habe ich gestern wieder an Rodbg

16. See Ebert, *Storm und seine Verleger*, passim.

geschrieben, das ihm eigesandte M.S. wolle mir aus der objectiviren-
den Ferne nicht mehr recht gefallen und stelle ich anheim es mir
zurückzuschicken. – Danach ist eine gewiße Ruhe bei mir eingekehrt.[17]

Rodenberg had meanwhile already rejected the story. This dismayed Storm, suggesting as it did that his powers had deteriorated so much that his "Schreiberei" was not good enough even
for a magazine. If this were the case, there was, he feared, no
prospect of financing his sons' studies in this way. Panic greeted
Hans's request for additional money: ". . . schnürte mir die Angst
die Kehle zu, die Angst daß ich Euch meine Söhne nicht ans Ziel
werde bringen können, ohne die kleinen Mädchen, die noch um
mich sind, ihres kleinen Erbtheils gänzlich zu berauben."[18] Unable
to walk to work without several stops because of breathlessness,
he feared a heart defect and insisted on Aemil examining him,
not once but several times.

By now fees were vital for specific projects. The fee from
Zerstreute Kapitel (1873) was to pay for Hans's doctorate, which
Storm assumed was in the offing, and for a trip to the author
Julius Schindler's castle near Salzburg. This trip, which was
intended to restore his Pegasus's "silver wings" and make "the
silver fountains of inspiration" flow again,[19] in fact precipitated
a financial crisis. Sons had to wait for basic articles like winter
overcoats. Storm spoke of a bitter struggle for existence.[20] He still
had to tout his wares about, and although the fees writers could
demand for novellas rose after 1870, editors and publishers found
excessive his demands for products which, in their eyes, were
slight or mediocre. They turned him away or beat him down. As
he was demanding a rate higher than that of Keller or Auerbach,
Albert Payne, the proprietor of the *Salon*, refused to confirm his
editor Julius Rodenberg's agreement to pay Storm 150 talers for
Beim Vetter Christian (1873). Westermann and Keil also declined.
Storm despaired: ". . . wie gern ließe ich mein armes Gehirn mit
poetischen Arbeiten in Ruh; aber des Brodes wegen zwinge ich
mich dazu, und wenn ich mich redlich müde gearbeit, – dann ist
es doch umsonst; denn meine Kräfte sind dahin."[21] In the end he

17. Storm to Ernst, 16 May 1871.
18. Storm to Hans, 22 May 1871, *Stargard*, p. 39.
19. Storm to Hans, 25 May 1869, *Stargard*, p. 13.
20. Storm to Ernst, 2 October 1871.

settled for a lower fee from Payne, 113 talers. At the time he was terrified of being asked to repay part of the sum embezzled by his court secretary; Hans's treatment for alcoholism also had to be paid for. But it was a sign of the times that Payne lost his editor as well as readers and contributors. Storm did not publish there again.

Fortunately Adolf Glaser, the editor of *Westermanns Monatshefte*, although not generally impressed by Storm's products, had a high opinion of *Viola tricolor* (1874). Although he judged the fee demanded steep in relation to its length, he recommended acceptance. The balance of supply and demand was shifting in Storm's favor. He himself drew up the contract. Henceforth it was crucial to him that he should be paid promptly, whether in a lump sum or in installments, and should not have to wait until a work began appearing. He also attached great importance to having the right to proceed to book publication with a minimum of delay.

Financial pressures ensured that he was always keen to have something on the stocks and despaired when he did not. The moment *Viola tricolor* was finished, he began work at the end of October 1873 on *Pole Poppenspäler*. Promised to the *Deutsche Jugend*, it was already more than half finished by the beginning of December. He was anxious to secure himself a niche in this magazine in case his artistic powers really were failing. Despite this boost to his earnings, he considered 1873 a bad year and was forced to take out further bank loans. Concern about his failure to build up sufficient capital with which to finance his daughters' education and provide them with dowries mounted, and fears of leaving his dependents penniless were never far away, either. Yet, despite all his judicial duties and the seasonal disruptions, he still completed *Pole Poppenspäler* by the end of January 1874. He immediately began work on *Waldwinkel* (1874). In his view, his survival ("wenn ich bürgerlich weiter existiren will") depended on completing it in time to catch the launch number of Rodenberg's new magazine, the *Deutsche Rundschau*.[22] Hans's treatment for syphilis in a Kiel hospital consumed more money. To Karl he wrote: "Ich habe ein Gefühl des Unglücks in mir, wie

---

21. Storm to Karl, 26 April 1873.
22. Storm to Hans, 27 June 1874.

noch nie; bald müssen diese Leiden durch meine Kinder aufhören oder ich gehe zu Grunde."[23]

By the mid-1870s he had at last secured himself two well-paying outlets, the *Deutsche Rundschau* and *Westermanns Monatshefte*. Their publishers, the Paetels and the Westermanns, were also rival book publishers. *Westermanns Monatshefte*, modeled on Harper's *New Monthly Magazine*, had four sections: one devoted to natural science, one to literature, history, and geography, one to art, theater, and painting, and one to novellas. Politics, mathematics, and theology were excluded. In 1872 it had under 4000 subscribers; by 1877 that figure had risen to 15,000, with sales highest in South Germany.[24] The *Deutsche Rundschau*, founded in 1874 and edited by Julius Rodenberg, was more up-market in price, format, and content. Targeting the *Bildungsbürgertum*, it adopted a National-Liberal position which soon hardened into a pronounced anti-socialist one. By the end of the first year it was selling 9000 copies, and sales stabilized at about 10,000. The initial fee, the same for belletristic and scholarly contributions, was 300 marks per sheet (= sixteen pages). This *Doppelverlegertum* enabled Storm to calculate his earnings on the basis of a part formal, part tacit agreement about the rate to be paid per sheet. Had rival authors been able to provide equally marketable goods and charged lower rates, he could have been turned away or beaten down. But from the mid-1870s the demand for good-quality novellas outstripped supply. Editors could not afford to lose the top names to competitors. There was scope for Storm to play off the two camps against each other.

In theory he might have settled into a hard-working, if monotonous routine, supplying editors with stories of above-average quality. With the handsome financial returns he could have secured himself and his family a comfortable lifestyle. This did not happen. His creative imagination refused to function with mechanical smoothness. The balance between financial and emotional pressures, psychosomatic state and creativity was a delicate one. If the scales tilted too far in the direction of worries and physical ailments, his creative powers deserted him.

After his father's death in 1874 and amid mounting concern

23. Storm to Karl, 10 April 1874.
24. See Ebert, *Storm und seine Verleger*, pp. 55ff.

that Hans might need to be confined to a reformatory or asylum, depression, anxieties and nervous complaints made him repeat his Heinean leitmotif of *gesanglos und beklommen*. He lamented: "Mir fällt, halt, nichts ein. Und mir sollte gern was einfallen; denn die Kasse wird leer."[25] Fortunately, instead of paralyzing his creative powers, his fears about the future of his youngest son Karl produced *Ein stiller Musikant*, a piece of perfect wish-fulfillment. But it was written so quickly – in two months – that Storm asked for the manuscript back in order to revise it. This was to become a common practice. Having hastily completed a story, he would try to set his artistic conscience at rest by consulting friends at proof stage. He had to trust that the time lapse between initial completion and the return of the proofs had sufficiently distanced him from the work for him to be able to recognize and remedy weaknesses. Further changes could then be made for the book version. In fact they were often necessary if editors had insisted on passages being removed or reformulated which might antagonize readers. But by then it was often too late to repair basic design faults. Realizing that editors would not reject manuscripts once a rate had been negotiated, only Storm's artistic conscience stood between him and offering works which might be less than perfect. Furthermore, as long as publishers were prepared to pay a certain rate for products of the requisite length, he had little incentive to prune. The textual density of the best of the earlier works was often lost.

In order to be able to satisfy editors' demands and generate regular additional income, he needed a regular supply of material which could be processed fairly rapidly. Sometimes he embarked on stories armed with nothing but the fond hope that an idea or motif would come to life in the act of writing. In an ideal world he would have abandoned such projects once he realized that he had miscalculated. But he could not afford to do so. In fact, he discarded very little. The sense of writing *invitis musis* grew. The period of time also tended to shrink between chancing on a motif, indicating to editors that they could include a work in their schedules, and completing it. Thus *Psyche* (1875), which was triggered off by a notice in a newspaper, was begun at the beginning of March and sent off as early as 25 April 1875. The quality suffered.

25. Storm to Karl, 20 October 1874.

The later 1870s deepened this vortex of pressures and anxieties. On the one hand, the fees he could command encouraged a new optimism. They had risen from 100 talers for *Im Schloß* (1862) to 300 talers or 900 marks for *Waldwinkel* (1874). Editors were, he wrote, on their knees begging for contributions; the new magazines had increased demand while the productive forces were visibly shrinking.[26] To Heyse he wrote: "Ich denke, es ist nicht unbillig, daß dafür die Buchhändler einen entsprechenden Theil ihres reichen Verdienstes überlassen; und ich habe große Lust, sehr viel mehr zu fodern, als ich bisher gefodert und ohne Weiteres auch erhalten habe . . ."[27] His problem remained that of being able to cater for demand. His worries about Hans intensified: "Es ist keine Sorge mehr, es ist ein Entsetzen, das mir mein Blut vergiftet hat, ich bin dem gegenüber völlig rathlos."[28] A urethral discharge, for which Karl was treated in the summer of 1875, added to his worries, and he found it an ordeal just to discharge his judicial duties. Nevertheless he simply could not afford "to let his imagination continue to be a sick bird dragging its wings along the ground."[29]

In retrospect one can see that the original motif for *Aquis submersus* (1876) captured his deepest concerns. But he began the novella in a mood of near despair, simply to prove that he could still write. He described himself as crawling from page to page.[30] Although the fee, 1800 marks, represented another large rise, the relief was short-lived. It became clear that Karl was suffering from syphilis and that it might be a case, not of a recent infection, but of an advanced stage in an untreated or poorly treated infection dating back to the early 1870s. Henceforth Storm sought to convince himself that Karl's fears of possible future developments were unfounded and that any infection had been cured. An expensive visit to Hans in Würzburg in August in an attempt to help him complete his studies, left him suffering from all sorts of ailments. Fear about Hans was, he wrote, the ghost standing behind everything.[31]

A second visit to Würzburg in early 1877 imposed further

26. Storm to K.T. Pyl, 7 April 1875, *Briefe* 2, p. 101.
27. Storm to Heyse, 20 March 1875, *Storm-Heyse* 1, p. 87.
28. Storm to Karl, 24 January 1875.
29. Storm to Heyse, 16 April 1876, *Storm-Heyse* 2, p. 11.
30. Storm to Karl, 22 January 1876.
31. Storm to Heyse, 20 Decmber 1876, *Storm-Heyse* 2, p. 25.

financial strains. It also made writing impossible. He described himself as bearing two crosses[32] and wrote to Karl: "Nun höre mich! An jeden zehn Talern, die ich jetzt für Euch aufbringe, hängt Angst u. Nahrungssorge; denn Hans hat mich arbeitsunfähig gemacht u. vollendet jetzt sein Werk, woran du hoffentlich nicht noch helfen wirst."[33] He sold bonds and went further into debt. During the summer of 1877 the pretence had to be kept up that Karl was being treated by his uncle Aemil for a chronic throat infection. Storm's "black, winged worries" grew.[34]

But at least he had completed *Carsten Curator* in late August. This work was the turning point with regard to fees. Storm decided that the time had come to try to get his fees on to a different footing. In a letter to Rodenberg he threatened that if his demands were not met, he would in future keep anything he wrote for inclusion in his posthumous works.[35] He then went on to talk business. Although by rights he should have first offered his new novella to Westermann, he was, he wrote, offering it to the *Rundschau* since he was convinced that Westermann would not accept it at the price, 3000 marks. However, before sending it to Rodenberg, he wanted to know whether he could indeed count on that fee from him. Of course he knew that if Rodenberg gave him a positive answer, he could put pressure on Westermann. It is not clear whether he actually needed to. At all events, the latter accepted his demands. To his brother Aemil he wrote of the huge fees on which he could now count.[36] But the reassuring knowledge that he could command a fee of 3,000 marks for a work of two sheets did not allay his fears: "Aber was verschlägt das bei den wahrhaft ungeheurn Ausgaben für meine Kinder ... Nun die großen Honorare endlich kommen, bin ich alt und meine Schaffenskraft ist zu Ende."[37] Again the "silver springs" dried up.[38]

Karl moved to Berlin in the summer of 1877, and medical and tuition fees had to be paid. Lisbeth was studying at the conser-

32. Storm to Karl, 25 March 1877.
33. Storm to Karl, 31 March 1877.
34. Storm to Erich Schmidt, 16 August 1877, *Storm-Schmidt* 1, p. 53.
35. Storm to Rodenberg, 6 June 1877, STSG, vol. 22, 1973, p. 51.
36. Storm to Aemil, 21 February 1877.
37. Storm to Otto, 30 September 1877, in private possession, copy in Storm Society Archive, Husum.
38. Storm to Heyse, Easter 1877, *Storm-Heyse* 2, p. 26.

vatory in Stuttgart, while Lucie had been sent to the Mannhardt Institute, a boarding school in Hanerau. In September, however, Storm was still looking in old chronicles for a subject to work on over the winter. He eventually found the motif which grew into *Renate* in a back number of Biernatzki's *Volksbuch*. To his dismay, Hans, having at last finished his exams, failed to return home and went instead to Rotenburg in Hanover on a wild spree with a fellow student. His creditors began to dun Storm.

Storm worked on the novella from early November 1877 to the end of February 1878: "Jede halbe oder Viertelstunde, wo's nur einigermaßen geht, setze ich mich hin und bringe einen Brocken zu Papier, zuletzt wird's unmerklich mehr und mehr, und eines schönen Tages – siehe da, es ist fertig."[39] In the manuscript he labelled the story "Letzte Novelle." His heart pains, stomach disorders, nervous complaints, and fears of imminent death persisted. He complained of a strange smell and wondered whether his brains were rotting.[40]

A chance remark by Ernst during a trip they made together to Schwabstedt on court business provided the starting point for *Zur Wald- und Wasserfreude* (1879), a story about a music-hall-type girl ("das reine Tingel-Mädchen") and her father with his *Gründerzeit* sentimentality and speculative ventures. The subject failed to develop as Storm had hoped, and the many sketches and draft versions only document his attempts to get the flawed recipe right in the course of composition. Even after revisions at proof stage and further changes to the revised proofs he still dreamt of having time the following summer to make changes for the book version. By then he was, of course, struggling to complete another work.

Zur Wald- und Wasserfreude precipitated the bitter exchanges with Westermann that had been brewing since the last great rise in the rate paid to Storm. Whereas it should strictly have gone to the *Rundschau*, he offered it to Westermann for 3000 marks – even though it was shorter than *Carsten Curator*. It was rejected. Further friction resulted from Westermann's refusal to continue printing separate or collected editions of the stories before they appeared in the collected works. In his view the demand for them did not warrant it. Storm, on the other hand, could not

39. Storm to Karl, 25 November 1877.
40. Storm to Hans, 30 March 1878.

afford to lose this extra fee, and a reference to his "künstliche in die Höhe getriebene Honoraragitation" stung him into spelling out magazines' dependence on good-quality novellas. He reminded Westermann of the fee paid for *Carsten Curator*.[41] Once Paetel had also rejected his demands, Storm abandoned his bluff and admitted that he could not afford to put aside works for posthumous publication since his future literary earnings had been built into his calculations about how to finance his retirement. He offered the *Rundschau* an arrangement whereby he would receive 2500 marks for a novella of forty pages plus or minus three pages. For any deviation either way, the fee would be 1000 marks per sheet. When this proposal was rejected, he dropped his demands to 2000 and 600 respectively.[42] Paetel at first rejected both the revised proposal and the price calculated for the novella on this basis, but in the end he agreed to Storm's wishes on both scores. This became the basis on which fees were calculated. Because Paetel was keen to acquire the right to publish separate editions, a pattern soon became established: Paetel would publish two works in separate miniature editions and also together in an octavo collection designed for the lending libraries. In due course they would be included in the collected works published by Westermann. Storm attached great importance to layout, format, and binding, and was particularly anxious that any book should catch the Christmas market.

Im Brauer-Hause (1879) may reflect his serious concern with the problem of superstition, but it never shook off its anecdotal origins. Similarly, *Eekenhof* (1879), which was inspired by a chance reference to Chamisso's poem "Der Geist der Mutter," may have drawn on his preoccupation with incest, but it too lacked intellectual and artistic organization. The public's taste for historical novellas and chronicles was a temptation which Storm did not always resist.

Having for decades struggled to combine his judicial and literary activities – hewing wood and catching butterflies[43] – he had long toyed with the idea of retiring. The booming market for novellas; his own heightened output; fears that proposed judicial reforms would entail additional work and worry; his mother's

41. Westermann to Storm, 10 July 1878 and Storm to Westermann, 23 September 1878, in Ebert, *Storm und seine Verleger*, pp. 99ff and appendix.
42. Storm to Paetel, 7 October 1878, ibid., pp. 52ff.
43. Storm to Schmidt, 13 September 1878, *Storm-Schmidt* 1, p. 99.

death in 1879; receipt of his share in his parents' settlement and in the sale of the family home; his wife's wish to be near her sister – all these factors inclined him to take retirement, sell his house, and build himself a spacious villa on a plot which he had already bought in Hademarschen. By 1880 Hans was a well-paid ship's doctor; Ernst was almost qualified, although his engagement to a 17-year-old from a modest family caused some concern; Karl was living as a music teacher in Varel in Oldenburg; Lisbeth was married to a Protestant pastor in Heiligenhafen; Lucie was engaged to a pharmacist – even if it was worrying that he was a Catholic and had no pharmacy. Storm had reason to believe that he would be able to recoup the cost of his villa and the money frittered away by his sons, provide his younger daughters with an education and a dowry, and leave his wife with no financial worries after his death. Unhindered by professional duties, by Husum's social round and all his memories, he could enjoy a new lease of life.

However, his muse, far from being reinvigorated, seemed struck mute. Having lost his job on his first ship, Hans had to be brought home from Hamburg. When Storm's creative powers returned, *Der Herr Etatsrat*, on which he worked during the winter of 1880/81, was hardly one of the ideal creations which he had envisaged. Hopes that Hans would leave his second ship at Rotterdam in good health and with some capital proved misplaced. Instead he had to be brought home from a doss-house in Hamburg. The ten-year-old pattern was repeated of being like a man condemned to the gallows and only capable of snatching short breaths of air as the final execution was postponed.[44] Once again Aemil had to reassure him that he was not suffering from a heart defect. Suffering from insomnia and incapable of working, he feared that this might indeed be the beginning of the end.

Fortunately, his son-in-law in Heiligenhafen, Pastor Gustav Haase, provided him with a fleshed-out plot for a novella in which he could treat the father-son problem. *Hans und Heinz Kirch* (1882) was written from mid-October to the end of February, 1882. Having intended it for the *Deutsche Rundschau*, he switched to *Westermanns Monatshefte* once he realized that its length could earn him an additional 700 marks. On discovering that the length of column had been altered from forty-six to fifty

---

44. Storm to Heyse, 28 February 1881, *Storm-Heyse* 2, p. 68.

lines, he demanded – and got – the difference. Perhaps because of its length and the resultant large fee, 3091,30 marks, Westermann or, in Storm's view, the new editor, the novelist Friedrich Spielhagen, expressed the wish to vet Storm's works rather than automatically accept whatever he sent in. This threatened to reintroduce the element of uncertainty which he had found so hard to bear before the mid-1870s. It could have played havoc with his calculations. In the end, he settled for a compromise: the editor could ask for changes, but it was understood that the works themselves would not be rejected *in toto*.[45]

Storm's health deteriorated during the eighties. The chronic digestive and intestinal disorders linked to his anxieties and nervous disorders worsened. Trips and holidays during the summer months were seen as means of boosting his health in time for his main creative period during the autumn and winter. At Christmas he always took a break for the festivities, while a visit in January to Husum, staying either with his brother Aemil or the Reventlows, became part of the annual schedule. He would then return to Hademarschen to finish whatever he had started in the autumn. This proved a good *modus vivendi*. Financial and emotional pressures did not lessen. Hans lost his practice in Frammersbach in the Spessart and moved to Wörth; Karl's syphilis entered a new phase as gummas appeared on his legs; after an adulterous affair, Lisbeth's husband was forced to find a new church;[46] Lucie, once her engagement had been broken off, became prone to nervous disorders; finally, his wife began exhibiting signs of depression reminiscent of her state in the late 1860s. Fears of senility, total unproductivity and death recurred.

Through the winter of 1882/83 Storm struggled with the novella *Schweigen*, one of his most disturbing stories. He would have burned it but for his financial straits.[47] Having finally finished it, he complained: "Leider will sich Neues nicht gestalten, was doch nicht nur sehr tröstlich, sondern auch für meine dieß Jahr außer-

---

45. See LL 3, pp. 795f.

46. Peter Goldammer provided me with details of an entry in vol. 17 of Julius Rodenberg's *Tagebuch* in the possession of the Goethe-Schiller-Archive in Weimar. On 7 June 1894 he writes: Einen recht traurigen Besuch hatt' ich gestern: die *Tochter Theodor Storm's*, eine Frau, tief in Schmerz, hoch in den Dreißigen jetzt u. von nicht unsympathischer Erscheinung, mit einem Pfarrer verheirathet, der ihr vor zehn Jahren – die Treue gebrochen hat u. seitdem unerbittlich vom geistlichen Consistorium verfolgt wird, wie wohl sie seinen Fehltritt ihm längst verziehen hat. Des Amtes entsetzt, hat er bald hier, bald dort, u. in den letzten

gewöhnlich strapazirte Caße sehr nothwendig wäre."[48] Even though *Zur Chronik von Grieshuus* (1884), had been in his mind for some time, the prospect of a famous actor doing a reading from it in Vienna put him under great pressure to finish the first part to meet a tight deadline. He so rushed the second part that he asked for the manuscript back and submitted a new version. Scarcely had he finished, than he began a new work, *Florentiner Novelle,* based on a motif in a story by a relative of the Mannhardts. He abandoned it in favor of a story recounted by his son Karl about a fellow student. It could be worked up with a minimum of effort. But, recognizing *Es waren zwei Königskinder* (1884) to be slight, he sent it to the less prestigious magazine *Vom Fels zum Meer* in Stuttgart, where it earned him 1200 marks. He need not have had any such scruples: Paetel was annoyed that he had supplied a competitor.

At a dinner held in his honor in Berlin in 1884 he vented his displeasure at remarks attributed to the novelist Georg Ebers who had allegedly said that for him writing a novella was a relaxing break from the serious business of writing novels. Storm claimed that he commonly spent five months on a novella; in the draft of his speech he even spoke of eight.[49]

Unable to find a subject for the winter, in *John Riew'* (1885), he unsuccessfully tried to fuse two independent motifs which he had earlier noted down as potential subjects. In 1885 he made preparatory studies for *Der Schimmelreiter*. Fortunately he did not attempt to rush it, and his search for less demanding motifs took him to a collection of legends from the Neckar Valley. *Ein Fest auf Haderslevhuus* (1885), perhaps the nadir of his writing in the 1880s, was written in four months in the summer of 1885. By that time he was suffering from terrible stomach pains and

---

beiden Jahren bei der hiesigen Arbeitercolonie des Pfarrers Diestelhang eine dürftige Stellung gefunden, aus der er aber jetzt auch wieder vertrieben werden soll. Abgewiesen von all den hohen u. höchsten Stellen, an welchen christliches Erbarmen walten sollte, wendet sie sich mit ihren vier Kindern Hilfe suchend an die alten Freunde ihres Vaters. Aber was vermögen die für sie zu thun? Es schnitt mir durchs Herz, wie sich ihre Verzweiflung, ohne zudringlich zu sein, äußerte. Keine Novelle von Storm vermöchte so tragisch zu wirken, wie dieses Schicksal seiner Tochter.

47. Storm to Karl, 25 May 1883.
48. Storm to Hans, 27 May 1883.
49. See *Storm-Heyse* 3, pp. 247ff., and *Storm-Schmidt* 2, pp. 170f.

diarrhea – the first signs of his stomach cancer. His wife was clinically depressed. Attempts by two of his daughters to steady Hans proved futile and they had to be ordered home. *Bötjer Basch* (1886) was again a stop-gap.

When approached by Karl Emil Franzos about contributing to the new magazine *Deutsche Dichtung*, Storm at first declined. But he needed money to pay for Elsabe's music studies in Weimar and Lucie's treatment in an expensive clinic in Kiel. He was also contemplating moving back to Husum at a time of falling house and land prices. Recognizing the potential of a story he heard from a relative, he therefore supplied *Ein Doppelgänger* (1887). It earned him a welcome 2446 marks. That autumn and winter he was gravely ill. Hans died in early December. Although still bed-ridden, he began *Ein Bekenntnis* (1887) in the new year. Adolf Glaser, who was again editor of *Westermanns Monatshefte*, felt that Storm's work had deteriorated: he had begun to "speculate" with his writing and to turn out two works per year instead of one. Yet as a promotional asset ("ein Gegenstand der Reklame") he was indispensable. He had admirers who found everything he wrote unsurpassable, and, even though his stipulations were hard, one could not reject them.[50]

Storm wrote *Der Schimmelreiter* in 1887/88. After stomach cancer had been diagnosed in the spring of 1887, he became depressed and was unable to write until the family arranged for a fake medical examination. Believing the growth benign, he was able to complete the novella in February, 1888. He died on 4 July.

6.5   Hoffmann and Heine: Critical Strategies

In the Poetic-Realist aesthetic the harmonious, closed work of art mirrored the supposed stable harmony of the ideal state and society which, it was claimed, was emerging in Germany. After the mid-1860s Storm no longer shared this optimism. His need to question the realities of Bismarckian Germany led him to seek a more open form and alternative techniques. He adopted the techniques of E.T.A. Hoffmann and of the Heinrich Heine of the *Reisebilder*. *Empfindsamkeit*, irony, satire and parody returned. Although the plan to write a loose cycle of stories under the title

---

50. See Ebert, *Storm und seine Verleger*, p. 64.

Zerstreute Kapitel was ultimately abandoned, parts of the original plan such as the novella *Eine Halligfahrt* and *Der Amtschirurgus – Heimkehr* allow one to glimpse an unfamiliar Storm.[51]

Eine Halligfahrt captures many of his reactions to developments in Schleswig-Holstein since his return in 1864; it also documents his "mid-life crisis." Instead of relying on a tight, single plot working to a climax and *dénouement* and having a hero and heroine with elaborate social identities, it follows the Heinean recipe: in the course of a trip to an older cousin on a *Hallig* or holm, a fictional narrator allows himself a wide range of reflections, historical reminiscences and moods. Finally, after the cousin's death, he presents this latter-day Kreisler's account of his last violin performance in the presence of a young woman, Eveline.

The vision of a German Hellas in the north was a key component of national-liberal cultural ideology. Yet, at the very moment when German unification is being achieved, the cousin retires from the civil service and withdraws to rented rooms on a holm. Odysseus opts to leave Ithaca. This modern Robinson Crusoe (LL 2, 54) shipwrecks himself. His holm becomes his "little land of freedom" (LL 2, 46). He cannot stomach his "regierungslustige Mitkreaturen," these "Geheime-Ober-Gottweiß-was-Räte" (LL 2, 50). In the manuscript the text went on: "Ich kenne eine ganze Blumenlese davon, die alle einen subalternen Geruch mit sich herum tragen . . ."[52] He is not prepared to risk being caught up in the cogs of this state machinery nor to live with Hoffmannesque puppets, who clumsily throw their weight about and derive their sense of identity solely from their rank and status. In the first version he retires when still young because he cannot stand being praised in public by a superior in a way unseemly for a grown-up person. Instead of identifying with any eagle or bird of prey – the Prussian eagle? – the cousin identifies with the sparrow: ". . . er gleicht dem Menschen, an sich ist er ohne Wert, aber er trägt die Möglichkeit zu allem Großen in sich" (LL 2, 47). The Martje Flors story (see LL 2, 51f.)

---

51. See LL 2, pp. 789ff; B. Litzmann, "Heine in Storms 'Halligfahrt.'" in B.L., *Beiträge zur Literatur- und Theatergeschichte*, Berlin, 1918, pp. 430–37; T. Kuchenbuch, *Perspektive und Symbol im Erzählwerk Theodor Storms*, Dissertation, Marburg, 1969, pp. 91–187; I. Schuster, "Theodor Storm und E.T.A. Hoffmann," *Literaturwisssenschaftliches Jahrbuch*, 11, 1970, pp. 209–23.
52. Kladde, SHLB.

so beloved of Storm as a symbol of courageous, if non-violent, opposition to tyranny, returns (LL 2, 51) – and is implicitly directed against the occupying Prussians. Instead of proclaiming the permanence of the new Empire, the novella stresses the transience of all things. Seneca is commended for declaring that things are best preserved in the past (LL 2, 43). The Rungholdt story of a once proud, heathen town engulfed by the sea both echoes the transience theme and may hint at the future rebirth of states like Schleswig-Holstein. Legend, we are told, has it that the cocks still adorn the weather-vanes and that the bells still ring (LL 2, 44).

The text reaffirms Storm's vision of Germany as a cosmopolitan *Kulturnation*. The holm has a place for Claude Lorrain, Ruysdael, Beethoven, Jean Paul, Goethe, Mozart, Spohr, Schumann, Eichendorff and statuettes of Venus. This rich cultural tradition cannot be dismissed as flotsam and jetsam, mere antiquaria (LL 2, 48). At a time when ethnic nationalism was rife, the text comments *à propos* of a Beethoven sonata: "– Ist doch Musik die Kunst, in der sich alle Menschen als Kinder eines Sterns erkennen sollen!" (LL 2, 65).

In the original version the text reiterated the reflections on the deeper causes of the Franco-Prussian War which Storm had expressed in letters (see p. 158). The uncle went on: "Ich hasse den Krieg, weil er wie nichts Andres, den Menschen zum willenlosen Werkzeug der Natur erniedrigt . . ." He challenges the view that war is a "Stahlbad für die Völker," contrasting the devastation caused by the Thirty Years War and the Wars of Liberation with the real achievements of the German people: work. Peaceful work, he claims, not war, made Germany strong. In the manuscript "work" is even underlined. He closes with the words: "Mögen, wenn dieß Blutbad ausgeschüttet ist, die klugen Lenker der öffentlichen Dinge sich nach einem festen Frieden umthun!"[53] Rodenberg rejected the work. Before submitting it to *Westermanns Monatshefte*, Storm omitted this entire passage. It was accepted.

The second great thematic strand is what I have called the mid-life crisis. In physical terms the cousin is a self-portrait: "der kleine schmächtige Mann mit den tiefliegenden Augen und dem

---

53. In rejecting the contemporary glorification of the Wars of Liberation, the cousin cites the ending of F.C. Schlosser's *Geschichte des 18. Jahrhunderts*. Vol. 7, part 2, Heidelberg, 1848, portrays the war against Napoleon as a war fought for

vollen weißen Haupthaar" (LL 2, 46). He takes up his violin one last time when inspired and encouraged by the youthful Eveline. She, for her part, is criticized for her behavior. After that he abandons any hope of again enjoying youth, passion, and creativity, and puts his violin away into its "coffin." This is no magic island full of alluring music like Circe's, no Cythera. Indeed the text plays with readers' expectations that love will develop between the young narrator and Susanne. Despite every encouragement to fall in love, they manage not to do so. Traditional motifs are parodied. Thus the boat in the dark boathouse is on its stocks, and Susanne declines the narrator's invitation to join him in it. He is preoccupied with thoughts about the tyranny of public opinion, which decrees that nobody sporting a Friedrich Hecker hat and moustache, i.e. the "uniform" of democrats in 1848, can possibly prosper as a lawyer (LL 2, 57). The manuscript originally added "among his conservative fellow countrymen."

Before writing *Eine Halligfahrt* Storm had completed another of the chapters intended for the cycle: *Der Amtschirurgus – Heimkehr*. Here autobiographical and local-historical elements allow him to indulge in veiled criticism of contemporary trends and to restate subversive religious views. The opening section is full of allusions to the topsy-turvy world, to human beings' inability to see reality as it is and their tendency to shape it to meet their needs. Who are mad, those who supposedly embody reason or those classed as outsiders and eccentrics? The text relies on the Heinean technique of contamination by association. Thus it asks whether the surgeon-barber was really such a fool if on certain days he proclaimed himself Crown Prince of Prussia from an attic window of the Town Hall. Was he not perhaps a prince in that far-away, but much greater and much more beautiful realm where Cinderella once ascended the throne (LL 4, 160)? His imprecations

---

freedom but which despots, aristocrats, and diplomats, who had always been opposed to freedom, exploited in order to reimpose the old yoke and add new burdens: "Alles was vom Mai 1814 an, in Europa geschah, hängt daher in Beziehung auf den Kampf des demokratischen Princips mit den aristokratischen Vorurtheilen und Privilegien, des diplomatischen Trugs mit den Rechten der Völker, die man zum Schein einräumte und in der That durch Polizei, Autokratie und Büreaukratie ärger als jemals beschränkte, so innig mit den Begebenheiten des Jahres 1848 zusammen, daß wir nicht wagen, es davon zu trennen und also zum Schlusse nur noch einige wenige Andeutungen über die Geschichte der Jahre 1814 und 1815 unserem Werk beifügen wollen" (p. 1171). One sees the link with Storm's general emphases.

and uninhibited frankness about civic dignitaries are commended
for having destroyed in the narrator as a boy any respect for the
"Autoritäten des Staatskalenders" (LL 4, 159). Like the cousin in
Eine Halligfahrt, the surgeon-barber retires from human society,
preferring the company of his rats. Storm required the reader to
read between the lines and respond to his cues. Unfortunately
these techniques, which had been part and parcel of oppositional
literature before 1840, had been outlawed by the Poetic Realists.
The palates of most middle-class magazine readers were by now
adjusted to other fare.

The section on Storm's schooldays is full of barbs directed
against the educational changes introduced by the Prussians (see
pp. 146). The new grammar-school curriculum is obliquely tar-
geted:

> Freilich, unser Schultisch war derzeit nur mit geistiger Hausmannskost
> besetzt: wir kannten noch nicht den bunten Krautsalat, der – "Friß
> Vogel oder stirb!" – den heutigen armen Jungen aufgetischt wird. Ich
> habe niemals Kaviar essen können, und – Gott sei Dank! – ich habe
> ihn auch niemals im Namen der "Gleichmäßigkeit der Bildung" essen
> müssen; diese schöne Lehre beglückte noch nicht unsere Jugend. (LL
> 4, 165)

Storm's speech at the annual speech-day for sixth-formers treats
the decline and fall of states; his poem a year later focuses on the
Jewish patriot Mattathias. Many readers would know that although his struggle failed, his son Judas Maccabee created a
separate Jewish state.

Great care was needed in presenting the poem "Crucifixus." In
1867 Storm had imagined it suitable for a volume designed to
raise money for Ferdinand Freiligrath who had returned to
Germany. The editor rejected it. It was now smuggled in here as
a critique of anti-semitism. It was further defused by following
it with the remark of his friend "Alexander," i.e. von Wussow,
himself an anti-semite, that this was just one point of view. It
runs:

> Am Kreuz hing sein gequält' Gebeine,
> Mit Blut besudelt und geschmäht;
> Dann hat die stets jungfräulich reine
> Natur das Schreckensbild verweht.

Doch die sich seine Jünger nannten,
Die formten es in Erz und Stein,
Und stellten's in des Tempels Düster
Und in die lichte Flur hinein.

So, jedem reinen Aug' ein Schauder,
Ragt es herein in unsre Zeit;
Verewigend den alten Frevel,
Ein Bild der Unversöhnlichkeit.
(LL 4, 168)

Jesus Christ's death on the cross, which, according to Christian teaching, reconciled God with sinful mankind, is presented as a symbol of irreconcilability. Virginally pure nature would have obliterated the memory of this barbaric crime had not the church insisted on making it the cornerstone of a scheme of grace and redemption which denies mankind's ability to progress, unaided, to *Humanität*. In terms of whether material could be published or not, commercial considerations now weighed as heavily as did the constraints imposed by the state authorities. Storm knew that critical reflections on Christianity, if they were to have a wide influence, had to find their way into the large, popular magazines; but he also knew that, for that to be possible, they would have to be doctored and camouflaged.

The hymn to transience and mortality which follows returns to Storm's grammar school days. The values commended in Hölty's poem "Üb' immer Treu' und Redlichkeit" are implicitly contrasted with the situation in Prussia-Germany: "Wir ahnten damals noch nicht, daß die Redlichkeit nur soweit geübt werden dürfe, als sie nicht verboten ist. Jetzt weiß ich es und begreife nur nicht, warum man die Kinder Dinge lernen läßt, die ihnen später so gefährlich werden können" (LL 4, 170). This in its turn leads to the comment: "Wir kannten weder die Schöne griechischer Götterbilder, noch andererseits jenes cäsarische Wesen, in dem Bilde des jemaligen Herrschers der aufstrebenden Jugend ein drohendes Symbol der Gewalt entgegen zu halten" (LL 4, 170f.). Storm sailed even closer to the wind when the text questions the Prussian "liberation." The narrator writes of a classmate killed in 1850: "'Niemand hat größere Liebe denn die, daß er sein Leben lässet für seine Freunde.' Für seine Freunde; möge das dein Los gewesen sein!" (LL 4, 172).

Once one is attuned to the techniques and strategies of these pieces, one sees that the same principles apply to the collection of autobiographical pieces in *Von heut' und ehedem* (1873). They are not self-indulgent evocations of Woldsen glories. The past's richness is rather a reflection of the present's emptiness. The first piece describes as typical of "today" an actual incident involving Constanze at Hanover railway station in 1863. A young officer, who had offered her his help as she struggled with all the children, disappeared once he learned that she was traveling third class.

In the early 1870s Storm began to move back beyond the later eighteenth century to the seventeenth and early eighteenth centuries. He saw them as key periods in the struggle to achieve Enlightenment and *Humanität* and sought to convey the slow and painful emergence in North Germany of a humane world out of dark, medieval conditions. Remarks on professions until recently deemed dishonorable – like that of the knacker or executioner – provided the prelude to the evocation of a barbaric execution which took place in Husum at the turn of the nineteenth century, the last of its kind. This in its turn leads to the comment:

Hoffentlich werden auch die wenigen noch übrigen Fronvesten des deutschen Reichs in nicht zu ferner Zeit einen ebenso tröstlichen Umbau feiern (as in the case of the Husum one), wenn auch die Strafgesetzgebung des Norddeutschen Bundes ihre sinkenden Fundamente noch einmal zu unterbauen versucht hat; und, die nach uns kommen, werden dann auch bei diesen Mauern stehen bleiben und sich das für sie Unbegreifliche zu beantworten suchen, wie jemals einem Menschen das Abschlachten eines anderen von Staats wegen als eine amtlich zu erfüllende Pflicht hat zugemutet werden können; denn nicht auf Seiten des Delinquenten, sondern auf Seiten des Henkers liegt für unsere Zeit die sittliche Unmöglichkeit der Todesstrafe. Als ein sicheres Zeichen aber für das endliche Verschwinden derselben dürfen wir wohl den an sich unheimlichen Umstand begrüßen, daß, während im übrigen das Gerichtsverfahren in die Öffentlichkeit hinausdrängt, dieser furchtbare Akt, der wie nichts Anderes des freien Himmels und des zustimmenden Zeugnisses der Nation bedarf, neuerdings im Gegenteil der Öffentlichkeit entzogen und als ein Schauderstück für wenige Eingeweihte in die beklemmende Enge der Gerichtshöfe hineingeflüchtet ist. (LL 4, 260)

But Storm had to accept that editors and public had no appetite for such fare. If he were to earn top-rate fees, he had to get back into the mainstream as far as novellas were concerned.

6.6   Images of Love and Sex

The years after 1865 were years of crisis for Storm in the areas of love and sex. His own frustrations, together with reflections provoked by Darwinist theories, prompted him to reassess his cult of love. *Draußen im Heidedorf* (1872) can profitably be considered against this background.

Storm could have written a story about a middle-class male who is married off by his parents to a wealthy girl and then destroys his marriage and comes to grief as a result of his passion for an unmarried woman loved since childhood. But such a plot would have posed great psychological, ideological, and aesthetic problems for Storm. Equally, even if the topic had been presented with a punitive moral slant, his middle-class public would not have taken kindly to the depiction of an adulterous middle-class husband who squanders his wife's fortune, imperils the future of his child, and commits suicide when half demented by frustration and despair.

It was altogether easier to treat the problem in terms of a case that Storm had investigated in a farming community. Things unacceptable in a middle-class context could be projected onto a remote, wild world of farmers, superstition, Slovak women, and bogs. Storm's critical distance *vis-à-vis* the peasant world, when cemented by his use of a fictional narrator and the presentation of the story in terms of a judicial hearing, enabled him to treat Hinrich Fehse's "fate" as a genre or case study. By choosing not to use *Stimmung* to sensitize his readers' *Gemüt*, he discouraged empathy and instead encouraged a critical attitude. This self-imposed asceticism was a valuable experiment. But at this stage he could only apply it to subjects which were an arm's length away. He could not have presented his personal preoccupations or a middle-class love story in this way. In *Viola tricolor* he returned to *Stimmung* and pathos. In contrast, by the time he came to write *Der Schimmelreiter*, he was able to combine elements marked by this distance with scenes suffused with *Stimmung*; by then he also did not need to abstract from his own life-long concerns. Ultimately he was not a writer able or willing to impose on himself Flaubertian impassivity and "objectivity." He would still have endorsed the sentiments expressed to Turgenjev in 1864: "Md Bovari habe ich auch gelesen; der Verfasser ist ein feiner Beobachter oder vielmehr Anempfinder und hat in der Passivität des Vortrags eine gewisse Ähnlichkeit mit Ihnen; aber es ist mir doch zu stofflich, das Vereinzelte zu wenig zu lebendigen Scenen verabschiedet; ich bedarf aber in der Novelle ein wenig drama-tisches Leben."[54] Such case studies were as alien to him as they were to the German classical-idealist tradition. The technique of simply observing scenes, reporting gestures and words, and presenting without comment the accounts of the protagonists, bred a welcome tautness and produced scenes of great drama, but it did not allow him to pursue other key concerns. Even where it points toward works like *Renate* and *Der Schimmelreiter* in its study of superstition, *Draußen im Heidedorf* lacks many of the other ingredients of the greater works.

Peasant characters speak in a language intended to come much closer to everyday speech than the diction of Storm's middle-class heroes and heroines. Peasant language is set apart from the language of the narrator, a judge, who accompanies his one use of an everyday idiom with an added "wie man bei uns sagt" (LL 2, 76). This juxtaposition highlights a perceptible condescen-sion on his part and also underpins notions of peasant life being cruder, more violent, and more passionate than middle-class life. In theory Storm could have exploited the clash between the norms and assumptions inherent in middle-class language and the narrator's judicial function, on the one hand, and the conditions, motives, and language of the farming community on the other. But that would have taken him beyond his ideological limits and outside the socio-economic system which, despite his criticism, he upheld.

Disillusioned by contemporary trends and overwhelmed by private worries, he was under great psychological pressure to create stories with happy endings. Thus, in the novella *Beim Vetter Christian* (1873), the eighteenth-century patrician world evoked in earlier works – but with the negative elements removed – is projected into the present. In this humorous idyll Homeric epic features blend with rococo stylistic devices like the smiling little

54. Storm to Turgenjew, 9 December 1864, in Laage, *Studien*, p. 91.

guardian angel that flies above the heroine's head (LL 2, 124). The only disruptive element is provided by a standard comic jealous spinster. In this cozy theodicy all her machinations only contribute to the general good.

Even if one accepts the conventions of the idyll, it is still revealing that Storm, the former champion of passion and of the rights of young people *vis-à-vis* their parents, here adopts a highly conservative stance on such matters. The heroine's name, Julie Hennefeder, captures the new emphasis on maternal domesticity: "Julie war keine schlanke Idealgestalt; sie war lieblich und rundlich, flink und behaglich, ein geborenes Hausmütterchen" (LL 2, 106). Innocence of heart, health, kindness, modesty, practical skills at mending armchairs and bottling preserves – these are the commendable attributes of a spouse with whom the virginal Christian can enjoy paradisical happiness. His sexual electricity (LL 2, 102) will be contained within marriage. The Biblical Fall is reversed as this Adam and Eve pick apples in the garden; later the moon shines down on them in the garden "as it did through Adam's trees thousands of years ago" (LL 2, 129). Storm's fears about his own sons and their sexual contacts are banished from this paradise.

The family gathering is presented as an Homeric occasion. What, before 1865, could easily have typified a stiff, hierarchical society, becomes, in the context of the early 1870s, a comfortable, intact world. Here the Prussian bureaucrats, the colleagues hanging themselves, the swindling secretaries and bankrupts of the contemporary Husum scene disappear. The final line underlines the cozy intimacy that the text seeks to create: "Und also, lieber Leser, gehab' dich wohl" (LL 2, 130). Despite all this the Martje Flors leitmotif still recurs (LL 2, 115).

In *Viola tricolor* (1874), Storm presented a husband, his young second wife and his daughter from his first marriage resolving problems in their relations. The straining for poignancy and sublime intensity produced a work which today smacks of kitsch but appealed to contemporaries including Fontane. Traditional aesthetic assumptions, according to which climaxes had to be conveyed with appropriate rhetorical emotion, led to passages like the following:

"O, Ines!" rief er. "Wenn erst aus deinem eignen Blut ein Kind auf deinem Schoße liegt."

Sie machte eine abwehrende Bewegung; er aber sagte: "Die Zeit
wird kommen, und du wirst fühlen, wie das Entzücken, das aus
deinem Auge bricht, das erste Lächeln deines Kindes weckt und wie
es seine kleine Seele zu dir zieht. – Auch über Nesi haben einst zwei
selige Augen so geleuchtet; dann schlug sie den kleinen Arm um
einen Nacken, der sich zu ihr niederbeugte, und sagte: "Mutter!" –
Zürne nicht mit mir, daß sie es zu keiner Anderen auf der Welt mehr
sagen kann!" (LL 2, 140)

Storm's obsessions and the resultant one-sided perspective
ruled out any probing study of the issues at stake.

Written for the magazine *Deutsche Jugend*, *Pole Poppenspäler*
(1874) illustrates the values Storm was keen to purvey to Imperial youth. It remains true to his alternative history, portraying
the fates of *die kleinen Leute*, and, in the case of the puppeteer
Joseph Tendler, the losers, those overtaken by socio-cultural developments. It reaffirms the goodness of human nature, the need
for non-authoritarian behavior, and the importance of love tri-
umphing over considerations of class, status, and honor.

At a time when the paths of artisans and middle-class Germans were taking them in different directions, the novella re-
states the ideal of an 1848 democrat, holding up for emulation a
society where there is close contact and mutual respect between
these classes. Paulsen, a master and a town councillor, is loved
and respected, like his wife, by the middle-class narrator, who
learns from him things which play no part in his formal education (LL 2, 165). In Stifterian fashion, Paulsen's story captures his
own gradual recognition of what is important in life. Having
been affected by his story, the narrator communicates it and its
values to his magazine readers in the hope that it will also mold
their values. Youth must be entertained, but it must also be
edified. The puppet plays performed by Tendler, the father of
Paulsen's wife, reflect past periods' treatment of topics like threats
to marital virtue and fidelity, sexual chastity, perdition and
damnation. In contrast, Storm's novella associates itself with the
Enlightenment tradition of children's stories represented by C. F.
Weiße's *Kinderfreunde* (LL 2, 193). In the modern, literate age the
magazine has superseded the puppet-theater. It must communicate values appropriate to a modern, humanitarian society.

The theme of alienation returns. Paulsen overcomes a boyhood fascination with the unreal world of the puppet plays and
recognizes that his love for Lisei is what is truly important. In

this he differs from so many earlier Storm heroes. In contrast to earlier stories, too, the novella not only affirms the ideal of love; it also shows characters determined to achieve this ideal. Paulsen's relationship with Lisei affords both of them a unique sense of security symbolized in the way they snuggle up together in the chest (LL 2, 188f.). Whereas their disappearance and Paulsen's breaking of the puppet's nose – with its Freudian significance? – could provoke parental wrath and corporal punishment – Lisei's mother advocates whipping the pair! – clemency prevails. Just as material damage is repairable, so too human nature needs understanding and love, not castigation. Any sexual contact between the children is, of course, edited out of the picture, even though Storm's "incest complex" (see p. 21) may be at work here.

The second half of the story juxtaposes the authorities' behavior toward those deemed suspect riff-raff and the standards of Paulsen, Lisei and the widow of Paulsen's master. Storm engineers a situation in which the reader's sympathies are on the side of the individual, not authority. In this the novella anticipates *Ein Doppelgänger* (1887). Once Tendler has been arrested on false suspicions and thrown into a stinking prison, his daughter, having had her passport confiscated, cannot hope to find accommodation despite the bitterly cold weather. As a Catholic, she prays to the wooden crucifix in hope of finding there help and consolation; but, as one now expects of a Storm story, the text suggests that help can come only from other loving, kind human beings and that her true savior is Paulsen. He, unlike so many other Storm heroes, heeds the quiet revelation that his salvation depends on his love for her. In contrast to Elisabeth and Reinhardt in *Immensee*, both have the courage (LL 2, 208) to defy society's prejudices. They achieve happiness. Like Veronica, Lisei no longer goes to confession (LL 2, 210).

In an age depicted as having become coarse and rough Tendler is ridiculed and driven into silence; but his burial, which certain elements in the town intended to be the final humiliation, is discreetly presented as an apotheosis. Damnation, devils, hell, and heaven have been replaced by a commendation of love and humane *Nächstenliebe*.

In his next work, *Waldwinkel* (1874), the pendulum swung back to a pessimistic vision of love and sex. In it Storm tests the viability of the *seuls sur la terre* motif, i.e. his ideal of two lovers isolated in a natural, Rousseauist paradise away from the pressures of state and society. Conscious that a story about a scholar in his early forties who sets up a love nest with a lower-class seventeen-year-old ward was a base (*niederträchtig*) topic and could cost him his reputation,[55] Storm abandoned the technique employed in *Viola tricolor*, i.e. working outward from within, in favor of working inward from the outside and adopting a romance-like presentation. The motifs would then, he hoped, only gleam through the outer veil (LL 2, 859f.). The novella contrasts an idealist, Richard, with a series of realists: first, Fritz, the archetypal bureaucrat, a corpulent, comfortable mayor with wife and children who toils away at his files, unaware of the glorious spring outside; then the forester, trader, and inn-keeper (LL 2, 227ff.), all of whom exhibit varying degrees of cynicism and resignation. Engrossed in their petty concerns, they lack any sense of wider responsibility to their fellow human beings and show no understanding whatsoever for national, democratic strivings in the immediate post-1815 period. They refer (LL 2, 229) to the student conspiracy "als sie die Könige all' vom Leben bringen wollten." Junkers who participated in the "Wartburgstanz" of 1817 were, in their view, only obeying cranky whims. The long years of solitary confinement to which Richard was sentenced by the Prussians mean nothing to them.

An idealist in love, too, Richard finally emerged from prison, only to find his wife living with a baron. Having killed the latter in a duel and eventually divorced his wife, he drifted restlessly. The novella, which is in many respects a reply to Stifter's *Die Narrenburg*, asks whether love between him and a harshly treated, lonely orphan, Franziska, might not bring them mutual happiness. But, from the start, the text puts a question-mark behind the idea. Encircled by a twenty-foot-high wall and with its windows all on one wall, the *Waldwinkel* is more of a prison than a refuge/love nest and is known in popular parlance as the *Narrenkasten*. Written from a perspective which largely favors the hero, the text emphasizes a link between Franziska and the Biblical serpent (*scientes bonum et malum* [LL 2, 225]). Later Richard discerns in her eyes the serpent's shimmer (LL 2, 252). Throughout love and sex are presented from a Darwinist standpoint. Thus Franziska's features suggest a bird of prey (LL 2, 225), and notions

55. See LL 2, 863ff.

of a struggle for existence, of the instinct of self-preservation, for predators and prey, and of young males struggling with older ones for possession of the female are prominent. The text even hints at a war between the sexes and suggests that a man can only win a woman's passionate love if he breaks the independence of this "enemy" (LL 2, 240f.).

For a while the *seuls sur la terre* ideal seems viable: "Wenn gar so schwül der Duft auf ihrem Wege stand, ergriffen sie sich wohl an den Händen und erhoben schweigend die glänzenden Augen gegen einander. Sie atmeten die Luft der Wildnis, sie waren die einzigen Menschen, Mann und Weib, in dieser träumerischen Welt" (LL 2, 250). But the text cleverly hints that, unknown to Richard, Franziska is soon secretly seeing a sexually attractive young forester and is torn between passion for him and a need for material security. Richard, with his past experiences, does not respond to her talk of marriage and by making out state bonds in her name, weakens her dependence on him. By the time he is keen to marry and return to the world, the prospect of losing her sexual partner and having to minister to an aging husband tilts the balance for Franziska. The text discreetly suggests that this ailing, middle-aged man cannot satisfy her sexuality. The lovers flee with the bonds, and Richard has to learn to forget and be forgotten.

In this series of experimental works *Psyche* (1875) represents another new departure. In its would-be profundity it is typical of the worst of Wilhelminian "classicizing" writing. The issues it treats are not unimportant, even if they are hardly original: the question of whether Imperial culture will be purely Germanic (a veiled anti-Wagner polemic lurks in the background) or whether it must be a synthesis of Christian and classical, Germanic and Latin elements; whether the subject-matter of literature, as of sculpture, must be contemporary (see also p. 232); whether treatment of classical motifs must be "idealistic" rather than "realistic." But the treatment is hackneyed and pretentious; dialogues and narrative are often kitsch.

This reworking of Apuleius's tale of Amor and Psyche allows Storm to express a patriarchal view of sexual relations and gender roles. A "rosebud," Maria, is cured of her bold, tomboyish spirit when she proves unequal to the stormy waves and has to be rescued by a young sculptor. Having bathed naked, she is torn between *pudeur* and love for her unknown rescuer. The bud unfurls and a young woman pining for love emerges. This flower of German womanhood is neither a Walkyrie nor – despite her name – a Virgin Mary, nor a seductive Venus. The experience of such virginal beauty and vitality is the revelation enabling the scuptor to unlock "das schlummernde Geheimnis aller Schönheit" (LL 2, 331). His sculpture treats the incident in a classical guise. While breaking with classical-idealist conventions and depicting the rescuing river-god as a handsome young male, it still "idealizes" the subject matter. Even then some visitors still find elements too naturalistic (LL 2, 335), and the text is critical of those who, instead of undergoing the true aesthetic experience, indulge in tittle-tattle about possible models and actual experiences (LL 2, 335). Fortunately Storm did not pursue this vein.

7

Catering for the Wilhelminian Public: Criticism and Conformity

7.1 Continuities and Changes

The audience at which Storm pitched his fiction in the 1860s had not disappeared by the later 1870s. After 1866 liberals and democrats may have indulged in self-criticism and sometimes accepted their unfitness in matters of grand politics and state-craft; but they did not renounce all their previous convictions. There were still large areas of common ground between them and Storm. He could see himself as appealing to values which corresponded to innate human qualities and which until recently had been in the ascendancy. The liberal, Enlightenment elements in the National-Liberal consensus did, however, decrease in relative importance. Younger generations of middle-class males grew up whose formative experiences were not the frustrations of the Metternich period, the euphoria and disappointment of 1848/49, the years of reaction in the 1850s, or the constitutional struggles of the 1860s. They had been molded by a string of wars and a period of economic dynamism. They benefited from the new situation in terms of job prospects and general expectations. As the feudalization of the middle classes deepened, they gravitated upward toward the upper classes. They saw their status and privileges threatened, not by the aristocracy, but by the proletariat. They had never felt the lower classes to be allies, whether actual or potential, in an emancipatory struggle. Their minds were fallow ground for Social Darwinism.

In terms of expectations and horizons the two generations had different backgrounds and starting points. For Storm's generation the overwhelming emotion was satisfaction at having progressed so far from the 1830s and 1840s. For people formed by years of economic dynamism and national expansion, their parents' contentment with the status quo came to seem stuffy and provincial. Many of Storm's generation had grown up in a still largely rural country. Unless they had lived in the pockets of early industrial growth or economic dislocation, they had hardly been confronted with the factory proletariat before 1848. Themselves products of small, pre-industrial towns with their traditional network of artisans, laborers and servants, many of them found it difficult to think in terms of the large-scale capitalist ventures that emerged in the 1870s and 1880s. On the other hand, the inner logic of capitalism and of this vast accretion of national power, coupled with growing social and economic tensions, generated pressures and demands for further expansion: in the 1880s the clamor for colonial and imperialist ventures grew. In the administrative and professional infrastructure of the state the influence of liberal-democratic ideas shrank as 1848ers retired and died, to be replaced in the 1880s by an influx of conservative civil servants. Liberal professors like Virchow and Mommsen were replaced by a different breed.

After 1875 the themes which constitute the great continuities in Storm's fiction remain, but in modified forms. His hostility to the aristocracy persisted; but he could not forcefully articulate this criticism in fictions with a contemporary setting. Furthermore, however anxious he was to dislodge the aristocratic component, he had no desire to bring down the whole sociopolitical edifice in the process. Perhaps even more important than his own subjective position was the perception of others: he could not afford to be thought of as aiding the socialists. The middle classes' attitude toward the aristocracy had changed. In a society where becoming an officer in the reserve, having oneself photographed in uniform, and having one's rank printed on one's visiting card were the crowning ambition of many middle-class sons, Storm had to tread carefully. He tended therefore to move into past periods since it was altogether less dangerous to reinforce hostility to the Junkers and the aristocratic principle by depicting Junkers in past centuries mistreating their serfs and resisting all attempts to liberalize and humanize society than it was to show their descendants engaged in the equivalent contemporary actions. Like his contemporary C.F. Meyer, he recognized that historical subjects, besides being popular, provided him with a useful mask and preserved the conventional distinction between art and life.

In his later works direct contemporary criticism of the nobility is limited to *John Riew'* (1885) where the aristocrat's offense – picking up a lower-class girl and slinking off back to his estate having made her pregnant – hardly exhausts the problem of the aristocracy in Wilhelminian Germany. By projecting the emancipatory struggle for humanitarian principles back into the past, Storm may have secured himself a means of suggesting the need for continued struggle in present and future; but this ploy meant that he portrayed struggles between aristocrats and aspiring, educated, or would-be educated and professional members of the third estate. In Bismarckian Germany any searching critique of the aristocracy had to assume new forms. The problem was that criticism of the nobility and of the feudalization of the middle classes could now hardly be kept separate. Storm could not afford to pursue that topic even with the radicalness of the original version of *Immensee* and of *Auf der Universität*. In *Der Herr Etatsrat* the criticism of life in a student corps focuses on drinking, duelling and general dissoluteness. It does not dwell on other anti-democratic, anti-humanitarian behavior. Heinrich Mann's *Der Untertan* is still far away.

The same considerations apply to another of Storm's lifelong preoccupations, the relationship between individual and society/state. He may have resisted the elitist individualism of the type advocated by Paul Heyse and stressed the need to uphold institutions and binding legal arrangements like the family; but his concern was to safeguard the welfare of individuals threatened by libertarian actions, not to enhance the power of the state.[1] He never adopted the view that the state's demands transcended the rights and aspirations of individuals or that individuals only acquired a true identity by being parts of this greater whole. Resistance to alienating social norms and pressures remained the distinctive feature of his heroes and heroines. However, as with his critique of the aristocracy, this resistance had to be projected backward. He could not show present-day individuals locked in bitter struggle with the state. To have depicted persecuted Catholics or harried socialists would also have put huge strains on his own principles.

There is no suggestion in his later work that national power is a positive value and that national struggles are life-enhancing. It is true that he indulges in some ethnic stereotyping in the novella *Es waren zwei Königskinder*(1884) where the tragic hero inherits a less than happy genetic make-up from a Swabian father

1. Storm to Heyse, 21 January 1875, *Storm-Heyse* 1, p. 100.

and a French mother. But his tragedy springs essentially from his class prejudices *vis-à-vis* a girl of inferior status and education; from his sense of disgrace at having been humiliated at the police station after insulting a soldier when he was drunk; and from his fear of getting a criminal record and finding himself in the newspapers.

Having always refused to exalt material values at the expense of civilian ones and criticized the ethos and practices of the Prussian army, Storm did not revise his judgement in a state where the officer class was erected into a privileged "estate" and where the army virtually became a state within the state. Yet, with rare exceptions, one has to look at the way in which he depicts armies and war in past ages to recognize how far removed his stance was from the dominant one.

7.2   The Uses of History

Until the mid-1860s Storm had subscribed to the liberal belief in the irresistible march of progress. Events made him revise his expectations and modify his categories. He had to recognize that elaborating and implementing enlightened ideas and principles had been a long and painful process in the past and that the struggle would be equally painful in the future. At the same time he recognized the importance of stimulating in his readers a sense that history was an ongoing process and that prevailing arrangements did not represent some final state of affairs. It was also crucial to resist the attempts being made to usurp the Enlightenment principle of progress and equate it with the accretion of national power. Above all Storm refused to make literature a reflection of political and diplomatic history with their concentration on the doings of the great and powerful. He rejected this perspective "from above" and its tendency to equate might with right and the real with the ideal. The eighteenth-century middle-class novel and drama had challenged the aesthetic hierarchies buttressing the social and political hierarchies. By resisting any refeudalization or re-aristocratization of literature and treating the lives of characters who did not walk the boards of official history, he could preserve a perspective favorable to the under-privileged.

Many penetrating observations have been made on the subject

of Storm's sense of the transience of all things, and critics have rightly highlighted his concern with preserving the memory of the past. However, by interpreting this as a private, existential concern, they often obscured its function as part of Storm's attempt to keep alive the memory of those individuals whose lives and actions found no place in official histories or in older literature. While other writers were concentrating on the great artistic and intellectual "geniuses" and "heroes," indeed naming ages after them, Storm regarded as equally heroic the struggles of lesser mortals either responding to nascent progressive ideas or themselves seeking to elaborate such ideas and articulate their own frustrated aspirations despite inner inhibitions and external obstacles. Their struggle corresponded to the attempts being made in the present by individuals like himself to safeguard alternative principles in a hostile environment. He wrote history against the official grain. His "heroes" are figures like a minor painter (*Aquis submersus*), the daughter of a sick farmer (*Renate*) or a dikegrave in a small Frisian community (*Der Schimmelreiter*).

Given the social distribution of literacy – or rather the socio-political organization of illiteracy – in past societies and the monopoly of the powerful and rich over the labor of artists and writers, few records remained of plebeian lives and struggles in memories, chronicles, documents, and paintings. While any orally transmitted records that had survived were liable to ideological distortion, it was especially when plebeian characters found their way into official histories that they were made to serve the interests of the dominant social group. Much of nineteenth-century critical exegesis had been devoted to getting beyond eighteenth-century notions of deceiving priests and charlatan prophets in order to illuminate the process whereby often meagre historical data was transformed into myth and legend. Developing this primitive sociology of knowledge, Storm would himself attempt to illuminate this process.

Storm had to revise his analysis of the mechanism by which enlightened, humanitarian principles emerged in the course of history. He no longer believed that ethical and intellectual progress had been one long harmonious natural process. Indeed what is striking about works written from the mid-70s onward is the injection of a new element of bitter, often bloody struggle. Faced by similar setbacks in terms of his liberal- Protestant view of the course of history, C.F. Meyer had adopted a position akin to

Storm's in his verse epic *Huttens letzte Tage* (1871). In *Das Amulett*(1873) and *Jürg Jenatsch*(1874) he set enlightened figures in a world of fanaticism and *Realpolitik*. After 1875, Storm, too, began to depict past champions of humanitarian principles struggling, sometimes for their lives, in feudal, aristocratic societies. He showed them confronted with barbaric behavior and caste exclusiveness on the part of the aristocracy and intolerant dogmatism on the part of the church – while also having to combat their own ingrained political subservience and orthodox Christian values. In addition, they had to contend with subservience, superstition, and petty-minded egoism in the very people whom their reforms and enlightened principles were intended to benefit.

In *Aquis submersus, Renate, Eekenhof,* and *Der Schimmelreiter* Storm portrays these heroes/heroines as isolated individuals with little, if any, institutional support and little backing except from close relatives and isolated enlightened persons. In *Aquis submersus* the hero Johannes is not only physically crushed by the system; he is also defeated ideologically.[2] Initially he believes that he can overcome aristocratic caste prejudices and live happily with his boyhood sweetheart, the aristocratic Katharina, if not in feudal Schleswig-Holstein, then in Holland where state and society have progressed further toward democracy. However, if even the first part of his memoirs ends with his hopes dashed, the second part shows him endorsing the orthodox Lutheran categories that underpin the socio-political status quo.

The 1870s and 1880s, decades in which the state and influential pressure groups were developing unprecedented skills in influencing public opinion, sharpened Storm's awareness of the obstacles facing those individuals who, in any age, attempt to formulate alternative ideas and to organize support for them. His position as one of a dwindling number of democrats in a world dominated by contrary forces helps explain his predilection for epochs like the second half of the seventeenth century and the early eighteenth century in Schleswig-Holstein, when Enlightenment could be shown struggling to assert itself in a world still dark and brutal. Isolated attempts to challenge the feudal system and orthodoxy could still be easily defeated. The most individu-

---

2. See D.A. Jackson, "Die Überwindung der Schuld in 'Aquis submersus'." *STSG*, vol. 21, 1972, pp. 45–56.

als could hope for was to create some private refuge, as in *Renate*. But, as in *Zur Chronik von Grieshuus,* war and violence constantly threatened to destroy it. At the same time, if an individual aristocrat's attempts to challenge the feudal system founder, his practical achievement in eradicating wolves from the area remains. Concentrating solely on the defeat of progressive individuals might have encouraged pessimism and resignation. Readers had to be provided with a historical perspective and a sense that, whatever the setbacks, important advances had nevertheless been made since the times evoked in a particular novella.

The use in one and the same story of various historical periods offered one solution to this problem. A framework set in the present with a "modern" fictional narrator could be juxtaposed with a past historical epoch and past fictional narrators. The latter could either exemplify past mentalities or – a more challenging option – the conflict in one and the same person between traditional positions and forward-looking ones. Had Storm suggested that all was sweetness and light in the present, he would have played into the hands of those who, while ready to concede abuses in the past, maintained that they had now been rectified. By often choosing as his modern reference point a date in the pre-1848 period, he could suggest that much had still to be done. Readers left, so to speak, on the threshold of a truly humanitarian age, might be stimulated to ask why this potential had not been realized.

Thus, in the framework of *Aquis submersus*, the Protestant church, as symbolized by the pastor father of the narrator's friend, seems on the way to becoming untheological and humane. A society can be glimpsed where human beings accept humanitarianism and have left behind notions of sin and guilt. The wars and class divisions of the inner story seem a thing of the past. Why then, readers in 1876 might be prompted to ask, had they just lived through a series of bloody wars and why did they still not enjoy the benefits of a democratic, humanitarian state and society? This strategy of juxtaposing old and new times also allowed Storm to suggest that institutions and mentalities once dominant had either disappeared or were crumbling and that ideas branded godless and evil in past epochs were now part of the moral and intellectual consensus among educated people. This process could not be permanently halted.

In the later 1870s and 1880s Storm's confidence in the forward march of enlightened ideas was, however, further eroded. He was forced to recognize that progressive ideas were not making the inroads which he had earlier predicted. As the lower classes drifted either to socialism or remained solidly conservative, he inclined to the view that there was perhaps a deep-seated superstitious and irrational streak in people. Thus from *Renate* onward he depicts situations where people living in the present are still as bigoted and credulous as their ancestors despite the fact that enlightened aspirations have stirred and in some cases even triumphed many years before. Public opinion is shown transforming into malefactors and devilish figures those who deserve to be considered the benefactors of humanity. This problem lies at the heart of *Der Schimmelreiter*. By 1888 Storm had come a long way from his Vormärz vision of the *Volksseele*. Then it had seemed as if democratic writers only had to unlock and articulate the positive aspirations of the popular soul. At the end of his life he had no illusions on this score. The old order could perpetuate itself so successfully only because its ideology and propaganda were congenial to innate human tendencies. Once again one can see this as reflecting Storm's own sense of isolation and impotence in a world split between conservatives and socialists. The *Volk* had failed to respond in the prescribed way. The conclusion which he drew from this was not that his ideology needed revising; instead he found the lower classes themselves lacking. While not abandoning a belief in some overall principle of progress, he tended to see history more and more as a manichean struggle – often in one and the same person – between the forces of light and darkness.

7.3 Presenting the Middle Classes

In the 1850s and 1860s German liberal writers were preoccupied with achieving German national unity and promoting a capitalist economy. The middle classes had to be presented positively as the motors of change. In Britain, in contrast, where a national capitalist economy had been established much earlier, state and society were sufficiently stable after the 1840s and the accommodation between landed aristocracy and industrial meritocracy also sufficiently secure for middle-class writers to be able to criticize defects without fearing that they would bring down the whole system in the process. They could criticize the moral deficiencies of individual hard-hearted, utilitarian capitalists, and even dwell on suffering and hardship. But the solutions they advocated were a humanized capitalism, Christian charity and philanthropy, and working-class self-help. Property and private ownership of the means of production were left intact. The labor movement was gradually integrated into the parliamentary system and remained under Liberal tutelage.

In Germany, although demands for a national, capitalist market had been met by the early 1870s, the integration of the proletariat into the system had not been achieved. Democrats, who had seen themselves as spearheading the struggle for humanitarianism, found themselves outflanked by the socialists. The latter claimed to have donned the mantle of humanitarianism and communitarian ideals. They demanded more than mere formal legal and political rights; their criticism was directed not just against the aristocracy and the church, but also against the middle classes. A democrat like Storm was in a dilemma. Unwilling to adopt National-Liberal positions, he was equally not prepared to make the transition to democratic socialism. It was one thing to criticize the middle classes from within a middle-class framework; it was another to move outside these bounds and call into question his own relatively privileged social, political, and economic position. He was too convinced of the educated middle classes' ethical and intellectual prowess to be able to conspire for their downfall.

The Bismarckian establishment's anxieties about the permanence of the empire complicated matters. Obsessed with threats, real or imaginary, it denounced Catholic, Polish, and French elements and, of course, socialists. But this only increased these groups' alienation and, by heightening tensions, magnified the doubts it was intended to remove. Sensitivity grew about artistic depictions deemed to undermine the status quo. In compiling the second edition of his lyric anthology Storm ultimately did not include Freiligrath's "Ein Dampfer auf dem Rhein" even though he recognized it to be a "really significant" *Zeitgedicht*.[3] One did not, however, have to preach revolution to arouse hostility. Indeed, the authorities could deal with crude, frontal attacks, which also would not grace the pages of popular middle-class magazines. Those most suspect were writers catering for

3. Storm to Heyse, 22 February 1874, *Storm-Heyse* 1, p. 69.

the middle classes and identifying with a great many of their norms while at the same time offering disturbing images of middle-class society.

The attacks on Storm for betraying poetic realism (see pp. 230f.) may have been couched in aesthetic terms, but socio-political issues were at stake, too. When friends like Wilhelm Petersen and Wilhelm Jensen reproached him with pessimism, what was also at issue was his judgement on Wilhelminian Germany. *Carsten Curator*(1878) sent uneasy tremors through friends and relatives. Earlier Storm had been convinced of the "divinity" of the family. He had seen it affording support, security, and consolation. But here there is no human redeemer. Neither wife nor father can save Heinrich from his inherited weaknesses. Father and son must each bear his cross. Carsten becomes the long-suffering man of sorrows who sacrifices his only beloved son in a vain attempt to save his daughter-in-law Anna. He agonizes as his son, like Jesus Christ on the cross, clings to a pole above the swirling flood and – again like Christ – calls out for his father (LL 2, 518f.). The strain and shock induce a stroke. But it was especially the depiction of Heinrich which disturbed friends like Erich Schmidt. In his view, there was no place in literature for such a figure. He reminded Schmidt of those traveling salesmen who swindled people and then squandered their earnings in St Pauli (i.e. the red light area of Hamburg). The final section on Anna's spiritual development and the grandson's sound genetic make-up had clearly not compensated for all the unsettling reflections provoked by the work. Storm knew that if magazine readers were to share Schmidt's sentiments, he could abandon any ambition of being a regular contributor to prestigious magazines like the *Deutsche Rundschau* and *Westermanns Monatshefte*. No editor could afford to tolerate an author whose works subscribers found unappetizing, embarrassing, or sordid.

Carsten Curator was followed in 1881 by *Der Herr Etatsrat*. Storm chose as his "hero" a dike-inspector of aristocratic rank who exploits his son, denies him any proper education, turns him into an alcoholic, receives the news of his death with total unconcern, and refuses to pay his debts. Described in turn as a bear, a beetle, and a primeval monster emerging from the beach, he neither feeds nor educates his daughter, allows her to be corrupted and seduced in the family home by the scoundrely Käfer (=beetle), and feels neither remorse nor sadness when she dies in childbirth. Coarsened as a corps student, he indulges in perverse, blasphemous bouts of drinking and music-making in front of his "altar." They invariably end with him writhing about on the floor, like a beetle on its back, drunk and in a state of undress. He treats young girls like whores or vaudeville girls, sings coarse student songs in their presence, and incites them to drink his punch. Notions of progress and evolution are stood on their head. *Bildung* is here a hollow perversion. The gap yawns wide between the hero's rhetoric and bombast and his moral depravity. His language has no connection with contemporary reality and practice – except to mask and ignore them.

Storm chose a narrator who himself is not a subversive outsider, but an educated professional man. As a "decent" young man, he fails – like a Henry James character – to register the full horror and significance of things unthinkable and unmentionable in polite society. Indeed it is only because a neighbor sneaks in through a gap in the garden fence and peeps in through an uncurtained window that the hero's orgies are known of at all. But if this device spared Storm being too explicit, the conflict between the narrator's schoolboy notions of individual enterprise, heroic courage, and idealism, and the reality of the Etatsrat's family life could hardly have induced in the reader a sense that all was well in middle-class society. The behavior of other circles in the town and at the university must have been equally disquieting. The distance between what the narrator sees and grasps and what the text itself suggests protected Storm against the charge of explicit prurience but it did nothing to reassure readers or suggest that the incidents in the story were atypical. In a key scene (LL 3, 54) the narrator attempts to find out more details about the Etatsrat's daughter, Phia, whom the other young ladies in the town treat like a pariah. His sister immediately leaves the room, and an aunt remarks: "Das sind keine Dinge für die Ohren einer jungen Dame." Storm was faced by a dilemma: on the one hand, these things had to be exposed and victims presented as victims needing love and support, not as moral reprobates to be shunned. On the other hand, he knew that his public would not tolerate uncloaked presentation of such issues, especially not in popular magazines which could fall into the hands of young ladies. Storm's Poetic-Realist reliance on concrete, "poetic" techniques of presentation may have debarred discussion of such issues; but the techniques were themselves part of the problem: they were the only tolerated means of adumbrating such topics at all.

Westermann insisted on changes to the manuscript "in usum delphini oder delphinarum,"[4] and the various versions document the stylistic consequences of such censorship. Thus originally Storm wrote: ". . . bis der Herr Etatsrath, immer noch bei Gesang und Spiel, zuletzt in greuelvoller Nacktheit (amended to Unbekleidung) dasaß" (LL 3, 783f.). In the magazine version this read: ". . . bis der Geist aus einigen weiteren Gläsern den Herrn Etatsrath über alle Schwere und Unbequemlichkeit des irdischen Leibes hinausgehoben hatte" (LL 3, 783). For the final book version he amended the passage again, but only to "bis er zuletzt in greuelvoller Unbekleidung dasaß" (LL 3, 13). In the manuscript the Etatsrath's behavior at Phia's funeral was described with stark brevity: "Als man sich dem Platz des Herrn Etatsraths näherte, winkte er herablassend mit der Hand. 'Sie hat sich noch recht schönes Wetter ausgesucht zu ihrem letzten Gange!' rief er dem Gefolge zu und stieß dann wieder seine blauen Wolken in die Luft. Hierauf betrat der Zug den Kirchhof und der Sarg mit den beiden Kindern wurde eingesenkt" (LL 3, 792). This was softened for magazine publication. The final book version was, however, still much more conciliatory than the original:

> Als der Zug unterhalb des Altanes angelangt war, scheuchte der Herr Etatsrat den blauen Tabaksqualm zur Seite, indem er herablassend gegen das Gefolge grüßte. "Contra vim mortis, meine Freunde! Contra vim mortis!" rief er und schüttelte mit kondolierender Gebärde seine runde Hand; "aber recht schönes Wetter hat sie sich noch zu ihrem letzten Gange ausgesucht!"
>
> Der Zug hatte bei diesen Worten bereits die Kirchhofsschwelle überschritten, und bald waren die beiden armen Kinder in die für sie geöffnete Gruft hinabgesenkt. (LL 3, 56)

In similar fashion Storm toned down the depiction of the lifestyle of a student corps (see LL 3, 767f.).

At a time when middle-class minds were concerned about the rise of socialism, it was unwise to draw too much attention to middle-class failings. Yet *Hans und Heinz Kirch* (1882) does precisely that. In the character of Hans Kirch it criticizes the human bankruptcy of petty-bourgeois social ambitions; in the

---

4. See LL 3, pp. 770f.

figure of his son-in-law the aspirations and lifestyle of an "upwardly-mobile" bourgeois; and in the figure of the pastor humbug and windy patriotism. But the most telling indictment of this society is the fact that a father and sister are shown literally denying the very existence of their son and brother because he does not conform to their standards of respectability, professional success, morality, and good manners. The text suggests that this son denied for thirty shillings is the true, contemporary Son of Man.

It was equally bold on Storm's part to choose as his heroine a barmaid-cum-prostitute in a harbor pub. Wieb is contrasted with Hans Kirch's eminently respectable daughter. A lower-class Mary Magdalen/Virgin Mary, who in all her degradation retains a purity of heart, was an affront to conventional standards. But – and this is crucial – the text distances itself from any socialist critique by introducing (LL 3, 128f.) an obnoxious Social Democrat. Such specific labeling is unique in Storm's work. The novella relies on an appeal to the reader's human feelings and a call for a change of heart. Wieb does not become a socialist; instead this victim of middle-class norms is shown caring for old Kirch. Her "true Christianity" does not affect the son-in-law's socio-economic position; nor does it alter the ongoing social production of other victims like herself.

7.4 Critic and Custodian of Conventional Morality

Since the self-identity of the middle classes was so bound up with their organization of family life, work, and business, any mirror held up to them was expected to confirm the moral excellence of these arrangements. Writers indulging their private subversive ruminations in scholarly tomes or even in expensively priced books were one thing; putting question marks behind conventional norms and infringing taboos in magazines which lay about in drawing-rooms was another. The effect of works on impressionable young ladies became a prime concern. It had, after all, long been wives and daughters trapped in the home who had been the main consumers of literature. To be deemed unsuitable reading for them was the death sentence on any magazine contributor. Parents had to be convinced that in presenting a tasteful, expensive miniature volume at Christmas or on some festive occasion, they were not introducing corruption into an innocent daughter's heart.

In an age without radio and T.V. and still dependent on candles and lamps, reading was still a social, family activity. Indeed, if literature was to perform a democratic, humanitarian function, it could not retire from middle-class drawing- or living-rooms to the salons and cafés of bohemian and artistic cliques. Elitist notions of art for the few, of a literature uncoupled from social reality were alien to Storm. But the corollary was that literature had to remain suitable for general consumption. A story had to offer something to everyone. Young people had to be catered for as well as discriminating, highly educated listeners. Given the classical-idealist definition of art it was possible to accept such constraints and still tackle disturbing topics – on condition that one abided by certain rules. Provided that women, young people, and children were not offended or directly confronted with incidents and characters which could shake their "idealistic" view of the world, adult males could savor other, more subtle dimensions built into a work of art. Storm, for example, wrote of Heyse's atheist work *Kinder der Welt* (1873) that the intellectual content was so absorbed into the plot and the depiction of characters that many a lady would have read the novel without becoming conscious of it.[5] Not that this was any guarantee against readers denouncing works or others feeling bound to alert potential readers to what in their view were pernicious ideas. No matter what precautions one took, one could not satisfy the bigoted – as Storm found in the reaction of Friederike Hornung to *Aquis submersus* (see LL 2, 927f.). Even readers like Heinrich Keck, the Husum headmaster, branded Heyse's novel "pure godlessness" and declared in a review in the *Deutsches Literaturblatt* in 1885 that *John Riew'* and *Ein Fest auf Haderslevhuus* were among those of Storm's works which were not suitable for the family table and for domestic reading.[6]

The strictness with which middle-class society demanded at least outward observance of moral conventions paradoxically promoted a readiness, both conscious and unconscious, on the part of many readers to collude with authors seeking to broach

5. Storm to Heyse, 9 July 1873, *Storm-Heyse* 1, p. 60.
6. Storm to Heyse, 9 July 1873, *Storm-Heyse* 1, p. 61; *Deutsches Literaturblatt*, no. 39, 26 December 1885.

taboo topics. Provided authors did not provoke moral indignation, they could survive; indeed they were welcome. But it was a thin line. Storm himself both criticized and upheld prevailing moral standards. His novellas may, for example, have urged understanding and sympathy for certain categories of people conventionally deemed dishonorable and immoral, but on other issues his stance was much closer to accepted norms. Moreover, as a citizen living with his family in Husum and Hademarschen, he was as much subject to society's constraints as any other inhabitant. Whatever his subjective position on certain issues, he could not afford to see a member of his family fall foul of established morality and become a social pariah. In such a climate it is often difficult to distinguish between an individual's personal convictions and the stance necessitated by fears of social consequences. There was always a real possibility of guilt by association. "Shame" could blight whole families.

Storm's letters to his son Karl in the early 1870s abound in the words *bürgerlich* and *Bildung*. Thus Karl was to lodge with an educated, middle-class family rather than with respectable artisans. In fact the difference in cost prevented this. He was to pay regular social visits to educated families since this would enable him to acquire general *Bildung* and meet women very different from those with whom students normally came into contact. He was always to go suitably attired, i.e. wearing kid-gloves![7] Visits to the opera and theater, like reading the works of Goethe and Schiller, would further facilitate entry into this world. Beneath it lay one of sordid lodgings, student pubs and prostitutes, one which could blight health, finances, and future career. Despite his attachment to the world of respectable artisans and his understanding for *die kleinen Leute* theirs was not the world Storm envisaged for his children. Nor was it the world into which they would sink if they fell off the middle-class ladder to respectability.

Once Karl became a music teacher in Varel, Storm was concerned that he should consort with civil servants and their families and not relegate himself to second- or third-class society.[8] Thoughts of the very different fees he could charge went hand in hand with the conviction that one could only lead a full and beautiful

7. Storm to Karl, 8 October 1873.
8. Storm to Karl, 18 March 1879.

life in such circles. Whatever the abuses and depravity to be found there, they were, in Storm's eyes, the exception, not the rule. When rumors circulated that Karl had behaved in an unseemly fashion to young girl pupils, Storm knew that he would have to bring a court case to clear his reputation. Otherwise Karl could have fallen outside the pale of decent society – and become a further burden on his finances. As it was, provided his syphilis was kept a guarded secret, he could maintain a modest standard of living and accumulate capital for the future.

Hans's alcoholism not only threatened to exclude him from respectable society; it could also prejudice his sisters' marriage prospects. In addition, it consumed money which could have swelled their dowries. Whenever any of his daughters attempted to run Hans's household, Storm remained fearful of exposing them to his drunken bouts and degradation and conscious that their reputation could be affected. Although for a few brief years in the early 1880s Hans was largely able to support himself as a doctor and, well away from Husum and Hademarschen, was less of a social liability, Storm could not shake off the fear that his condition would worsen and that he as his father would have to settle further debts and pay hospital or asylum bills. If, as seemed likely at the end of his life, Hans were to marry a working-class girl, he could also be held legally responsible for supporting any dependents.[9]

The possibility that his daughters might fail to retain middle-class status bred chronic anxieties. Without dowries or capital they could be forced out of the world of middle-class respectable leisure and supervisory domesticity. His obsessions with predatory male sexuality and fears of seduction, pregnancy, and *déclassement* made him adopt an increasingly conservative definition of women's role. Aware of the problems facing any young woman who did not make the smooth transition from virginal "rosebud" to salon rose, matron and mother, he encouraged both Lisbeth and Elsabe to study music even though this strained his finances. Haunted as he was by fears of dying a poor man, he could then at least die with the reassuring knowledge that they were in a position to fend for themselves. Further, as music teachers, they would maintain close links with the world of *Bildung* and respectable society. But, ideally, he envisaged them married.

9. Storm to Karl, 6 June 1886.

Having given up her studies and married, Lisbeth revealingly commented that her true vocation was to be a housewife.[10] Storm would have been horrified had he lived to see his daughter Gertrud forced to open a boarding-house like Marthe in *Marthe und ihre Uhr*.

In his earlier novellas he may have stressed the overriding rights of love and the need to resist parental pressure; but in the 1870s and 1880s his practice was very different. Thus he was uneasy about granting the very formal and proper request of a young man, Hermann Kirchner, to be allowed to make his daughter Lucie's closer acquaintance. Even though Kirchner seemed a decent young man, Storm did not want to see his daughter married to a pharmacist without his own business – or a Catholic. On the other hand, he did not want to seem "the barbaric father, who destroys everything from the outset."[11] His brother Otto was instructed to allow Lucie to see Kirchner a few times "natürlich wie jeden andern jungen Mann und ohne nähere Beziehung." Otto was always to accompany her home!

Storm's growing conservatism is evident in letters to Hermione von Preuschen in which he declares it to be far more important for a woman to be domesticated and pay extreme care to her appearance than to strive for intellectual or artistic development and independence.[12] Men, he alleged, paid more attention to a woman's hair and dress than to anything else.[13] When, after the ending of her engagement, Lucie voiced ideas of going to Berlin or Paris, he would not countenance the idea. Instead his daughters were farmed out to relatives and friends to adorn their drawing rooms and learn womanly ways. If finances permitted, they were allowed to spend the season in places like Erfurt. There they could hope to make a suitable match. Strict, unwritten social rules had to be observed. Thus a young lady could act as a lady's companion and governess without losing social status and any hope of finding a bridegroom – but only if she received no salary and remained one of the family. In contrast, as an employee, one

10. Lisbeth to Karl, 6 June 1879, SHLB.
11. Storm to Otto Storm, 23 September 1878, in private possession, copy in Storm Society Archive, Husum.
12. Storm to H.v. Preuschen, 16 December 1873, *STSG*, vol. 22, 1973, p. 69.
13. Storm to H.v. Preuschen, 27 December 1878, ibid., p. 81.

was excluded from the family and polite society.[14] Any young lady studying with a view to supporting herself in the future was liable to be deemed *persona ingrata* in respectable circles. Despite all the letters of recommendation provided by her father, who personally travelled with her to Weimar to facilitate her entry into polite society, Elsabe experienced this reaction. Storm commended her for accepting it.[15] On the other hand, he was horrified at the thought of Lucie becoming a sales assistant in Bad Kissingen. That was simply unthinkable for a daughter of Theodor Storm![16] It is little wonder that, frustrated at every turn, Lucie developed all sorts of nervous complaints and had to be treated in an expensive clinic in Kiel. The reassuring confidence that Lisbeth, his eldest daughter, was happily married also turned out to be misplaced. After an adulterous affair with a parishioner, his son-in-law, Gustav Haase, a free-thinking Protestant frustrated with the lack of intellectual stimulus in Heiligenhafen, found himself forced to move to an even more uncongenial post in rural Grube. It is, of course, possible that Storm may never have known of the true reason for the move; but it is most unlikely. It is much more probable that positive comments on the new post and a total absence in his letters of any references to the adulterous affair reflect an attempt on his part to safeguard at least something of his family's reputation.[17]

In a climate where one was compelled to guard one's reputation jealously, people tended to become self-appointed custodians of morality on the look out for the failings of others. Storm was no exception. Writers made disapproving noises at each other's lapses from good taste. Moreover, a gentle or not so gentle word before publication might save a colleague and friend greater discomfiture later. The best defense was often attack. Thus Storm argued that the works of Heinrich von Kleist and Gottfried Keller were more "suspect" than his own and found scenes in Keller's and Heyse's works ugly and unappetizing.[18] He could not stomach a drama by Ada Christen on sexual love between mother and son, and was nonplussed by homosexual poems.[19] Keller, Storm,

---

14. Storm to Petersen, 3 June 1881, *Storm-Petersen*, pp. 100ff.
15. Lisbeth had experienced the same fate in Stuttgart. See Storm to Schmidt, 9 March 1878, *Storm-Schmidt* 1, p. 87.
16. Storm to Lucie, 30 November 1883, SHLB.
17. See chap. 6, note 46.

and Heyse would disagree as to whether they had succeeded in transforming life into art and lent artistic acceptability to something which in its raw state was simply sordid. Moral and aesthetic judgements were often inseparable. Thus Storm attributed Keller's lapses to the fact that he was a bachelor with a rumored drinking problem and could not count on the advice of a wife or female audience. He did not fight shy of tackling him on specific works.[20] Partly riled, partly wrily amused by Storm's prim moralizing, Keller paid him back in kind when his *Der Herr Etatsrat* appeared.[21]

Assessing what readers would tolerate was by no means easy. Storm paid careful attention to women's reaction to new works when he read them out in the home or in a social gathering. Even if the verdict was only that a work was charming or delightful,[22] such a reaction was reassuring. Friends like Erich Schmidt or Wilhelm Petersen were invaluable in pointing out artistic shortcomings; but they were just as important as sounding-boards by which Storm could gauge the educated public's likely responses to a work. In fields like politics or religion he had learned over the years what was permissible. But in addressing topics like marriage, the family, and sex he often found himself in a minefield of his own making. The problems which were preying on his mind and drove him to write drew him into areas where his antennae for sensing danger failed him. Not that he was careless. It was simply that he could not anticipate every reaction. He might go to great pains to present a disturbing topic in terms that he considered beyond reproach, only to find readers took offense at things that he had not even regarded as potential risks.

Although in the late 1870s and early 1880s he was preoccupied with Karl's fears of the tertiary stages of syphilis, Storm could not discuss the matter with anyone except his wife, his doctor brother, Aemil, and his son Hans. Himself a doctor, Hans had both had the disease and taken a keen interest in it as a student.

---

18. See, for example, Storm to Heyse, 24 June 1872, *Storm-Heyse* 1, p. 44, and Storm to Schmidt, 15 March 1881, *Storm-Schmidt* 2, p. 35. See further J. Michielsen, "Theodor Storm als Kritiker Paul Heyses." *STSG*, vol. 26, 1977, pp. 57–66.
19. Storm to Heyse, 13 December 1882, *Storm-Heyse* 3, pp. 39, 203f.
20. E.g. *Das Sinngedicht*. Storm to Keller, 15 March 1881, *Storm-Keller*, pp. 74f.
21. Keller to Storm, 25 September 1881, ibid., pp. 101f.
22. See *Storm-Esmarch*, pp. 65, 115 and *Storm-Schmidt* 2, pp. 51, 79.

He, like Aemil, would treat his brother. If letters referring to
Hans's alcoholism had to be burned and compromising passages
made illegible,[23] the stigma attached to syphilis was even greater.
A known syphilitic in a family could destroy its reputation. Aemil
was sworn to secrecy, Karl was to bring medicines and creams
home with him in order to avoid having to buy them from the
local pharmacist. His mercury-inhalation treatment was presented
as a cure for a chest and throat infection.

Topics like syphilis were as taboo in art as they were in life.
On the other hand, Storm had such a need to tackle the problem
of Karl's obsessions that he sidestepped the topic of insanity
produced by tertiary syphilis and substituted for it fears about
the recurrence of mental illness after a mental breakdown. In
Schweigen (1883) the latter's possible manifestations are, however,
conveyed in forms equally applicable to syphilis. But moral taboos
and inhibitions even affected Storm's treatment of mental illness.
Rudolph's original breakdown had to be attributed to the pressures
of a new job and readers convinced that he is cured from the
outset. His subsequent psychological disturbance is presented as
resulting purely from his inability to confess his breakdown to
his fiancée/wife. Once he brings himself to do so, he immediately
knows that he is indeed cured and has nothing to fear. There
is no possibility of mental illness recurring given the blessings
of marriage. Because it no doubt came close to what often actually
occurred, neither Storm nor his readers would have tolerated a
novella in which a mother seeks a healthy, well-balanced bride
for her son in the hope that she could prove his salvation. If
deception with regard to mental illness was taboo, concealment
of a son's past syphilitic infection was "unthinkable" – precisely
because, one also suspects, it did so frequently occur, bringing
in its wake disastrous results. Storm himself attributed a string
of stillbirths and infant deaths in Otto's family to congenital
syphilis. Rudolph may confess his mental illness to his wife, but
a hero confessing to a venereal infection and receiving understanding and support was another matter.

Women's liberation became an issue in the 1880s. In Storm's
case fears about assertive women lent a new attractiveness to the
ideal of the pale, innocent virgin, which he had rejected in his
earlier works but which had returned in the early 1870s. In *Ein*

23. Storm to Heyse, 9 May 1879, *Storm-Heyse* 2, p. 45.

Fest auf Haderslevhuus, he presented these issues in a medieval setting. C.F. Meyer had led the way with his *Die Hochzeit des Mönchs'* (1884) and its early-Renaissance setting, and he returned to the theme in *Die Richterin* (1885), which is set in medieval Switzerland. Storm's text presents a younger man married to a widow determined that her second husband will satisfy her sexual needs and do her bidding. The sex scenes are as explicit as Storm could afford to be. In theory, the text could have presented the husband Rolf's "romantic" love for an innocent girl, Dagmar, as an ideal alternative which founders on the reef of social, moral, and legal obstacles. But Storm's obsession with any pre- or extra-marital sex and with the danger of transmitting venereal diseases was such that Rolf's passion for this frail, would-be Isolde wreaks havoc and death in a family already decimated by the plague(!). The text suggests the folly of Dagmar's wish to emulate the girl in Hartmann von Aue's *Der arme Heinrich* who hopes to restore her sick master to health by sacrificing her own body (LL 3, 409). To make the subject poetic, to turn life into art, Storm added sentimental, operatic elements, as he had done in *Schweigen*.

In some areas Storm was concerned to promote a revision of moral value-judgements and social behavior and had a clear vision of where the problem lay. In others, however, his criticism of attitudes and arrangements was much more entangled with the norms of the educated middle class to which he belonged. Given the social pressures on him, his partial collusion with the system and the drawbacks of his Poetic-Realist techniques, Storm's actual, as opposed to his hoped-for, critical impact was small.

8

Literature at the Crossroads

8.1 Heredity

As a theme, heredity, like milieu, tends to be associated with the naturalist movement, especially the novels of Emile Zola and the dramas of Henrik Ibsen. As such it belongs to the attack on bourgeois society mounted in the late 1870s and 1880s. In this version it spread to German literature in the mid-1880s. However, the heredity theme first appeared in Germany in the later 1860s and 1870s. In its social-Darwinist form it legitimated German ascendancy: in all areas of life the victors were those who had best adapted to the struggle for life and in so doing guaranteed humanity's progress. However, socialists soon grasped the theory's potential for justifying their own struggle; the dominant classes became the dinosaurs retarding the emergence of progressive world-historical forces. Particularly threatening to the self-identity of the middle classes was the fact that socialists now leveled against them the charge of corruption, degeneracy and effeteness that for so long had been their own rallying cry in the struggle against aristocratic pre-eminence. But, in the 1870s this subculture still could not compete with the official ideology. Plays, novels, and stories depicted ascendant nations, empires, states, classes, and individuals. Their virility highlighted the decadence and degeneracy of their counterparts. By projecting onto the lower orders the "negative" manifestations of heredity – or rather, of things presumed hereditary – such as alcoholism, mental disorders, and sexual licentiousness, one reinforced stereotypes and justified continuing political and sociopolitical discrimination.

On the other hand, such topics became highly charged once they were explored in the context of middle-class life and once responsibility for negative, inherited traits was laid at middle-class doors. Of course, moralists could exploit their deterrent effect by depicting the dire consequences of departing from the straight and narrow; but they had to be careful not to suggest that these traits were widespread or that middle-class mores and norms might even promote them. It was unwise to suggest that individuals might lack the free will with which to avoid or at least ultimately overcome such dangers. Equally unsettling was the thought that hereditary traits might at any moment irrupt into the lives of respectable, "moral" individuals.

Heredity would not, however, have loomed so large in Storm's later fiction had he not been confronted with its real or presumed role in the histories of the Storm, Woldsen, and Esmarch families. He attributed both Hans's alcoholism – which he tended to link with allegedly inherited mental defects – and Karl's proneness to morbid ruminations to its mysterious workings.

If nature was no longer deemed good or perfectible and if individuals were thought to be at the mercy of uncontrollable hereditary urges, this clearly had implications for Storm's humanitarianism. Having dismissed Christian notions of fallen nature and original sin, he was now under pressure to reinstate in a medical, scientific form the notion of the sins of the fathers being visited on the third and fourth generations. From birth individuals might be dominated by inherited traits and urges which, instead of piloting them to happiness, drove them to destruction and ruined the lives of those who came into contact with them. Nature, which was to have underwritten the onward march to *Humanität*, even threatened to prevent mankind consolidating any gains made. In his blackest moods Storm feared that nothing could contain these elemental forces. Heredity threatened to become the new blind Fate: "Das nicht bloß poetische, sondern sich fortwährend vor unsern Augen abspielende wirkliche *Schicksal* liegt in der *Vererbung*."[1] The fact that alcoholism could supposedly miss a generation but then afflict a particular person in the third generation while leaving others untouched, conflicted with all notions of reason, justice, and scientific predictability.

Alcoholism, syphilis, and mental illness affected the very core of Storm's humanitarianism: his cult of marital love. He had always seen a fulfilled marital relationship as the means of overcoming the existential loneliness to which human beings were exposed as isolated individuals. The supreme tragedy of hereditary or transmissible diseases was that individuals suffering from

1. See LL 4, p. 511.

them could not lightly embark on marriage or be encouraged to do so. Yet without this "refuge" those in most need of its benefits would be driven further into misery and isolation. Had Storm been convinced that these diseases were incurable, his position would have been easier. But his continuing confidence in the recuperative power of physical nature when aided by medical science and by caring love encouraged hopes that individuals could make a complete recovery. He was torn between fear and longing, hope and misgivings. As the father of three sons, he dreamt of self-sacrificing women "redeeming" his sons; on the other hand, as a father of a bevy of daughters, he could not in all earnest recommend his sons as prospective son-in-laws if this risked wreaking havoc on an innocent girl and her family. The problem had affected him directly: Adolph Möller (see p. 170) had cited him as a referee when seeking a girl's hand, and Storm had felt bound to report Möller's drinking problem to her father.[2]

Storm's later stories attempt to reconcile his beliefs about the workings of heredity with his humanitarian ideals. The resulting tension distinguishes him from the naturalists in whose works heredity often acts as a demonic force overpowering individuals. There heredity is often used to refute an idealist, spiritual view of human nature and promote a crude determinist materialism. But just as Storm never abandoned his brand of Poetic Realism, so too he sought to envisage humanitarian responses strong and flexible enough to contain, perhaps even conquer, these destructive forces. The qualities that earlier had been expected to promote a neo-Grecian world beyond sin and guilt, were now, in modified form, the sole hope of ensuring at least a limited degree of human happiness.

Storm's definition of love shifted during the 1870s and 1880s. From Julie Hennefeder (*Beim Vetter Christian*) onward, kind, practical, maternal, domesticated women, not passionate ones, are seen as ideal partners. In the novella *Schweigen* (1883) the dark-eyed aristocratic amazon with her taste for playing the leading lady and mocking at men who get stuck during rehearsals (LL 3, 133) is not a suitable match for a son with a history of mental illness. I have already suggested that behind Rudolph von Schlitz's (!) fear of recurrent mental illness lurks Karl Storm's

2. Storm to Möller, 10 September 1871, SHLB.

fear of recurrent syphilis. A healthy, practical maternal wife from a simple rural vicarage, who is accustomed to looking after a semi-paralysed brother, was the ideal spouse for such "wounded" Tristans: "durch die scheue Jungfräulichkeit des Mädchens war wie aus der Knospe etwas von jener Mütterlichkeit hervorgebrochen, in deren Obhut auch der Mann am sichersten von Leid und Wunden ausruht" (LL 3, 137).

Schweigen has an optimistic ending. In contrast, the hero of *Carsten Curator* seeks in vain to overcome in his son traits inherited from his mother and compounded by the time and circumstances of his conception. After a champagne ball Carsten's teenage wife, a nonchalant speculator's daughter with Lolita/ Lorelei traits, is caught up in sexual fantasies about a dashing French officer. Himself full of frustrated sexual desire, Carsten profits from this lust. He later ruminates: "Meinst du . . . daß die Stunde gleich sei, in der unter des allweisen Gottes Zulassung ein Menschenleben aus dem Nichts hervorgeht? – Ich sage dir, ein jeder Mensch bringt sein Leben fertig mit sich auf die Welt; und Alle, in die Jahrhunderte hinauf, die nur einen Tropfen zu seinem Blute gaben, haben ihren Teil daran" (LL 2, 478). The text speaks of merciless natural forces (LL 2, 517). What so disturbed contemporaries was the suggestion that love and a secure family life could not rescue Heinrich. All the father's and wife's sacrifices are in vain. The text also questions notions of moral responsibility, guilt and punishment by implying that Heinrich has simply not inherited the moral fiber needed to lead a "respectable" life. Even if the grandson does not inherit his father's characteristics, the heredity lottery remains.

In *John Riew'*, Riew' initially dismisses the claim that everything – illness and sickness, virtue and vice – is determined by heredity, and finds absurd the suggestion that the son of an old lag should be dealt with more leniently than a criminal with an honest father. However, the doctor corrects him: ". . . den mitschuldigen Vorfahren müßte gerechter Weise doch wenigstens ein Teil der Schuld zugerechnet werden, wenn auch die Strafe an ihnen nicht mehr vollziehbar oder schon vollzogen ist" (LL 3, 376f.). In his view, alcoholism is essentially an hereditary disease and the most that can be hoped for is that constant care and attention will prevent the fearful seed developing. Once forced to drink alcohol by Riew', Anna becomes an easy prey for the aristocrat. On the other hand, there is nothing inevitable about her suicide. She is driven to it by a socially conditioned sense of shame and contagious disgrace, and by her anticipation of the prejudice which her illegitimate child will encounter. Riew' himself declares: ". . . Schande ist nur unter den Menschen und verweht in einem guten Leben" (LL 3, 380). His tragedy is that of a decent, kind, if limited character who, as a hard-drinking sailor, cannot imagine the consequences of his actions. But it is his reaction to his "guilt" which is crucial: he resolves to do his utmost to help and to prevent the boy succumbing to the same disease. Mindful of the reaction to *Carsten Curator*, Storm was careful to affirm the principle of hope: ". . . die Hoffnung ist die Helferin zum Leben und meist das Beste, was es mit sich führt . . . " (LL 3, 388).

But Storm's ambivalent position persisted. He could write to Erich Schmidt of Hans: "Diese Dinge, welche dem armen Jungen, vielleicht nicht ohne culpa patris, von kindauf anhaften, fordern den, der sie kennt, andrerseits auch zu einem milderen Beurtheiling des Menschen Hans auf, und rufen mein, des Vaters, ganzes Erbarmen auf."[3] At the same time he could not abandon the notion of at least some degree of free will and moral responsibility: "Ich will Dir nicht Alles zu Last rechnen, der Blutstropfen, der aus Großvaters Geschlecht kommt, mag einen Theil Deines großen Unglücks, Deiner großen Schuld und des mein Leben zerstörendedn Kummers tragen; aber darin liegt *Deine* Schuld, daß Du, obgliech Dir Deine Schwäche nicht verborgen bleiben konnte, Dich ganz darin hast gehen lassen, ohne auch nur den Versuch zu machen, Dich aufs feste Land zu retten."[4]

8.2 Tragic Guilt: Redefinitions

The issue of whether human beings could be held responsible for hereditary traits formed part of Storm's ruminations on the whoïe question of guilt. In his earlier works guilt lay with institutions and ideologies: they prevented human beings achieving true happiness. He had never adopted the view that individuals should relinquish selfish, particular interests and recognize the overriding demands of society or the state. Such an accommoda-

3. Storm to Heyse, *Storm-Schmidt* 1, 5 April 1877, p. 34.
4. Storm to Hans, 22 December 1878.

tion with the system was self-betrayal, "guilt." Punishment in such cases came not from some providential principle or moral world order: it came from the inner blight caused by denying the spontaneous, involuntary promptings of human nature. Storm staked everything on the goodness of human nature. In a post-Christian, democratic age, "sin" would be a historical memory.

After 1865 that confidence eroded. Constanze's death bred a sense of how the totally unpredictable could irrupt into individual lives and destroy them; he became aware that individuals might unwittingly provoke unforeseeable disaster; he realized that they could be caught up in situations where, whichever way they turned, they caused suffering to themselves or others; and he realized the extent to which individuals were frustrated in their aspirations, not just by external constraints, but also by physical disabilities and temperamental failings. As the painter Edde Brunken in *Eine Malerarbeit* admits, merciless Mother Nature did not always combine the parts very judiciously (LL 2, 10). Finally, as he himself grew older, Storm recognized the degree to which human begins as finite, mortal creatures are subject to ageing, to mental and physical deterioration, to the slow, insidious corruption of habit, to lethargy, and to the understandable desire for an easy, quiet life. The mental deterioration of his mother-in-law and his mother fueled in him, the inveterate hypochondriac, a sense of his own mental and physical deterioration.

The refusal of the middle and lower classes to conform to his expectations encouraged him to divide people into two categories. On the one hand, there was the small band of those striving for truth and humanity; on the other the vast majority trapped in their petty, egoistic concerns and clinging to their prejudices and superstitions. Individuals wanting to change the status quo would, he feared, find themselves locked in an exhausting struggle with such elements. His later novellas depict individuals groping their way toward enlightened ideas in the face of massive opposition. They have to contend with existing institutions, unenlightened ideologies and stifling socio-economic circumstances. In addition, they do not do it from some secure vantage point or armed with coherent categories and goals: they themselves have to haul themselves out of all kinds of ideological swamps and are in constant danger of sinking back into them. In addition, they have to contend with inherited physical disabilities, with illness and ageing. Storm rarely suggests that there is some final happy ending: any achievement is threatened by deterioration and change.

In the face of such sobering insights his novellas invite his readers to reconsider their notions of moral responsibility and guilt. High-minded, moral condemnation is as inappropriate as appeals to some inviolate universal reason or conscience. Trust in divine support and some afterlife may be the only hope left to people like Hans Kirch, and it would be cruel to destroy it. At the same time, the text suggests that this is an illusion and that Wieb alone is his consolation and support. Individual suffering and tragedy may be "relativized" in terms of a broader scheme of human achievement; but the suffering of the individuals themselves is not diminished. Suffering is not the salutary or ennobling preliminary to the final reward of a Christian afterlife or some classical-idealist realm of spiritual freedom. The finality of mortal life is upheld. Guilt is redefined in relation to what is truly human in oneself and others.

If the suffering and the tragedy remain, so too does quiet, unaristocratic heroism on far-from-grand stages; and so too do the human qualities of love and devotion to which Storm attached such importance. While bringing out the often tragic nature of human life, the novellas do not encourage a cynical view of the futility of human efforts to achieve enlightened institutions and ideas; nor do they suggest that sordid pettiness is universal. Instead they suggest the achievements possible notwithstanding formidable handicaps and obstacles. Despite all their individual disabilities and shortcomings; despite the failings produced by the nature of society; despite the fact that they themselves sometimes despair of the sense of their actions, individuals are still shown making valuable, albeit small-scale contributions to the cause of humanity. Indeed – and this is not just a symptom of some trivializing tendency and parochialism in Storm – small-scale contributions may well be the true achievements, not the supposedly major exploits and accomplishments of the great "heroes" of history.

In a world where there were already enough impediments in the way of progress, one had to guard against the danger of falling back into the old notions of fallen nature, sin, and *vanitas vanitatum*. These were recipes for passivity. A tragic heroism had to be evolved which, while attaching full weight to negative insights, nevertheless succeeded in conveying a sense of purely human, as opposed to divinely based, dignity. If one can talk of existentialism in connection with Storm, it has to be of humanitarian existentialism. Works had to prompt readers to draw conclusions favorable, not hostile, to the enlightened, humanitarian cause.

On various occasions he defined his conception of guilt and tragedy:

Es ist ein eigen Ding, die specielle *Schuld* des Helden für das Tragische zu verlangen. Mir sagte neulich ein Bekannter, es gedenke ein quidam über mich zu schreiben (ein Pastor in Schleswig, mein ich) und dabei nachzuweisen, wie alle meine Personen ohne eigne Schuld untergingen. Ich muß nun auch nach meinem Sinn die Schuldfrage für das Tragische viel weiter fassen: der Held (lassen wir diesen Ausdruck) fällt eigentlich nie durch eigene Schuld, sondern durch die *Schuld* oder *Unzulänglichkeit* des Menschenthums, sei dieß Feindliche in ihm selbst gelegen oder in einem außer ihm bestehenden Bruchtheil der Menschheit, möge er gegen diese oder gegen sich selbst zu kämpfen haben und dadurch selbst oder mit seinem Glück zu Trümmern gehen. So ist es in "Aquis Subm" (wo ich an keine Schuld des Paares gedacht) so in "Renate," wo das Feindliche sowohl in die Seele des Helden, als in die Außenwelt gelegen ist und so die schöne Zeit der Liebe in Trümmer schlagt; im stillen Musikanten liegt das Tragische in dem unlösbaren Zwiespalt zwischen seiner höheren Erkenntniß u. Empfindg u. andrererseits seiner eng begrenzten practischen Fähigkeit, die er vergebens zu überwinden sucht etc. etc. Gehen Sie einmal diesen Spuren nach. Hierin finde ich seit lange bewußt das Tragische, u. finde das eigentliche tragische Schicksal in der Vererbung des Blutes.[5]

He wrote *à propos* of *Der Herr Etatsrat* and other novellas:

Für die Tragik, besonders in der epischen Poesie, eine *eigne* Schuld der betreffenden Personen zu fordern, beruht auf einer zu engen und – sit venia verbi! – etwas philisterhaften Auffassung des Tragischen; der vergebliche Kampf gegen das, was durch die Schuld oder auch nur die Begrenzung, die Unzulänglichkeit *des Ganzen der Menschheit*, wovon der Einzelne ein unablösbarer Theil ist, der betreffenden Person entgegensteht und der dadurch herbeigeführte Untergang, sei es der Person selbst, oder ihres eigentlichen Lebensinhaltes, das ist nach meiner Ueberzeugung das Tragische im rechten großen Sinn; und so habe ich es in "Carsten Curator," "Renate," "Aquis submersus"... aufgefaßt; der Untergang nur wegen eigner Schuld ist schon mehr

5. Storm to Schmidt, September 1881, *Storm-Schmidt* 2, p. 49.

eine pädagogische, polizeiliche oder criminelle Bestrafung. Freilich, ich weiß wohl, und sie können es mir einwenden, die Phia wenigstens wird nur mehr erdrückt, wo ist da der Kampf? Das ist schon richtig, sie fällt nur mit in das grausame Triebrad hinein; aber auch das möchte ich, besonders für die Epik, in Beschlag nehmen, wenn die Poesie ein concentrirter Spiegel des Lebens sein soll . . .[6]

The pattern is established from *Aquis submersus* onward. Readers are invited to endorse Johannes's early aspirations and condemn the society which thwarts them. In similar fashion, they are encouraged to recognize the tragic folly of Johannes, the hero of *Renate*, when he is misled by the orthodoxy of the time into denying his true salvation, his love for Renate. For his part, her father anticipates Hauke Haien in being a champion of enlightenment in a petty, superstitious society. A sick man, he dies alone and in agony, out in the bogs. The local people turn their would-be benefactor into one of the devil's own. In *Zur Chronik von Grieshuus* the hero may be unable to resist his choleric character; he may fail to change his grandson's character; and he may die in an accident while rushing to save him; in fact, his runaway horse may contribute to his death. Yet the practical manner in which he atones for his crime by ridding the area of wolves permanently benefits the whole community, and his achievement is not diminished by the fact that the wars go on and the feudal system survives. In *Ein Bekenntnis* the arrogant hero atones for his inability to grasp the true, Feuerbachian nature of love and the sanctity of human life by devoting the rest of his life to combatting illness in Africa.

Progress, Storm suggests, can only be achieved in painfully small stages. There will be setbacks, indeed reversions to unenlightened conditions. But the struggle must go on. The principle of hope must be upheld. In the Wilhelminian Empire he saw no other way forward.

8.3 Aesthetic Crisis

During the 1850s and early 1860s Storm had believed his aesthetic techniques well suited to communicating his humanitarian

---

6. Storm to Heinrich Schleiden, 9 November 1881, City Archive, Hamburg, copies in SHLB.

message. But his Poetic-Realist variant of the classical-idealist aesthetic was based on confidence in socio-political and economic trends and a positive view of human nature. Once these certainties crumbled, the ideological crisis soon brought in its train an aesthetic one. In a very real sense, he experienced in his own person the death throes of the old classical-idealist creed. At the time of his death German literature was moving beyond it into naturalism, symbolism and impressionism. At times philosophy had challenged the primacy of art (see p. 32), and history and science also had their devotees; but, until the 1880s, few challenged the classical-idealist aesthetic itself. Historians have written a great deal on the disparity between Imperial Germany's advanced economic and technological achievements and its backward-looking social and political structures. What is just as remarkable is the discrepancy between the complex problems of the 1870s and 1880s and the traditionalism of Imperial art and literature. At a time when trends in politics, economics, technology, science, and intellectual life had fractured the system of interlocking worlds and disciplines on which the old aesthetic had been based, its disciples still strove to preserve the trinity of the good, the true, and the beautiful.

Storm's later works attempted to uphold the old conception of art and its function. The more other bastions fell to undemocratic, unenlightened forces, the greater was his need to believe in its impregnability and see himself as its faithful defender. The triumph of Bismarckian politics, of Darwinist science and sociology, and the emergence of grave socio-economic tensions lent even greater urgency to the need to believe that art could nonetheless prevail in the end. But to do this it had, he believed, to remain true to its own specific nature and principles. Reality had to be subjected to the unique treatment which transformed it into *Dichtung*. Among the pitfalls to be avoided was that of letting pessimistic moods produce a distorted picture of reality. Related to this was the need to avoid attaching undue importance to what was sordid or disturbing in reality.[7] Storm also regarded it as a damning verdict on his powers if friends found his works *rührend* rather than *erschütternd*. If he had failed here, he had certainly not achieved his more ambitious goal of a third possibility somewhere between the two: "den Leser in einer herben

7. See LL 2, 955f.

Nachdenklichkeit über die Dinge des Lebens zurückzulassen."[8] He was dismayed if critics like Fontane praised him for providing a series of genre-pictures but did not recognize any organizing center in a work.[9] The cumulative effect of these individual criticisms was to make him feel that he had failed in the basic task facing any *Dichter*: he had not transformed life into art. If readers regarded his works as *peinlich* or *unerquicklich*,[10] the fundamental reason for this, in his eyes, was that raw material, ideas and motifs had got stuck at various intermediate stages in the transformation. He feared that because of this his works could not affect readers in the prescribed way and could not have their hoped-for humanizing effect. Last but not least, he risked forfeiting the public's favor if his creative powers had indeed deserted him.

The hostile reaction to one work in particular, *Carsten Curator* (1878) (see p. 208), opened Storm's eyes to what critics and public would accept and what they would not; it generated in him misgivings about his artistic and moral fitness. The terms in which he couched them are part and parcel of the classical-idealist tradition. Thus he accused himself, first, of having lacked the distance from the subject matter and the serenity needed to create a true work of art. Secondly, he had used material that was morally and poetically ugly without either magnifying it to such terrifying proportions that it was worthy of art, or alternatively using humor to turn it into the grotesque. As a result, it remained simply sordid and embarrassing. Thirdly, in Heinrich, he had created a character who was not misdrawn if one took reality as the yardstick, but who could have been less common without any loss to the thrust of the novella and at great gain to the poetic quality of this *Dichtung*. Fourthly, he had undermined confidence in the positive nature of reality: "Im Leben und in der Poesie können wir das Glück entbehren, aber nicht die Hoffnung."[11]

In *Renate* he retired to altogether safer ground. An already

8. Storm to Schmidt, September 1881, *Storm-Schmidt* 2, p. 50.

9. Fontane to Storm, 28 October 1884, *Storm-Fontane*, p. 136.

10. See J. Hillier, *Theodor Storm's Novelle Carsten Curator; an evaluation of the terms "Befreiungungsdichtung" and das "Poetische,"* doctoral thesis, Leicester, 1973.

9. Storm to Schmidt, September 1881, *Storm-Schmidt* 2, p. 50.

10. Fontane to Storm, 28 October 1884, *Storm-Fontane*, p. 136.

11. See LL 2, p. 956.

structured account allowed him to elaborate dramatic, poetic scenes and convey a positive message about the advent of Enlightenment in a superstitious, bigoted world. Love triumphs in the end. The novella may contain illness and suffering, but there is no sordid heredity, no vice, no degradation. The presentation of the fanatical pastor Petrus Goldschmidt avoids being simply ugly and sordid. The distance between life and art is maintained.

The compulsion felt to poeticize, in the sense of putting a subject into the literary mode, meant that in *Zur Wald- und Wasserfreude* (1879), a story about a vacuous *Gründerzeit* speculator and his daughter, Storm introduced a witch-like old woman in the woods with an array of animal pelts and poisonous love-potions. Similarly, Gottfried Keller's reaction to such a minor work as *Im Brauer Haus* (1879)[12] exemplifies how this generation reinforced each other in traditional aesthetic categories. Thus his first impression had been that the brewery business was too prosaic. However, Storm had compensated for this by the tight composition and the good peripeteia. In Keller's view everything was pertinent and fitted in harmoniously. Continually Storm was under pressure to treat idyllic, anodyne subjects. Thus he wrote *Die Söhne des Senators* in response to Petersen's complaints that he was writing depressing, somber stories: "*Er* will alte freundliche Rokoko-Geschichten von mir, wo er den Toback unserer Altvordern riecht."[13] On receiving the manuscript, Petersen still suggested that vulgar elements should be removed. Inevitably such a climate reinforced all Storm's own Poetic-Realist norms and heightened his doubts about the way in which he was moving almost against his own conscious will and certainly against his traditional, rather than his better, judgement.

Given the appetite of critics and public for optimistic works, it was tempting to abandon disturbing topics and provide a reassuring, idyllic version of reality. Such a course also corresponded to Storm's need to imagine satisfactory outcomes to his own family problems. This option had, however, at least three main drawbacks. First, it avoided the intellectual and artistic task of showing humanitarian principles a match for disturbing aspects of reality; secondly, it represented a retreat from any belief in art's supreme powers of transformation; and, thirdly, it proved

---

12. Keller to Storm, 20 December 1879, *Storm-Keller*, p. 63.
13. Storm to Heyse, 22 October 1879, *Storm-Heyse* 2, p. 53.

to be impossible to put into practice. Despite the pressures to maximize his literary earnings, Storm often could not turn on his creative imagination at will. If he chose to write on, mechanically, he was liable to find himself confronted with the very criticism he was anxious to avoid. What compounded his problems was the fact that the emotional pressures which did activate his creative imagination often related to his sons' problems. Depicting them brought him back into the danger zone. Even if he allowed wishful thinking to produce optimistic solutions, he still had to depart from an inauspicious starting point. Moreover, to overcome that handicap, he had to be able to call on the creative resources which he feared he no longer possessed.

Another means of avoiding potential friction was to retire to some historical, exotic, or imaginary setting and period. The distance between art and life was then easier to maintain. By choosing an exotic setting or past society about which the public knew little, one could also avoid the rigor which any convincing treatment of contemporary issues demanded in terms of information and insight. A browse in several histories or chronicles might suffice. However much the Imperial public may have relished historical novels and novellas, the verdict today on all but a few of these works has to be very critical. Authors often indulged in hackneyed dramatic scenes and lyrical climaxes. Both narrative and dialogue were full of archaic words, endings, and syntax. The classical-idealist aesthetic's emphasis on timeless, universal human traits and problems itself encouraged the tendency to impose a veneer of historical color while conveying very little of the specific mentalities and problems of past ages. In stories like *Eekenhof* or *Ein Fest auf Haderslevhuus* Storm himself was a prime offender. Even in much greater works like *Aquis submersus* or *Zur Chronik von Grieshuus* the style often verges on the spurious.

In *Psyche* the hero, a sculptor, declares to his friend:

Warum in so entlegene Zeiten greifen? Als wenn nicht jede Gegenwart ihren eignen Reichtum hätte!
Warum? Erneste! Du sprichst ja fast wie, ich weiß nicht, welcher große Kritikus über Immermann's Tristan und Isolde. Was geht den Künstler die Zeit, ja was geht der Stoff ihn an? – Freilich, aus dem Himmel, der über uns Lebenden ist, muß der zündende Blitz fallen; aber was er beleuchtet, das wird lebendig für den, der sehen kann, und läge es versteinert in dem tiefsten Grabe der Vergangenheit. (LL 2, 320)

The stilted classical language indicates where the blame for many of these historical fiascos lies. Storm failed to recognize that the classical-idealist aesthetic was the product of a specific historical, cultural juncture. Paradoxically, by laying claim to a unique identity and mode of operation, literature did not guarantee itself a pre-eminent position in disseminating modern values and shaping sensibilities; it tended to take up a position where it could not come to terms with modern life. The distance insisted upon between art and life, instead of protecting literature's scope for maneuver, led to it promoting an increasingly ossified, iconographic version of reality. An aesthetic which had seen the separation between art and life as a means of safeguarding literature's enlightening, humanizing function and its ability to mold society, had failed to recreate society in its ideal image. Now it was in the interest of those defending the status quo to insist on the prescribed distance from "common reality" while suggesting that "true reality" was indeed captured in Poetic-Realist depictions of contemporary reality. A literature was legitimated which abstracted from the illiberal, inhuman features of state and society and created a sense of harmony when none existed.

The hopes Storm attached to retirement and the move to a spacious villa in Hademarschen were themselves classical-idealist ones. Such an environment would, he hoped, transform the quality and content of his art. He would be able to rise above sordid subjects. The hope persisted that art could still achieve the classical wholeness and greatness that his generation had dreamed would come with German unity. In fact the first product of his retirement was anything but serenely noble or sublime. The novella *Der Herr Etatsrat* scandalized friends and readers alike (see p. 210) with its depiction of the ravages caused in his family by a former dike inspector. Storm had imagined that he had protected himself against critical strictures. Indeed he had a copy-book defense at hand, namely that, by adding humor, he had transformed the morally ugly – which was inadmissable in art – into the grotesque – which was.[14] His critics were not convinced. They still found the novella unwholesome. Storm's crime was to have shown the innocent daughter, Phia, seduced in the family home and then dying in childbirth, while her

14. See LL 3, pp. 775ff.

unconcerned father prospers in his depravity.

When he found himself adopting a psychological, realistic approach in his presentation of the father-son conflict in *Hans und Heinz Kirch*, Storm did not see this as a promising new departure but rather as further evidence of his waning powers. In his eyes, it was only by meticulously collecting details about an actual family in Heiligenhafen, soberly chiseling away at his block, and calling on all his accumulated expertise, that he could hope to conceal a lack of youthful freshness. Whereas naturalist writers would pride themselves on their preliminary field-work and documentation, Storm belonged to another tradition. *Stoff* had to be transformed and given artistic *Form* by passing through the poet's imagination; the creative imagination could not be dependent on existing material. Despite providing some idealistic uplift at the end, Storm again could not satisfy his critics. Perhaps the most uncomprehending and traditional of all the verdicts was that of Theodor Mommsen:

> Die schöne Trübe der Localstimmung empfind ich wohl, auch daß die Macht des Lebens derber als früher aus diesen Blättern einen ergreift. Aber, wenn ich es sagen soll, recht will es mir nicht glücken der bürgerlichen Tragödie gegenüber; wo einmal das Unheil waltet, wie hier, da soll es wenigstens die grimme Faust des großen Schicksals sein, die den Menschen zerschlägt, und davon finde ich hier nichts.[15]

Tactically it would have been advisable to avoid such subjects altogether. Yet such were the inner pressures on Storm that in *Schweigen* (1883) he nevertheless turned to the theme of recurrent mental illness (see p. 218). If one studies the draft versions, one can see what agonies he went through in his attempt to make the subject fit for art. The novella is a prime example of how Poetic Realism did not automatically ostracize certain topics; instead it brought in the censors through another door by insisting that the presentation should be consonant with its definition of art. It was forbidden to corrupt *Dichtung* by adopting the terminology or methods of medical science, psychiatry, or psychology. The naturalists were in this view sinning against art. Gottfried Keller praised Storm for having avoided these pitfalls and having

---

15. See Storm to Heyse, 2 October 1884, *Storm-Heyse* 3, p. 94.

provided, not a medical, psychiatric study, but "die poetische Darstellung eines seelischen Vorgangs."[16] Storm himself was appalled that Hermione von Preuschen should have felt it necessary to visit an asylum before writing a poem on mental illness: "Im Irrenhaus haben wir nicht die Studien für unsre Kunst zu machen, die Region wollen wir den Aerzten überlassen."[17]

Schweigen illustrates well the tension in Storm between the tendency to adopt an analytical, psychological method in treating disturbing subjects, and the need to uphold his concept of *Dichtung* by providing a positive message in the Poetic-Realist mode. The widening gap between ideal humanitarian solutions and the reality of his children's lives was paralleled by a similar one between his socio-political ideal and contemporary reality. He could only close the gap by abstracting from the complexities of life in the Second Empire and seeking refuge in solutions which were idealistic in both aesthetic and ethical terms. Far from becoming more realistic in subject matter and technique, Storm's works often became more idealistic, both in form and content, especially when the will to reaffirm certain human values and ethical principles was not matched in his intellect and creative imagination by convincing, realistic scenarios. At such times operatic and melodramatic elements had to compensate for "pessimistic" insights and a state of mind which he deemed inimical to the creation of true art or *Dichtung*. By intensifying the element of *Kunst*, he could, he hoped, perhaps neutralize the sordid, common features of the element of *Leben* and still transform life into art. Thus *Schweigen* balances the topic of serious mental disturbance with a *dénouement* taken straight from Weber's opera *Der Freischütz*. *Ein Fest auf Haderslevhuus* also ends in hackneyed melodrama. But the old harmony of *Form* and *Stoff* could not be maintained. The aesthetic world was as sorely out of joint as the socio-political and ethical ones. On the other hand, Storm could not jump over his classical-idealist shadow.

Paradoxically, Poetic-Realist ideals also underlay his resistance to pressure from Paul Heyse to apply rigid formal rules to the novella. Taking up Boccaccio's idea of the falcon, Heyse wanted every novella to be organized around a single clear theme. Although anxious to move the novella up-market and present it as

16. Keller to Storm, 19 may 1883, *Storm-Keller*, p. 139.
17. Storm to H.v. Preuschen *STSG*, vol. 22, 1973, p. 78.

the leading epic genre, Storm would have none of this. He glimpsed in a return to "the romantic novella" with its emphasis on epic action a way of overcoming his tendency toward psychological, analytic "realism."[18] It also promised to be a way of guaranteeing length – and income! This new technique – which he pursued in *Zur Chronik von Grieshuus* (1884) – might also allow him to present disturbing themes in a "poetic" form. In essence he reverted to his old technique of "situations." The difference was that now he did not texture them so densely, allowed for more dramatic, epic and linking passages, and provided more historical data. Such familiar themes as the struggle against hereditary characteristics or against aristocratic caste exclusiveness could not be dubbed sordid or tendentious if presented in this way. His friends applauded – even if they still tended to regard the "situations" as genre pictures. But while contributing to his final work, *Der Schimmelreiter*, this seam did not prove one which he could continue to work.

The literary scene was polarizing into those defending the old traditions and younger, self-styled revolutionaries advocating naturalism. Despite his loyalties to the old camp, the changing climate was not without its effect on Storm. In *John Riew'* he returned to a contemporary setting and the problem of alcoholism. But *John Riew'* ends optimistically, not in squalor and suicide. In 1886 Storm wrote:

> Daß in der Poesie Wahrheit sein muß, braucht man uns nicht zu lehren; aber Kunst und Natur decken sich nicht, die Wahrheit tritt in der Kunst anders in die Erscheinung als in der Natur. Wenn man die natürliche Wahrheit mit der bewundernswertesten Geschicklichkeit darstellt, so kann das, wo es am Orte ist, sehr anerkennenswert sein; aber mit einer Kunstleistung hat das gar nichts zu tun.
> Diese sogenannte neuere Schule, die wieder einmal aus Frankreich gekommen, durch einen Mann [=Zola], der zufällig auch ein recht großer Poet und bei dem das mitunter durchschlägt, verwechselt in ihrer Borniertheit die natürliche Wahrheit mit der poetischen.[19]

When in the following year he wrote the fragment *Wie wird man Schriftsteller von Beruf*, he defined the role of the *Schriftsteller* as being to proclaim beauty and duty – a typical Enlightenment

---

18. Storm to Petersen, 12 December 1882. See also LL 3, p. 845.
19. *Braunes Taschenbuch*, LL 4, p. 549.

formulation – and then substituted *Poet* for *Schriftsteller*. To the end, true to the German tradition, he regarded the *Poet* or *Dichter* as a higher species than the *Schriftsteller*.[20]

It is tempting to try to illustrate his modernity and closeness to naturalism by citing a later work like *Ein Doppelgänger*. However there is a danger of failing to recognize that the theme – the tragic career of an ex-offender whom society never allows to live down his shame – is presented from a very different standpoint from that often adopted in naturalist works. It is also crucial to recognize how much of the classical-idealist definition of "poetry" is still upheld in the form and the language. *Der Schimmelreiter* itself may contain naturalist themes like heredity and the power of milieu; it may rely on detailed, preliminary studies to achieve accuracy and authenticity; but both in ideological outlook and above all in technique, it does not belong to the world of Zola and the naturalists. It belongs to the Enlightenment tradition and employs the techniques of presentation which Storm had built up over a lifetime.

8.4 The Social Problem

By the later 1870s it was clear that the urban proletariat had not been integrated into the Bismarckian settlement. In response Bismarck adopted a twin-pronged policy: on the one hand, the draconian measures of the Socialist Law of 1878 and, on the other, social measures designed to tie the proletariat to the state. In the early 1880s insurance against industrial accidents and sickness was thus provided. However, the socialist vote continued to grow. In 1884, without any legal organization or election material, it reached a quarter of a million, and the number of socialist members in the Reichstag rose from twelve to twenty-four.

At first sight there is little to suggest that Storm was concerned about the so-called "social question" and socialism. Ferdinand Tönnies later referred to their discussions on socialism and democracy, but it is unlikely that either man greatly influenced the other even if it is tempting to look for parallels between

---

20. LL 4, p. 469.

Gemeinschaft und Gesellschaft (1887) and Storm's last works.[21] Storm had no direct experience of modern industrial technology or of the work and living conditions of the urban proletariat. In terms of his experience and sympathies he identified much more with small-town artisans and masters, servants and maids. His democratic vision had been built around the ideal of a close alliance between them and the educated professional middle classes. The new commercial-industrial bourgeoisie, in contrast, had always fitted rather uneasily into that scheme even during the years when Storm had set such hopes on capitalism's potential. The growing social tensions, the continued population movement from rural areas into the large cities, and the widely lamented atomization of society encouraged him to adopt a view of socio-economic conditions in the earlier decades of the century which, in its positiveness, was very different from the critical position adopted in the 1850s and 1860s. Then he had stressed the backwardness and stifling atmosphere of such pre-industrial, pre-democratic societies. Now, in contrast, he believed that in such societies the individual had at least been part of a close-knit, supportive community. It is typical of Storm's characteristic blend of democratic and profoundly conservative traits that he should have imagined that a solution to the socio-economic problems of the present might be found by combining the old patriarchal economic system with a degree of modernization and mechanization.

The novella *Bötjer Basch* bears witness to all these concerns. The story is built around the contrast between a stereotyped picture of capitalism and society in America and an equally iconic evocation of a German provincial town. Storm's stereotypes are much closer to those pervading Freytag's *Soll und Haben* (1855) than to Tönnies' definitions of community and society. The stability and order, the communitarian elements, traditions and culture of German provincial life are contrasted with a lawless, violent, chaotic America where egoistic individualism and ruthless acquisitiveness reign supreme in a bitter struggle for existence. The California gold rush is made to symbolize this spirit.

---

21. See Craig, *Germany, 1866–1945*, Oxford, 1978, pp. 140–49. See also R. Fechner, ed., *Der Dichter und der Soziologe. Zum Verhältnis zwischen Theodor Storm und Ferdinand Tönnies*, Ferdinand-Tönnies-Arbeitsstelle, Universität Hamburg, Hamburg, 1984.

In such a society the worst seeds in people germinate and luxuriate. They become drunkards, idlers, gamblers, and robbers, whereas an ordered framework could have contained these traits. In Germany such conditions are only preserved as historic memories in dramas like Schiller's *Die Räuber* (LL 3, 493). In the U.S. a motley mix of races create a situation akin to that at the building of the Tower of Babel (LL 3, 489). Any sense of human solidarity and of the need for good neighborliness, compassion, and support is destroyed. Here it would be absurd to tend flowers, to look after songbirds – certainly to teach them maxims like Hölty's "Üb' immer Treu und Redlichkeit/ Bis an dein kühles Grab." Such singing is made to symbolize both the German *Gemüt* and the sane, integrated psyche. It is only possible in the right conditions, given constant care and the right instruction.

The picture that the text paints of a small provincial town is based on pre-1848 Husum. It does not obscure social divisions; but it does evoke a fundamental social cohesion. Both the mayor – named after the actual mayor during Storm's childhood, Johann Christian Lüders – and the Landvogt are shown intimately acquainted with the inhabitants and their problems. In this they are implicitly contrasted with the remote, yet also interfering bureaucratic Prussian officials after 1866. Fritz, the cooper's son, plays with the mayor's son, while sons of officials, professional people, and tradesmen attend at least the lowest class of the grammar school together. In contrast to a work like *Auf der Universität* (1863), the text does not even hint at social tensions. The guild-system is presented as producing a supportive community between masters and journeymen. Thus Basch tells his journeyman of his marriage plans at the same time as he tells his sister; the journeyman later cooks for and consoles his widowed master. This society provides for the sick, the poor, and the elderly via the Bettelvogt, the Gasthaus zum Ritter St. Jürgen, and the support and pensions which patrician families give to former servants. It is suggested that a solution to loneliness, widowhood, and homelessness in old age could be for widowers like Basch to take in as lodgers or housekeepers elderly spinsters or widows like Riekchen Therebinthe.

The story is a parable or fable about the human condition and the ages of man. Storm constructs an idyllic, humorous epic of everyday provincial life in which potential tragedy, especially Basch's attempted suicide, and disturbing elements like his

confused mental state are finally overcome. Characters tend to
become types or symbols, even caricatures, described in terms of
a narrow range of fixed epithets. Indeed the use of topoi is part
of the attempt to suggest familiar, traditional values and stable
patterns. The three parcae and the three graces from whom Paris
had to choose have been replaced by "Mine, Line, Stine von
vierzig, neununddreißig und siebenunddreißig Jahren; sie waren
alle brave Mädchen; aber die braune Line war doch die bravste;
sanft, wirtschaftlich und von gutem Menschenverstande; dabei
ein wenig schelmisch" (LL 3, 461). Archetypal patterns and traditional gender roles are reinforced. Fritz Basch's insistence on
using Low German is part of the loyalty to traditional values.

The text documents Storm's continuing concern with the whole
problem of a "Prussianized," authoritarian upbringing and
education. The values inculcated at the grammar-school are criticized. The assistant teacher, an impractical man, chooses the name
Tiberius for his son. The boy turns into a malicious thief. The
teacher, who himself has features of a vulture, refers to his pupils
as vultures/gallows' birds (LL 3, 470) and reduces classical
education to a cult of heroes and classical maxims. He relishes
declining *pulso* (to beat) and has no time for German fairy stories. True education, the text suggests, is rather a question of
providing children with a loving, ordered environment, tolerating individuality, understanding frustrations, and trusting in
children's ability to ponder on the consequences of their actions
for others. Such an upbringing achieves more than one based on
castigation and commands. Thus Fritz's wild energy finds acceptable outlets; he learns to consider the welfare of others; he
recognizes the importance of maternal and paternal love; and he
realizes that there is more to life than independence and self-
sufficiency.

The story reiterates Storm's humanitarian stance. The depiction over the door of Basch's house of the omnipotence and
omnipresence of death "on land and sea" (LL 3, 459) does not,
whatever the inevitable end, capture the whole truth about mortal
life with its potential richness and happiness. Hence it is plas-
tered over until late in the story. Death itself can be calm and
peaceful. The text also affirms Storm's confidence in youth. Thus,
when Basch is suicidal, redemption comes from the young people.
In a scene which plays with Christian and classical associations,
Riekchen Therebinthe is transformed from a comic Medusa into

a Mary Magdalen who, finding her landlord alive, not dead, hurries away with the nightgown that she has brought to act as his shroud (LL 3, 503f.). Considerable space is devoted to the problem of aging and of deteriorating faculties, to isolation, confusion, and depression. The solution is found in a supportive network of close family and social ties. The maxim, Love thy neighbor as thyself, is stressed, not any socialist suggestion of irreconcilable class interests. This traditional community with its idyllic, Homeric traits can, it is suggested, survive if the trades become competitive by mechanizing production. "American" tools, and an "American" work-tempo – slogans of the 1880s – are necessary (LL 3, 505). But far from destroying the old communities, these practices can, it is hoped, be used to reinforce the existing system and preserve traditional values.

8.5 Social Stigma

It may seem surprising that despite his long experience of the Prussian judiciary Storm seldom explicitly criticized the Prussian penal system. His rejection of capital punishment (see p. 190) is a rare exception. At the same time he had persistently criticized Christianity for presenting human nature as sinful and incapable of achieving anything without divine grace. As far back as his days in Potsdam, he had recognized how poverty drove young people into crime[22] and in Heiligenstadt had commented in the case of a recidivist thief that a little sunshine could have perhaps nurtured a very noble human plant.[23] His later ruminations on the role of heredity and on individuals' inability to resist inherited traits clearly had judicial implications. In fact, in *John Riew'*, the doctor declares that the sons of lags should be dealt with more leniently than those from honest backgrounds (LL 3, 376f.). If milieu also played a crucial part in determining whether individuals offended or not, did it not have to be borne in mind in sentencing? Was it not desirable to switch the emphasis from punishment and retribution to prophylaxis and rehabilitation?

Seen from an establishment point of view, John Hansen, the

---

22. Storm to parents, 29 June 1854.
23. Storm to Constanze, 10 October 1863.

hero of *Ein Doppelgänger* (1887), is a dangerous, hardened criminal: he commits robbery with violence – in fact the blow to the head of the senator's servant could have proved fatal; he is a wife-batterer, lucky not to be charged with his wife's murder; and, despite his earlier punishment, he returns to crime, stealing wood and potatoes. Storm had to tread carefully if he wanted to suggest that the blame for John Hansen's career could be laid at society's door. The text adopts the well-tried Storm technique of maneuvering readers into unfamiliar positions. John's career is presented through the eyes of a lawyer-narrator, and the latter's sympathetic position is lent more explicit sharpness by introducing in the inner story a mayor who is highly critical of society's treatment of offenders. In addition, the text invites the reader to identify with the kind, humane forester who is married to John Hansen's daughter and who has an antipathy toward high-ranking civil servants and lieutenants. But ultimately readers had to be left to draw their own conclusions from the evidence presented in this "hearing."

The narrator attributes John's burglary with violence to his inability to find a channel for his energies after having been discharged from the armed service. Unable to find a job on a farm, he drifts to the town and gets into criminal company. Frustrated and bored, he is attracted by the element of sport and danger in the proposed burglary. Instead of simply sentencing him to six years in a convict prison, society, it is suggested, should have provided work and guidance in the first place. (Fritz Basch in *Bötjer Basch* and Hauke Haien in *Der Schimmelreiter* are also presented as frustrated young men in need of guidance and an outlet for their energies.) The forester's own son is described as having a wild, youthful nature which requires education and guidance (LL 3, 524). In fact, the story opens with the forester counseling a young trainee before sending him on to another colleague (LL 3, 517f.).

But it is society's treatment of John Hansen after he has "atoned" for his crime that incurs Storm's bitterest criticism. Nicknamed John Glückstadt after the prison where he served his sentence, he is henceforth dogged by the stigma of having been a convict. Society denies him the human right to lead a decent, honest life. He finds and remains in employment only because the mayor intercedes on his behalf; his fellow workers refuse to have anything to do with him and exclude him from their celebrations; and the midwife refuses to rush her coffee to deliver the child of a criminal. By refusing ever to let John regain his lost honor and become a happy, useful member of society, society traps him in feelings of bitterness and frustration which perpetually threaten to boil over into violence. His wound is kept open.

While his wife-battering is not played down, the text does suggest explanatory factors. Thus John's frustration intensifies when, from being an efficient foreman, he is condemned to become a stonebreaker; he returns home weary, having brooded on his "unatonable guilt"; his mother-in-law is suffering from gout; and his wife is exasperated by their young child's refusal to go to sleep (LL 3, 546f.). A bitter exchange ensues in the course of which she touches on his open wound and provokes him to physical violence. Far from suggesting that these people are violent monsters, an inferior species in the social-Darwinist scheme, the text brings out how circumstances promote such behavior. It also suggests that the working classes tend to be passionate and wild. Having to live from day to day, they cannot develop forethought and any sense of the implications of their actions; they do not learn from past experiences (LL 3, 548). Living by their hands and unable to vent their frustrations in words, they are soon sucked into physical violence. Such prejudices on Storm's part were at least intended to prompt the reader to take a more understanding view of working-class behavior. Violent though the marriage may be, it is based on true passion and tenderness. The text also underlines the fortuitous element in the "murder": Hanna, the child, has unscrewed the knob from the fatal bolt. At a deeper level, the sequence suggests that were the family to enjoy social esteem, secure employment, and decent surroundings, such crimes would be much less likely to occur. If workers were encouraged to plan for the future, they would behave differently: they could aspire to the world of *Bildung* eventually attained by John's daughter, Hanna.

One of the text's major achievements is to show how John himself helps destroy his happiness by remaining locked into notions of what is "honorable" and "dishonorable." He shares society's prejudices toward beggars (LL 3, 552), and it is his reference to his wife's own past which provokes her to refer to his criminal record. He behaves in similar fashion toward the elderly woman, Mariken, refusing to allow his daughter to eat any "beggar's soup" (LL 3, 560) even though she is desperately hungry. The text, on the other hand, stresses that there is nothing discreditable about his wife's past or about Mariken. The daughter of a poor schoolteacher, she became a domestic servant, married, lost her husband, and then, despite continuing in "honorable" work, gradually sank into poverty. She relied on food, warmth, and shelter from former employers whom she entertained with her stories. Eventually she is made homeless when the slaughterer builds himself a new house. Significantly there is no suggestion that the state should provide. It is Mariken who insists that Hanna is bought learning materials; she teaches her to read and write.

John Hansen certainly "atones" for his wife's death. However, the text does not suggest that suffering enobles or that he is granted divine grace and mercy. On the contrary, it suggests that what is far more important than any remorse or repentance is John's love for his daughter and his determination to provide for her. Here again the social criticism is at its most radical, because it is society which prevents him fulfilling this fundamental human need and duty without committing an offense. The gallows and the executioner's house no longer stand near the well down which he falls, but the symbolism suggests that contemporary society's treatment drives John Hansen down the well. In Dickens' novel *Hard Times* the same symbolism is used in connection with Stephen Blackpool.

The story, which pointedly alludes to the Christian story, develops sentiments first expressed in the poem "An deines Kreuzes Stamm o Jesu Christ" (see pp. 106f.). There Jesus Christ was addressed as only half a human being and the question asked whether he would have remained so pure had he had a wife and child to provide for. Here John becomes the true Son of Man ("ich bin ja nur ein Mensch" LL 3, 572) forced into crime by wanting, first, to provide his daughter with a warm bed like the manger Jesus Christ enjoyed and then to save her from starvation. He has to violate all his respect for private property in order to save her from being "crucified." This earthly father is the sole provider. The text suggests that were he to let his daughter starve, he would commit a far greater human crime than stealing potatoes. Equally, were he to let her go begging, he could set her on the road to ruin. His agony in the well lasts for days. Like Jesus on the cross calling for his father, he calls in vain for his daughter. There is no resurrection, only a bird of prey feeding off his stinking corpse (LL 3, 573ff.). Society, as the mayor comments, has hunted him like a prey and had its bloody sport with him (LL 3, 574). Such behavior, it is implied, is unworthy of civilized human beings in a humane society.

It may seem that society has progressed. Formerly people were executed for burglary with violence. Even in recent decades they were sentenced, like the old man in the story, to "slavery," i.e. were chained up and forced to push carts (LL 3, 550). It is a tribute to the resilience of human nature that he finally comes out of prison, finds work, and becomes the kindly old man loved by John's wife as a child for providing her with toys. But the reader is invited to ask whether contemporary society is in fact so much more humane. Wenzel, John's accomplice, a weak-natured lag with a drinking problem, is virtually condemned to a life of crime. Even though all his papers are in order and he has atoned for his crimes, the policeman marches him through the streets in full public view (LL 3, 568). He is sent from one authority to another. Such behavior is an affront to human dignity.

And yet Storm's ideological and aesthetic credo demanded that he provided the necessary "balance." The "horrors" of the inner story are relativized by the framework. After her initial education by Mariken and her adoption by a country pastor and his wife, Hanna develops into the ideal wife and mother. In fact at her forester husband's house in the country the Storm ideal is achieved of a fusion of practical, economic activity, and poetry. The *seuls sur la terre* motif of an earthly Paradise beyond guilt, sin, and suffering returns. But the harmony suggested in the frame cannot dispel a sense that all is not well in society. What, in concrete terms, are the solutions which kindly, humane middle-class folk like the lawyer-narrator, the forester, pensive folk, retired schoolmasters, and grandmothers (LL 3, 561) advocate and implement? Here the story is vague. Because he shrank from challenging the socio-economic structures of Wilhelminian Germany, Storm had only limited options: he could depict ideal solutions which often rang hollow, indeed smacked of opera, or he could persist with his old strategy of hoping that his readers, having been prompted to find the present situation intolerable, would themselves elaborate solutions. Underlying the story is his continued, albeit beleaguered hope that educated middle-class people would continue to champion *Humanität* and seek to uphold humane standards in state and society. Guided and encouraged by such people, the lower classes might adopt less violent, more providential behavior and gravitate toward the world of *Bildung*. It was a vague, unreal hope.

8.6 Annexation or Liberation of the Past? *Der Schimmelreiter*

Der Schimmelreiter embodies Storm's final humanitarian stance. It recapitulates themes and motifs familiar from earlier works. While retaining the epic and dramatic features of his later works, it achieves a density of thematic texture which they often lack. This has to do with the work's long gestation, and the fact that detailed, professional consultations were also a crucial part of the preparatory work.[24]

The complicated narrative framework is both medium and message. A first narrator writing in the present, i.e. the later 1880s, tells how, as a child "a good half century ago" (LL 3, 634), he first encountered a magazine story at his great-grandmother's. The narrator of this story, i.e. the second narrator, relates events which took place "in the third decade of the century" (LL 3, 634). He describes a nocturnal meeting with an uncanny figure on a white horse as he rides along a storm-swept dike. Having reached an inn and found himself in the presence of the dikegrave and his aides, he is told by the old village schoolmaster the story of Hauke Haien, the actual historical figure living in the middle of the eighteenth century out of whom the local community constructed the dike ghost. The schoolmaster declares that he has compiled his story from the accounts of reasonable, sensible men and their descendants during the forty years he has lived in this community (LL 3, 695). Yet, while distancing himself from it as superstition, he also includes material from the version of the story current in the community and associated with the dikegrave's housekeeper, Antje Vollmers (LL 3, 639).[25]

Storm's schoolmaster narrator is provided with a distinct personal identity which itself is inseparable from his socio-historical one. A former student of theology, he has portraits of his

---

24. See LL 3, pp. 1051ff.
25. See J.M. Ellis, "Narration in Storm's *Der Schimmelreiter*," *The Germanic Review*, vol. 44, 1969, pp. 21–30, reprinted in J.M.E., *Narration in the German Novelle*, Cambridge, 1974, pp. 155–68.

professors hanging in his room (LL 3, 679). In fact, his whole frame of mind reveals his theological pedigree. He subscribes to a form of Christianity which contains rationalist elements, whereas the rural population in general is orthodox or sectarian – but in either case superstitious. The schoolmaster is the product of an economically static, absolutist society. Looking back from the mid-1830s, he comments that around 1750 there was no talk in such communities of king or government (LL 3, 688). Although the implication is that things have changed in the interim, there are no signs of demands for reform, at least not in this community. What makes the story so fascinating and so typical of Storm is that, despite having been shaped by the institutions and ideologies of the *ancien régime*, the schoolmaster is shown groping his way toward different norms and ideals. Like other Storm heroes who are denied the support of progressive ideologies or socio-economic forces and dependent on their own resources, he cannot, however, resolve contradictions and overcome ambivalent feelings.

The novella illustrates how contemporary issues color presentation of the past. Thus the schoolmaster interprets Hauke in the light of the problems preoccupying him in his own society. In this the work resembles C.F. Meyer's *Die Hochzeit des Mönchs* (1884) with which Storm was familiar. There, too, the relation between framework and inner story explores the relationship between writer, narrator and patrons/public, and explores the connection between contemporary concerns and historical subject matter. In *Der Schimmelreiter* the criticism of Hauke Haien's father-in-law and the community around 1750 cloaks criticism of the dikegrave and villagers in the framework. Like Meyer's novella, *Der Schimmelreiter* brings out the limits set to any criticism of institutions and authorities.

The schoolmaster's attitude to Hauke is ambivalent through and through. A misshapen, frustrated bachelor, he only remained in this community as a result of an unsuccessful courtship (LL 3, 639). Presumably he was rejected because he did not have land and property and because his poorly paid job commanded little social esteem. For these reasons he is attracted to Hauke as an *alter ego*. Hauke is, after all, a dynamic figure who overcomes all sorts of handicaps to become an innovatory dikegrave. Above all, he enjoys the love and support of his wife, Elke. She stands by him even though he, too, does not have the property to which she could aspire as a dikegrave's daughter. One might therefore imagine that the schoolmaster would present Hauke as a perfect model. Yet, imbued with traditional notions of academic learning, he is suspicious of such an autodidact (LL 3, 639); himself brought up to know his place in society, he cannot wholeheartedly endorse Hauke's ambition. Any attraction felt for emergent notions of individual self-fulfillment is balanced by older norms which condemn such behavior as megalomania and hybris (LL 3, 725). Confidence in human nature and the power of human reason to solve practical and theoretical problems plays no part in a system where orthodoxy and sectarianism both reinforce notions of human powerlessness and the frailty and folly of human works. If the schoolmaster is fascinated by Hauke Haien's refusal to be cowed into submission – behavior that contrasts with his own inability to do more than voice indirect criticism – this does not preclude guilty feelings of self-reproach for himself being so resentful and critical of the community's shortcomings. He projects onto Hauke his sense of guilt at such unchristian feelings.

Nor, despite moving in this direction, does the schoolmaster progress to a purely humanitarian position. He rejects belief in the devil incarnate, in ghosts and supernatural portents, but he continues to describe himself as "ein ehrlich Christenherz" (LL 3, 645); he endorses the view that the mentally deficient child, Wienke, represents divine punishment (LL 3, 645); and he cannot decide whether Elke's recovery was due to Hauke's prayer or to the doctor's medicine (LL 3, 715). Above all, despite all the doubts projected on to Hauke, he cannot break away from the belief in divine providence and a moral world-order. If reality is the court of divine justice, he has no alternative but to regard the bursting of the dike and Hauke Haien's death as the result of divine retribution. He builds Hauke's death into the scheme of guilt, sin, and atonement.

Despite the schoolmaster's emphases, the text itself contrives to depict Hauke as a true humanitarian hero. As in *Auf dem Staatshof*, Storm cleverly engineers a distance between his narrator(s) and the meanings conveyed by the text. Hauke is without ideological support from outside – as a child he simply has a primer and the Bible to read (LL 3, 639); without a mother's loving guidance; without any initial encouragement from his father who cannot answer his questions, mocks his apparent presumptuousness, and even tries to break his interest in geometry in order to ensure that he follows in his steps as a small farmer (LL 3, 641). Nevertheless he prevails because of his natural disposition and inherited talents. Thus he teaches himself Dutch in order to study a Dutch Euclid; he consolidates his talent for geometry by conducting practical experiments and scientific observations – things not encouraged in this community; he resists the fear aroused by gruesome stories, insisting instead on searching for rational, scientific explanations for apparently mysterious phenomena. The fact that he finds the solution is cleverly shown when he later tries to counter the superstitious tales told his daughter by Trin Jans and explains to her that apparently strange human shapes are in fact those of birds (LL 3, 734). Like Fritz Basch he is frustrated as a youth, strangling the tom-cat (LL 3, 674f.). But the crucial thing is that he ponders on his action and takes steps to provide scope for his energies. Despite his poor prospects in a society where the size of land holdings plays such a major role and where offices are inherited on this basis, he succeeds – with Elke's support – in becoming dikegrave. He designs and builds a dike which profits and protects the whole community.

In intellectual terms he struggles through to positions where his Christian orthodoxy is under severe strain. Thus he questions whether God can work miracles, i.e. interfere personally with natural, scientific laws in response to prayers. He also questions the doctrine of divine omnipotence (LL 3, 715). Whereas the pious see storms and floods as divine visitations and even regard it as sinful to build dikes, he comes to regard his office as being to protect this community against the Lord God's sea (LL 3, 741). He adopts a form of pantheism: "Ja, Kind, das Alles ist lebig, so wie wir; es gibt nichts Anderes; aber der liebe Gott ist überall" (LL 3, 734). The step he has yet to take is to recognize that there is only nature.

In the novellas *Im Schloß* and in *Ein Doppelgänger* Storm had explored the working of the infant mind. Here, too, the scenes between Hauke and his mentally-deficient daughter, Wienke, illustrate how a childish or primitive mind interprets natural phenomena in animistic terms. The villagers and, to some extent, the magazine narrator retain such traits. At the same time the scenes stress Hauke's determination to provide even Wienke with true explanations. The tragic irony is that the superstitious community will not heed such words; Wienke cannot. The text conveys the Feuerbachian message that the only caring, "heavenly" father is an earthly one. While not being omnipotent and omniscient as Wienke would like to believe, Hauke is the only person who can protect the child – and the community. The parents and even Trin Jans can alone provide "divine" love while Hauke and Elke's "salvation" depends on their mutual love. The family may be flawed by inherited disease, but it still remains the only "holy family."

Scenes are included which illustrate the deep psychological appeal of specific Christian doctrines. Thus the novella echoes so many other Storm stories in evoking loneliness and human beings' need to bestow and receive love and affection. Having lost her son, the widow Trin Jans projects her needs on to a tom-cat – until more fulfilling, human objects can be found. Religion also affords surrogate solutions. Thus, after her father's death, Elke is shown needing to believe in a heavenly father and in an eternal life. However, like the earlier *In Urgroßvaters Haus* (LL 4, 170), the actual text suggests that of the two inscriptions described, it is the humanitarian one ("Hest du din Dagwark richtig dan,/Da kommt de Slap von sülvst heran," LL 4, 684) which is truer than the *vanitas vanitatum* message of "Dat is de Dot, de Allens fritt,/ Nimmt Kunst un Wetenschop di mit;/De kloke Mann is nu vergan, Gott gäw em selik Uperstan" (LL 3, 682). The need to believe in providence and a moral world order is especially strong. But if, on the one hand, such a belief absolves human beings of ultimate responsibility, it also perpetuates their sense of human impotence and denies them any true autonomy. The end of the story brings out how illusory this confidence in providence is. Those like the villagers who argue that divine punishment overtakes Hauke ignore the fact that Elke and Wienke also perish. What emerges from the novella is a godless world where everything depends on human qualities and "natural" factors.

At the end Hauke may, *in extremis*, relapse into Christian categories and express the hope that his own self-sacrifice can atone for his neglect of his duty and save the community. But the text conveys to the reader that his death has a different significance. Having first assured himself that the village is safe, Hauke plunges into the sea because, without Elke and his child, his life is meaningless. His end is in a sense a love-death.

For one last time Storm touches upon a central tenet of Christianity: the doctrine that Jesus Christ's sacrificial death redeemed sinful mankind. In the scene where the dike laborers are in the very act of sacrificing a young dog in order to cement the dike (LL 3, 721f.) the heathen roots of the belief in blood sacrifices are suggested. The thrust of the novella is to suggest that it is Hauke Haien's works, not his death, which are important. In the original ending the narrator progressed further along the road to a purely materialist view of human life by mockingly referring to the fact that the legend required "scattered atoms" (LL 3, 1061) to be reconstituted every time there is a springtide since otherwise there could be no phantom.

The novella lends no support to the idea either of a ghostly posthumous existence or of an orthodox definition of immortality. In contrast, it does reiterate Storm's affirmation of human love. Repeatedly the reader is discreetly shown how Elke encourages and protects Hauke and intervenes on his behalf. Her love is the cornerstone on which his success depends. She supports and consoles him during all the years of preparation and construction even though his self-sacrificial labors entail loneliness for her and even though she first has to come to terms with apparent childlessness and then with the fact of having a mentally retarded child. Hauke's commitment to her is made equally clear. Indeed the real human climax of the story is the scene where both of them finally admit to themselves and each other that Wienke is mentally retarded. In a society where childlessness or the birth of a physically or mentally handicapped child is attributed to divine displeasure, both parents have grappled in silence with feelings of guilt and anguished ruminations. In this scene the redemptive power of true human communication and confession is underlined: "Da warf sich Elke an ihres Mannes Brust und weinte sich satt und war mit ihrem Leid nicht mehr allein" (LL 3, 732). The sequence echoes the sentiments inspiring the poem "An deines Kreuzes Stamm o Jesu Christ" (see pp. 106f.). Marital love and communication alone provide true consolation and support. Hauke may still be unable to cast aside notions of guilt – even though he cannot imagine what their guilt may be; but he recognizes that their supreme human duty is to obey their natural instincts and love and support the child. Depictions of Hauke Haien as the *Gründerzeit*[26] tycoon or *Führer*-figure tend to ignore the picture of the loving father made happy by a mentally retarded child pressing close to his chest.

In its evocation of the "inadequacies" both of the individual
and of society in general, the novella links up to earlier ones in
paying special attention to the role of inherited traits. Hauke's
father voices the pessimistic notion (LL 3, 655) that deterioration
and degeneration occur in the third generation. Progress and
individual achievement will thus always be threatened. If Hauke
inherits positive talents from his father, Wienke inherits defec-
tive genetic material from her maternal grandfather. Illness, aging
and death also play a marked role, as they must in any serious
humanitarian vision of life. Hauke's own "guilt" is the result of
his illness. Strokes, cancer, and other forms of death all figure in
the story. What, however, is important is the human response to
them. Elke is shown concerned for her father; Hauke apparently
sacrifices his prospects in order to care for his ailing father; later
Elke takes in Trin Jans and cares for her; she in her turn cares for
Wienke. Storm's religion of humanity accepts the existence of
pain and suffering, but stresses the importance of seeking to
remove, minimize, or alleviate them by neighborly love and
concern. The novella echoes *Im Schloß* in showing that lame
animals and birds are also taken care of.

If such "natural," physical factors threaten human endeavor
and achievement, so too do the obstacles put in the way of re-
form-minded, enlightened figures by the rest of society. Ole Peters
does not epitomize "deeper" traditional and communal virtues:
he symbolizes petty, egoistic ambition and malevolent resentment toward a man who is intellectually his superior and who
also puts an end to his ambitions of marrying the dikegrave's
daughter. The opposition to Hauke's project is presented very
critically. Hauke Haien is not some brash, ruthless *Gründerzeit*
entrepreneur intent on his own individual profit; the dike scheme
is a cooperative, communitarian project built around "worker
participation." Since it will benefit everyone, everyone is expected
to participate in it in some way. Hauke is shown making every
effort to consult the community and involve them at every stage
– but to no avail. Democracy at this level is shown not to work.
The situation echoes Storm's own disillusionment with the refusal of the *Volk* and *kleine Leute* to follow the lead of the

---

26. J. Hermand, "Hauke Haien. Kritik oder Ideal des gründerzeitlichen
Übermenschen," *Wirkendes Wort*, vol. 15, 1965, pp. 40–50, reprinted in J.H., *Von
Mainz nach Weimar*, Stuttgart, 1969, pp. 250–68.

Bildungsbürgertum. That does not, however, mean that the novella commends some *Führer* principle or authoritarian alternative. The withholding of support and cooperation endangers the
scheme and the community; it breeds in Hauke undesirable
qualities and drives him back into the private domain. But, in an
imperfect world, such human impoverishment, alienation and
frustration of basic social needs have to be accepted as the price
of progress. Whatever tragedy befalls humanity's benefactors,
the important thing which should not be obscured – but tragi-
cally will be! – is that a worthwhile project goes ahead. Storm's
"existentialism" was a very humanitarian one.

The critical view which presents Hauke as arrogant and
imperious often rests on the assumption that, had he been more
sociable, spared the villagers' fears and superstitions, and argued his case with them more fully, they would have acceded to
reason and supported his schemes. Such notions of social harmony and rational cooperation for the common good do not,
however, correspond to Storm's mature reflections on the relationship between the enlightened individual and an alienated,
imperfect society. In his view there could not be any such harmonious relationship as long as anti-humanitarian ideologies and
institutions prevailed. Individuals who abandoned the struggle
to change society betrayed themselves and perpetuated the existing alienation; on the other hand, and this also entailed tragedy,
those who refused to conform and resign themselves to the status
quo, were either forced into isolation and frustration or ran the
risk of being victimized by the authorities and the public. To be
at one with this society was proof of alienation and self-betrayal,
true guilt.

The question of guilt is here treated for one last time. The text
suggests that Hauke's guilt is not hybris or undemocratic behavior; it lies rather in heeding the advice of the other members of
the dike committee, especially Ole Peters. It is the first and only
time he does so and it is against his own better judgement. Indeed
had he not still been weak from an illness and recoiled from the
prospect of more major works and renewed struggles with the
dike committee, he would never have done so. The relationship
between the individual and the community is again presented in
favor of the former. There is no suggestion that Hauke should
overcome his particular ambitions and recognize the wisdom of
existing arrangements. In heeding the counsel of the community,

Hauke betrays and destroys himself and his family; he also betrays and almost destroys the community entrusted to his care. In a godless world good and evil are redefined. It is no longer important whether actions please or displease a deity; on the other hand, it is crucial that they promote the welfare of the community. Duties are human, social ones, not divine, theological ones. If institutions and official ideologies do not provide enlightened, progressive goals and norms, then the small number of individuals who retain some critical independence must try to elaborate their own value systems in the light of the enlightenment traditions. In *Der Schimmelreiter* great stress is laid on performing the duties attached to one's office, especially if that office has service and protection of the community as its prime goal. Injurious actions or acts of omission and negligence (LL 3, 661) become crucial criteria. It is a conception of duty/guilt which is typical of somebody imbued with Enlightenment, Kantian notions of the moral imperative, and who believed that rational, humane civil servants could strive to promote the universal good. It is this duty which the dikegrave and his aides neglect in the outer framework. Their reluctance to get wet and cold is symptomatic of a wider failure to maintain and improve the dikes. Elke's father succumbs to the temptation of gluttony as a means of coping with his frustrations and loneliness. He, too, criminally neglects his duty. Guilt in Storm's scheme has nothing to do with pacts with the devil or forfeiting one's eternal salvation: it has to do with being indolent, apathetic, cowardly, concerned only for one's personal advantage and security. In an ironic anticipation of the much graver temptations which will face Hauke and with an equally ironic allusion to the Fall, the second narrator is shown telling of how he almost succumbed to the attractions of his friends' apples (LL 3, 635). Despite important business, he put off his departure because of the weather and would have turned back but for knowing that he had already covered more than half the journey. Like the dikegrave in the inn, he clearly likes his comforts and convenience. The implicit suggestion is that few human beings will exhibit the same determination to serve the community shown by Hauke.

Storm's experiences had taught him to beware of official heroes and saints. He refused to follow the suggestion of Mommsen and abandon his minor figures and bourgeois tragedies in favor of figures on grand historical stages. In commending the achievement of a petty, obscure dikegrave, *Der Schimmelreiter* is a democratic work. It suggests that enlightened, practical small-scale measures for the benefit of one's fellow human beings may be of greater long-term value than the exploits of those lauded by historians and the official media. But by 1888 Storm had long lost any confidence that reason and truth were values which would universally prevail once outmoded institutions and ideologies had been unmasked. The novella is preoccupied not only with the issue of how enlightened schemes and ideologies are formulated despite massive institutional and ideological opposition; it also offers pessimistic thoughts on the question of whether humane, critical ideas and the achievements of enlightened reformers can be preserved and disseminated. A lifetime during which he had seen his hopes dashed had not bred any great confidence about the power of *Intelligenz* and *Sittlichkeit* to determine the shape of events.

The second, i.e. the magazine narrator illustrates how the purveyors of magazine stories to the public either consciously neutralize or weaken the thrust of materials originally intended to promote a critical, humanitarian ethos; alternatively they may themselves be forced into accommodating public taste simply in order to get into print and safeguard something of the critical message. The schoolmaster himself has no access to the media. In the case of the magazine narrator – a professional writer or at least a contributor to such magazines – it is ultimately impossible to tell whether he allies with the schoolmaster but is also conscious of having to satisfy the editors, publishers, and readers of this magazine like, for example, the first narrator's senatorial great-grandmother. Such considerations might lead him to highlight the ghost-story element. Alternatively he may himself be inclined to superstition. The text suggests that fear, cold, tiredness, and a primed imagination soon lend ghostly shape to the seagulls brushing past him in the uncertain light (LL 3, 635f.). In the last analysis it is immaterial where he stands in terms of the effect on the public since in the years immediately after 1835 and the banning of the Young Germans there was simply no scope for magazine stories with a markedly critical, oppositional stance. In fact the magazine story (1838) which Storm himself read, not as a child, but in early manhood, is worlds away from the story the magazine narrator tells here (see LL 3, 1066ff.).

Storm realized that scholars may lay bare the essence of

religion, just as the schoolmaster devotes a lifetime to unmaking the *Schimmelreiter* myth; but their ideas may be confined to a small circle of educated readers. There is no guarantee that they will ever be disseminated to a wider public or translated into forms which are accessible to a popular audience. Equally, the popular soul, which in the 1840s Storm had imagined spontaneously generating ideas and motifs expressive of frustrated human needs, had long ceased to inspire any such confidence in him. In his old age he inclined rather to the belief that the lower classes had an innate capacity for superstition and that this made it easy for the dominant sections of society to promote their ideology and perpetuate human alienation.

The survival and dissemination of humanitarian ideas were as problematic to Storm as was the task of preserving the memory of champions of enlightenment. But for the fact that the schoolmaster devoted a lifetime to reconstructing it, Hauke Haien's life would have survived, if at all, only in superstitious local legends. While Gotthelf and Stifter had been preoccupied with how to ensure that future generations preserved the memory of past calamities produced by godless materialism, the problem for Storm was that, given the socio-political interests of the groups controlling the press, schools, and universities, champions of enlightenment in past centuries were either ignored and forgotten or their lives and message perverted. But for the fact that the first narrator encountered the story as a child and retold it fifty years later, any critical record of the historical Hauke Haien would have long been lost.

This question of the transmission of historical knowledge, of the creation of myths and of their socio-political function had always concerned Storm. What factors operated when historians, theologians, and writers compiled their canon of historical figures whose memory was to be preserved? What determined which "facts" were preserved, which forgotten? What deeds were highlighted, which played down? And what was the ideological purpose of these presentations? Did not myth and legend often usurp the place of historical fact in order to further specific ideological goals? Here he enshrined his final thoughts on the subject. As heir to a philosophic tradition which had sought to lay bare the kernel of historical truth underlying the gospels' accounts of Jesus Christ and to explore the factors generating supernatural myths and legends, it was fitting that he should see

Der Schimmelreiter as his last great challenge as a writer. On the basis of scant material afforded by a Vistula legend – one which the *Volkseele* could, however, have produced in any such coastal area – he had to work back from the ghost to the actual historical figure and explore the whole myth-making process. The schoolmaster refers to brutal men of violence and stubborn prelates being turned into saints. He hints that, whereas in earlier centuries the authorities brutally killed off champions of reason and truth like Socrates and Jesus, in modern times they could achieve the same end by turning them into ghosts, i.e. ensuring that the media and opinion-forming institutions devalued and distorted their stance, slandered or discredited them. Storm may not be identical with the schoolmaster, but there is surely a suggestion that Hauke Haien forms a trinity with Socrates and Jesus Christ as a searcher after truth. But there is perhaps another contrasting parallel between Jesus Christ and Hauke. Both men were turned into "ghosts." In Jesus's case the Church destroyed the impact of his humanitarian message by transforming a man into a god; in Hauke's case the significance of his life in humanitarian terms is perverted by turning him into a ghost. It is bitterly ironic that Hauke is transformed into a ghost by the very community which his labors benefit. He is turned into somebody who concludes a pact with the devil, is spirited to his death on a satanic beast and is then condemned to make a ghastly, guilt-ridden appearance whenever the dike is breached. The community itself does the establishment's work for it by turning him into a symbol of the sinful folly of purely human endeavor. If the latter has an interest in combatting enlightenment and *Humanität* and if superstitions spring eternally in the popular breast, how can isolated individuals hope to preserve and disseminate enlightened notions? By the end of his life Storm had few illusions.

8.7 Epilogue

In 1865, in the wake of Constanze's death and as part of the cycle "Tiefe Schatten," Storm wrote the poem "Größer werden die Menschen nicht." It had to wait for publication until the second volume (1913) of Gertrud Storm's biography. It runs:

Größer werden die Menschen nicht;
Doch unter den Menschen
Größer und größer wächst
Die Welt des Gedankens;
Strengeres fodert jeglicher Tag
Von den Lebenden.

Und so sehen es Alle,
Welche zu sehen verstehn,
Aus dem seligen Glauben des Kreuzes
Bricht ein andrer hervor,
Selbstloser und größer.
Dessen Gebot wird sein:
Edel lebe und schön,
Ohne Hoffnung künftigen Seins
Und ohne Vergeltung,
Nur um der Schönheit des Lebens willen.
(LL 3, 265)

By 1888 his humanitarianism had taken on a more somber hue.
Storm died on July 4. William I had died on March 3; Frederick
III, already suffering with cancer, died on June 15; he was succeeded by his son, William II. In 1890 the pilot, Bismarck, was
dropped. "At the end of his career, Bismarck had no other answer for the problems of his society but violence. His successors
proved to be no more fertile in expedients than he."[27] In the light
of subsequent German history, was Storm's *Husumerei* really so
blinkered?

Select Bibliography

This bibliography, which confines itself to material relating to Storm, covers books and articles that contain fuller information on works and issues discussed in the text or that I have found stimulating even if they present key topics and works from an angle very different from my own.

Bibliographies

Wooley, E.O. *Studies in Theodor Storm*. Bloomington, 1943, pp.106–141.
Teitge, H.-E. *Theodor Storm-Bibliographie*. Berlin, 1967.
Vinçon, H. *Theodor Storm*. (Sammlung Metzler, 122.) Stuttgart, 1973. (To be replaced shortly by a volume by W. Zimorski.)
The *Schriften der Theodor-Storm-Gesellschaft*, 1952ff., *Germanistik* and *The Year's Work in Modern Language Studies* all provide constant updates.

Unpublished Material

The Storm MSS – works and letters – are divided essentially between the Schleswig-Holsteinische Landesbibliothek in Kiel, the Archive of the Theodor-Storm-Gesellschaft in Husum and the Nissen-Haus in Husum. Many letters are still in private hands, and new material keeps coming to light. The Director of the State Library, Prof. Dr. D. Lohmeier, has in recent years had its holdings expertly catalogued. The new critical edition thus draws on many unpublished sketches and drafts. However, for reasons of space, it had to be selective. While the new critical editions of the correspondence represent a great advance, the problem remains that the letters Storm wrote to his fiancée/wife, parents, and children are still often only available in G. Storm's editions.

K.-E. Laage has provided a catalogue of the MSS of poems and prose works, "Der handschriftliche Nachlaß Theodor Storms. Katalog," in idem., *Theodor Storm. Studien zu seinem Leben und Werk*, Berlin, 1985, 1988[2], pp. 131–76.

Editions

Theodor Storm, *Sämtliche Werke*, ed. K.-E. Laage and D. Lohmeier, 4 vols., Frankfurt, 1987–88. This edition has made earlier ones redundant. However, as a handy, cheap edition with excellent apparatuses one can still recommend:
Theodor Storm, *Sämtliche Werke*, ed. P. Goldammer, 4 vols., Berlin and Weimar, 1956, 1967², 1972³.

Letters

I have asterisked the volumes in the new critical edition. Gertrud Storm's editions are to be handled with care.

*Theodor Storm – Hartmuth Brinkmann, Briefwechsel, ed. A.Stahl, Berlin, 1986.
Storm als Erzieher. Seine Briefe an Ada Christen, ed. O.Katann, Vienna, 1948.
Theodor Storms Briefe an Friedrich Eggers, ed. H.W.Seidel, Berlin, 1911.
Theodor Storms Briefe an seine Braut, ed. G.Storm, Brunswick, 1916.
*Theodor Storm – Ernst Esmarch, Briefwechsel, ed. A.T. Alt, Berlin, 1979.
*Theodor Storm – Theodor Fontane, Briefwechsel, ed. J. Steiner, Berlin, 1981.
"Theodor Storm und Karl Emil Franzos. Ein unbekannter Briefwechsel," ed. P. Goldammer, in *STSG*, vol. 18, 1969, pp. 9–40.
"Theodor Storms Briefe an Klaus Groth," ed. C. Jenssen, in *STSG*, vol. 4, 1955, pp. 31–77.
*Theodor Storm – Paul Heyse, Briefwechsel, ed. C.A. Bernd, 3 vols. Berlin, 1969–74.
Der Briefwechsel zwischen Theodor Storm und Gottfried Keller, ed. P. Goldammer, Berlin, 1960.
Theodor Storm – Emil Kuh, Briefwechsel, ed. E.Streitfeld, Habilitationsschrift, Graz, 1985.
"Theodor Storm. Briefe an Georg Scherer und Detlev von Liliencron," ed. F. Stuckert, in *STSG*, vol. 3, 1954, pp. 15–59.
Theodor Storms Briefe an seinen Freund Georg Lorenzen 1876 bis 1882, ed. C. Höfer, Leipzig, 1923.
*Theodor Storm – Eduard Mörike / Theodor Storm – Margarethe Mörike, Briefwechsel, ed. H. and W. Kohlschmidt, Berlin, 1978.
Theodor Storms Briefwechsel mit Theodor Mommsen, ed. H.-E. Teitge, Weimar, 1966.
*Theodor Storm – Wilhelm Petersen, Briefwechsel, ed. B. Coghlan, Berlin, 1984.
Blätter der Freundschaft. Aus dem Briefwechsel zwischen Theodor Storm und Ludwig Pietsch, ed. V. Pauls, 2d ed., Heide, 1943.

"Theodor Storms Briefe an Hermione von Preuschen," ed. G. Ranft, in *STSG*, vol. 22, 1973, pp. 55–94.

"Theodor Storm und Karl Theodor Pyl. Unbekannte Briefe," ed. K. Gassen, in *Pommersche Jahrbücher*, vol. 33, 1939, pp. 128–52.

"Theodor Storms Briefe an die Gräfin Emilie Reventlow," ed. F. Trömel, in *STSG*, vol. 25, 1976, pp. 25–47.

"Theodor Storm und Julius Rodenberg," ed. P. Goldammer, in *STSG*, vol. 22, 1973, pp. 32–54.

Theodor Storm – Erich Schmidt, Briefwechsel, ed. K.-E. Laage, 2 vols. Berlin, 1972–76.

"Theodor Storm und Heinrich Seidel im Briefwechsel," ed. H.W. Seidel, in *Deutsche Rundschau*, vol. 47, 1921, pp. 186–207.

Theodor Storms Briefe an seine Frau, ed G. Storm, Brunswick, 1915.

"Theodor Storm und Dorothea Storm geb. Jensen. Ein unveröffentlichter Briefwechsel," ed. G. Ranft, in *STSG*, vol. 28, 1979, pp. 34–97.

Theodor Storm, Briefe an seine Kinder, ed. G. Storm, Brunswick, 1916.

Theodor Storm. Briefe an seinen Sohn Hans, Catalogue no. 633, J.A. Stargardt, Marburg, 1985.

Theodor Storms Briefe in die Heimat aus den Jahren 1853–1864, ed. G. Storm, Berlin, 1907.

Theodor Storm und Iwan Turgenjew. Persönlichkeit und literarische Beziehungen, Einflüsse, Briefe, Bilder, ed. K.-E. Laage, Heide, 1967.

General Critical Biographical Works

Böttger, F. *Theodor Storm in seiner Zeit*, Berlin, n.d. (1958 or 1959).

Bollenbeck, G. *Theodor Storm. Eine Biographie*. Frankfurt, 1988.

Coghlan, B. and K.-E. Laage, eds. *Theodor Storm und das neunzehnte Jahrhundert. Vorträge und Berichte des Internationalen Storm-Symposions aus Anlaß des 100.Todestages Theodor Storms.* Berlin, 1989.

Fasold, R. *Theodor Storm*. Leipzig, 1988.

Goldammer, P. *Theodor Storm. Eine Einführung in Leben und Werk*. Leipzig, 1968, reprinted as the introduction to volume 1 of his four-volume edition.

Laage, K.-E. *Theodor Storm. Leben und Werk*. Husum, 1979.

——. *Studien zu seinem Leben und Werk*. Berlin, 1985, 1988².

Martini, F. *Deutsche Literatur im bürgerlichen Realismus 1848–1898*. Stuttgart, 1962, pp. 286–94, 630–64.

Pitrou, R. *La vie et l'oeuvre de Theodor Storm*. Paris, 1920.

Storm, G. *Theodor Storm. Ein Bild seines Lebens*. 2 vols., Berlin, 1912–13.

Stuckert, F. *Theodor Storm. Der Dichter im seinem Werk*. Halle, 1940: 2d ed., Tübingen, 1952.

——. *Theodor Storm. Sein Leben und seine Welt*. Bremen, 1955.

Tschorn, W. *Idylle und Verfall. Die Realität der Familie im Werk Theodor Storms.* Bonn, 1978.

Vinçon, H. *Theodor Storm in Selbstzeugnissen und Bilddokumenten.* Stuttgart, 1972.

Wooley, E.O. *Studies in Theodor Storm.* Bloomington, 1942.

Politics and Society

Ebersold, G. *Politik und Gesellschaftskritik in den Novellen Theodor Storms.* Frankfurt, 1981.

Eversberg, G. "Storms Reaktion auf die Wahlbeeinflussungsversuche von 1862." *STSG* 39 (1990): 69–74.

Fechner, R. ed. *Der Dichter und der Soziologe. Zum Verhältnis zwischen Theodor Storm und Ferdinand Tönnies.* Ferdinand-Tönnies Arbeitsstelle, Universitat Hamburg. Hamburg, 1984. (contains contributions by D. Lohmeier, H. Segeberg, J. Zander, R. Fechner, C. Bickel.)

Fisenne, O.C. "Storm als Jurist." *STSG*, 8 (1959): 9–47.

Jackson, D.A. "Theodor Storms Heimkehr im Jahre 1864." *STSG* 33 (1984): 19–44.

Jensen, J. "Nordfriesland in den geistigen und politischen Strömungen des 19. Jahrhunderts (1797–1864)." Neumünster, 1961.

Laage, K.-E. *Der kritische Storm.* Heide, 1989.

Löding, F. *Theodor Storm und Klaus Groth in ihrem Verhältnis zur schleswig-holsteinischen Frage.* Neumünster, 1985.

Lohmeier, D. "Theodor Storm und die Politik." *Storm und das neunzehnte Jahrhundert.* Pp. 26–40.

——. "Die Berichte der Husumer Behörden über Storms politische Haltung während der schleswig-holsteinischen Erhebung," *STSG* 34 (1985): 39–48.

Schriewer, F. "Theodor Storm in seiner politischen Welt." *STSG* 1 (1952): 27–40.

Schuster, I. *Theodor Storm. Die zeitkritische Dimension seiner Novellen.* Bonn, 1971.

Segeberg, H. "Ferdinand Tönnies 'Gemeinschaft und Gesellschaft' und Theodor Storms Erzählkunst. Zur literarischen Spiegelung eines Epochenumbruchs" in *Deutsche Vierteljahrsschrift für Literaturwissenschaft und Geistesgeschichte* 59 (1985): 474–96.

——. "Kritischer Regionalismus. Zum Verhältnis von Regionalität und Modernität bei Storm, *Storm und das neunzehnte Jahrhundert.* pp. 120–132.

Smeed, J.W. "Theodor Storm and His Reading Public: Some Cases of Editorial Interference and Its Effect." *The Durham University Journal* III (1960): 125–28.

Religion

Boll, K.F. "Theodor Storm, ein Kind seiner Zeit." *STSG* 10 (1961): 9–31.

Freund, W. "Theodor Storms religiöses Erleben." *Neue deutsche Hefte* 36 (1989): 3–23.

Jackson, D. "Storm at the Foot of the Cross." *Germanic Review* 59 (1984): 82–89.

——. "Theodor Storms Stellung zum Christentum und zur christlichen Kirche." *Storm und das neunzehnte Jahrundert*. Pp. 41–99.

Sievers, H. "Storms Gedanken über Unsterblickeit und Tod in ihrem inneren Zusammenhang." *STSG* 7 (1958): 18–42.

Stuckert, F. "Storms Religiosität." *Deutsche Vierteljahrsschrift* 19 (1941): 183–207.

Storm's Lyric Poetry

Boswell, P.M. *Theodor Storm* (Leicester German Poets). London and New York, 1989.

——. "Home and marriage. Theodor Storm's poetic realist love poetry," in *In Search of the Poetic Real. Essays in Honour of C.A. Bernd*, ed. J.F. Fetzer *et al*. Stuttgart, 1989, pp. 45–65.

Freund, W. ed. Theodor Storm, *Sämtliche Gedichte*. Munich, 1988.

Goldammer, P. "Erlebnis und Lebensgefühl. Die Lyrik Theodor Storms," *Neue deutsche Literatur* 4, no. 12 (1965): 98–106.

Goltschnigg, D. "Zu Theodor Storms Liebeslyrik," *Literaturwissenschaftliches Jahrbuch* 20 (1979): 299–305.

Lohmeier, D. "Das Erlebnisgedicht bei Storm." *STSG* 30 (1981): 9–26.

Martini, F. "Theodor Storms Lyrik. Tradition – Produktion – Rezeption." *STSG* 23 (1974): 9–27.

——. "Ein Gedicht Theodor Storms: "Geh nicht hinein." Existenz, Geschichte und Stilkritik." *STSG* 6 (1957): 9–37.

Müller, H. *Theodor Storms Lyrik*. Bonn. 1975.

Nicolai, H. "Theodor Storms Verhältnis zu Goethe. Zu Storms Auffassung vom Wesen der Lyrik." *STSG* 19 (1970): 9–24.

Sammern-Frankenegg, F.R. "Theodor Storms Gedicht "Crucifixus." Ein Vorwurf christlicher Unversöhnlichkeit." *Moderna sprak* 63 (1969): 34–42.

Schuster, I. "Zweierlei Lyrik: Theodor Storm und Robert Prutz." *STSG* 28 (1979): 98–108.

Sengle, F. "Storms lyrische Eigenleistung. Abgrenzung von anderen großen Lyrikern des 19. Jahrhunderts," *STSG* 28 (1979): 9–33.

Prose Works

General

Artiss, D.S. *Theodor Storm. Studies in Ambivalence.* Amsterdam, 1978.

——. "Theodor Storm: poetic realist or realist poet? Secret strategies of art and realism," in *In Search of the Poetic Real.* Pp. 23–32.

Bernd, C.A. *Theodor Storm's Craft of Fiction.* Chapel Hill, 1963.

——. *German Poetic Realism.* Boston, 1981.

Coghlan, B. "Theodor Storms Novelleneingänge: Ein Beitrag zur Darstellung seiner späten Erzählkunst." *STSG* 17 (1968): 72–76.

Coupe, W.A. "Der Doppelsinn des Lebens: Die Doppeldeutigkeit in der Novellistik Theodor Storms." *STSG* 26 (1977): 9–21.

De Cort, J. "Das Idyllische in Storms Novellistik." *STSG* 26 (1977): 22–36.

Freund, W. *Theodor Storm.* Stuttgart, 1987.

Kuchenbuch, T. "Perspektive und Symbol im Erzählwerk Theodor Storms." Dissertation, Marburg, 1969.

Pastor, E. *Die Sprache der Erinnerung.* Frankfurt, 1988.

Preisendanz, W. "Gedichtete Perspektiven in Storms Erzählkunst." *STSG* 17 (1968): 25–37.

——. "Theodor Storm: Novellistik im Zeitalter des Romans," in *Storm und das neunzehnte Jahrhundert.* Pp. 12–17.

Ritchie, J.M. "Theodor Storm und der sogenannte Realismus." *STSG* 34 (1985): 21–33.

Rogers, T.J. *Techniques of Solipsism.* Cambridge, 1970.

Royer, J. "Storms Verhältnis zum französischen Realismus des 19. Jahrhunderts." in *Storm und das neunzehnte Jahrhundert.* Pp. 133–44.

Sammern-Frankenegg, F.R. "Die dichterische Gestaltung der Liebesauffassung im Werk Theodor Storms." Dissertation. Vienna, 1965.

Smeed, J.W. "The Chief Ideas Underlying Poetic Realism in Germany. A Comparative Study of the Works of Keller, Storm and Stifter." Dissertation. Cardiff, 1953.

Zagari, L. and G. D'Onghia. "'Die häßliche Wirklichkeit.' Tre Novelle di Storm nel Giudizio dei Centemporanei." *Studi Germanici* 13 (1975): 33–44.

Specific works

(Listed alphabetically according to the title of the Storm text)

Kuchenbuch, T. "'Angelika' – oder die gescheiterte Auflehnung." *STSG* 21 (1972): 68–86.

Boswell, P.M. ed. Theodor Storm, *Aquis submersus*, Oxford, 1974.

Coupe, W.A. "Zur Frage der Schuld in 'Aquis submersus'." *STSG* 24 (1975): 57–72.

Jackson, D.A. "Die Überwindung der Schuld in der Novelle 'Aquis submersus'." *STGS* 21 (1972): 45–56.

Kaiser, G. "'Aquis submersus' – versunkene Kindheit. Ein literaturpsychologischer Versuch über Theodor Storm." *Euphorion* 73 (1979): 410–34.

Mullan, W.N.B. "Tragic guilt and the motivation of the catastrophe in Storm's 'Aquis submersus'." *Forum for Modern Language Studies* 18 (1982): 225–46.

Ward, M.G. "Narrative and ideological tension in the works of Theodor Storm. A comparative study of *Aquis submersus* and *Pole Poppenspäler*." *Deutsche Vierteljahrsschrift* 59 (1985): 445–73.

Fischer, L. "Lokalton, Sozialgeschichte und Macht des Schicksals. Etüde über Theodor Storms Novelle 'Auf dem Staatshof'," in *Literatur in der Demokratie. Für Walter Jens zum 60.Geburtstag.* Munich, 1983, pp. 390–400.

Freund, W. ed. Theodor Storm, *Auf dem Staatshof.* Stuttgart, 1983.

Freund-Spork, W. *Theodor-Storm: Auf dem Staatshof* (Reclams Lehrpraktische Analysen). Stuttgart, 1983.

Lohmeier, D. "Erzählprobleme des poetischen Realismus. Am Beispiel von Storms Novelle 'Auf dem Staatshof'." *STSG* 28 (1979): 109–22.

Hillier, J. *"Theodor Storms Novelle Carsten Curator: An evaluation of the terms 'Befreiungsdichtung' and 'Das Peinliche'."* Dissertation. Leicester, 1973.

Ellis, J.M. "Narration in Storm's *Der Schimmelreiter*." *The Germanic Review* 44 (1969): 21–30. Reprinted in J.M.E., *Narration in the German Novelle.* Cambridge, 1974, pp. 155–68.

Eversberg, G. et al., *Erläuterungen zu Theodor Storm: "Der Schimmelreiter."* Hollfeld, 1983.

Freund, W. *Theodor Storm "Der Schimmelreiter." Glanz und Elend des Bürgers.* Paderborn, 1984.

Frühwald, W. "Hauke Haien, der Rechner. Mythos und Technikglaube in Theodor Storms Novelle 'Der Schimmelreiter'," in *Literaturwissenschaft und Geistesgeschichte. Festschrift für R. Brinkmann.* ed. J.Brummack, et al. Tübingen, 1981, pp. 438–57.

Hermand, J. "Hauke Haien. Kritik oder Ideal des gründerzeitlichen Übermenschen." *Wirkendes Wort* 15 (1965): 40–50; then in J.H. *Von Mainz nach Weimar.* Stuttgart, 1969, pp. 250–68.

Laage, K.E. "Der ursprüngliche Schluß der Stormschen 'Schimmelreiter' -Novelle." *Euphorion* 73 (1979): 451–57.

Segeberg, H. *Literarische Technik-Bilder, Studien zum Verhältnis von Technik- und Literatur-Geschichte im 19. und frühen 20. Jahrhundert.* Tübingen, 1987, pp. 55–106.

Silz, W. "Theodor Storms *Schimmelreiter*." *PMLA* 61 (1946): 762–83; and in W.S. *Realism and Reality.* Chapel Hill, 1954, pp. 117–37.

Wagener, H. *Erläuterungen und Dokumente zu Theodor Storm: Der Schimmelreiter*. Stuttgart, 1976.

Ward, M.G. *Theodor Storm: Der Schimmelreiter* (Glasgow Introductory Studies to German Literature, 4). Glasgow, 1988.

White, A.D. *Storm: Der Schimmelreiter* (Critical Guides to German Texts). London, 1988.

Zimorski, W. *Theodor Storm. Der Schimmelreiter* (Bausteine, 659). Hollfeld, 1986.

Freund, W. "Rückkehr zum Mythos. Mythisches und symbolisches Erzählen in Theodor Storms Märchen 'Die Regentrude.'" *STSG* 35 (1986): 36–47.

Meyer-Krentler, E. "'Stopfkuchen' – 'Ein Doppelgänger.' Wilhelm Raabe erzählt Theodor Storm." *Jahrbuch der Raabe Gesellschaft* (1987): 179–204.

Doane, H.A. "Probleme der Kommunikation in Theodor Storms 'Hans und Heinz Kirch'." *STSG* 33 (1984): 45–51.

Grimm, G. "Theodor Storm: 'Ein Doppelgänger.' Soziales Stigma als 'modernes Schicksal'." in H.Denkler, ed. *Romane und Erzählungen des bürgerlichen Realismus. Neue Interpretationen*. Stuttgart, 1980, pp. 325–46.

Zimorski, W. ed. Theodor Storm, *Ein Doppelgänger – John Glückstadt*. Heide, 1986.

Freund, W. "Propaganda für die heile Welt. Harlans Verfilmung der 'Immensee' – Novelle von Theodor Storm," in *Literatur für Leser. Zeitschrift für Interpretationspraxis und geschichtliche Texterkenntnis* 3 (1988): 163–74.

——. "Zerstörte Idyllen. Zeitkritik in Storms novellistischem Frühwerk," in *Der Deutschunterricht* 40 (1988): 107–17. (Also covers *Auf dem Staatshof*.)

Jackson, D.A. "In the Lion's Den. Theodor Storm's *Immensee*." *Oxford German Studies* 14 (1983): 8–34.

McHaffie, M.A. and J.M. Ritchie. "Bee's Lake or the Curse of Silence. A Study of Theodor Storm's *Immensee*." *German Life and Letters* 16 (1962): 36–48.

Sammern-Frankenegg, F. *Perspektivische Strukturen einer Erinnerungsdichtung. Studien zur Deutung von Storms "Immensee."* Stuttgart, 1976.

Jackson, D.A. "Theodor Storm's Democratic Humanitarianism. The novella *Im Schloß* in context." *Oxford German Studies* 17 (1988): 10–50.

——. "Theodor Storm's *Marthe und ihre Uhr*." *Trivium* 19 (1984): 39–53.

Eversberg, G. "'Pole Poppenspäler' – zensiert." *STSG* 38 (1989): 55–62.

Jackson, D.A. "Theodor Storm's *Späte Rosen*." *German Life and Letters* 38 (1984/85): 197–204.

Miscellaneous

Ebert, M. "Storm und seine Verleger Paetel und Westermann." M.A. Thesis. Kiel, 1989.

Goldammer, P. "Storms Werk und Persönlichkeit im Urteil Th. Fontanes," *Fontane Blätter* 1 (1968): 247–63.

———. "Er war für den Husumer Deich, ich war für die Londonerbrücke. Fontanes Storm – Essay – und die Folgen," in *Theodor Fontane im literarischen Leben seiner Zeit. Beiträge zur Fontane–Konferenz vom 17. bis 20. Juni in Potsdam.* Berlin, 1987, pp. 379–96.

Häntzschel, G. "Theodor Storm als Anthologie-Herausgeber." *STSG,* 38 (1989): 39–51.

Lukàcs, G. "Bürgerlichkeit und l'art pour l'art. Theodor Storm," in G.L., *Die Seele und die Formen. Essays.* Berlin, pp. 119–69.

Mann, T. "Theodor Storm," in *Leiden und Größe der Meister.* Berlin, 1935, pp. 181–207.

Ranft, G. "Theodor Storm und Friedrich Hebbel." *STSG* 13 (1964): 7–27.

Roebling, I. "Liebe und Variationen. Zu einer biographischen Konstante in Storms Prosawerk." *Amsterdamer Beiträge zur neueren Germanistik* 17 (1983): 99–130.

Schuster, I. "Theodor Storm und E.T.A. Hoffmann." *Literaturwissenschaftliches Jahrbuch* 11 (1970): 209–23.

Zimorski, W. *Studien zur Kunst- und Künstlerproblematik.* Bouvier, 1988.

Index of Persons

Index of Storm's Works